English as a Second Language in the Mainstream:

Teaching, Learning and Identity

Edited by

BERNARD MOHAN
CONSTANT LEUNG
CHRIS DAVISON

Longman

An imprint of **Pearson Education**

Harlow, England · London · New York · Reading, Massachusetts · San Francisco
Toronto · Don Mills, Ontario · Sydney · Tokyo · Singapore · Hong Kong · Seoul
Taipei · Cape Town · Madrid · Mexico City · Amsterdam · Munich · Paris · Milan

Pearson Education Limited
Edinburgh Gate
Harlow
Essex CM20 2JE
England

and Associated Companies throughout the world

Visit us on the World Wide Web at:
www.pearsoneduc.com

First published 2001

ISBN 0-582-23484-0 PPR

British Library Cataloguing-in-Publication Data

A catalogue record for this book is available from the British Library

Library of Congress Cataloging-in-Publication Data

English as a second language in the mainstream : teaching, learning, and identity / edited by Bernard Mohan, Constant Leung, Christine Davison.
      p.   cm — (Applied linguistics and language study)
   Includes bibliographical references and index.
   ISBN 0-582-23484-0 (ppr)
   1. English language—Study and teaching—Foreign speakers.   2. Second language acquisition.   I. Mohan, Bernard A.   II. Leung, Constant, 1950–   III. Davison, Christine, 1958–   IV. Series.

PE1128.A2 E47227   2000
428'.0071—dc21   00-032740

Set in 10/12 Baskerville by 35
Produced by Pearson Education Asia Pte Ltd.
Printed in Singapore

APPLIED LINGUISTICS AND LANGUAGE STUDY

GENERAL EDITOR

CHRISTOPHER N. CANDLIN

Chair Professor of Applied Linguistics
Department of English
Centre for English Language Education & Communication Research
City University of Hong Kong, Hong Kong

Contents

List of Contributors

Mary Ashworth has taught elementary and secondary school and spent twenty one years before retirement training ESL teachers. Her work has included nine books, some ninety articles and keynote addresses. She holds an honorary doctorate of laws from the University of British Columbia.

Chris Davison is currently Associate Professor in English Language Education at the University of Hong Kong, on extended leave from the University of Melbourne. She has had many years' involvement in teacher education and language policy development and has published widely on the mainstreaming of ESL in Australia and the Asian-Pacific region.

Margaret M. Early is an Associate Professor in the Language and Literacy Education Department at The University of British Columbia, Canada, with a special interest in academic discourse socialization issues for school-aged children and teacher education. She has engaged in long-term action research projects in elementary and secondary schools.

Charlotte Franson is Lecturer in the School of Education at the University of Birmingham, with responsibility for the distance education programme, Bilingualism in Education. She has worked in the field of English language teaching in several countries and her professional interests are in second language education: teacher training, classroom practice and policy development.

Hugh Hooper has been involved in the education of ESL learners in a variety of capacities for the past twenty years. He most recently served the Vancouver School Board (in Vancouver, BC, Canada) as the District Principal for ESL programs. He has a special interest in teacher development and refugee students. Hugh is currently teaching highly gifted learners at Queen Mary Elementary School in Vancouver.

Constant Leung is Senior Lecturer at the School of Education, King's College, University of London. He has taught in schools and universities in Hong Kong and England. His research interests include second language pedagogy in the mainstream curriculum, second language assessment and language policy. Professionally, he has been active in the promotion of in-service teacher development.

Bernard Mohan is Professor in the Language and Literacy Education Department at the University of British Columbia. He has considerable experience in educational linguistics, language policy and teacher education in North America and the Pacific Rim. His publications include the areas of functional linguistics and language as a medium of learning.

Gloria Tang is Associate Professor in the Language and Literacy Education Department at the University of British Columbia, having previously been an English as a second/foreign language teacher and teacher educator for twenty years. Her research interests include language and content integration and second language pedagogy in linguistically diverse schools.

Alan Williams lectures in TESOL in the Institute for Education at La Trobe University in Melbourne, Australia. His teaching and research interests include content-based language teaching, methodology, curriculum and cultural learning in TESOL. He has worked as an ESL and mainstream teacher in schools in Australia, Canada and the United Kingdom.

Abbreviations

AMEP	Adult Migrant Education (English) Program (Australia)
BICS	Basic interpersonal communication skills
CALP	Cognitive academic language proficiency
CMEP	Child Migrant Education Program (later Child ESL Program) (Australia)
CSF	Curriculum and standards framework
DEET	Department of Employment, Education and Training (Australia)
DES	Department for Education and Science (England)
DFE	Department for Education (England)
DfEE	Department for Education and Employment (England)
EAL	English as an additional language
ELT	English language teaching
ESB	English-speaking background
ESL	English as a second language
ESL/D	English as a second language/dialect
ESP	English for specific purposes
KS	Knowledge structure
L1	First language
L2	Second language
LEA	Local education authority (England)
LEP	Limited English proficiency
LGA	Local government act (England)
LOTE	Language other than English (Australia)
NESB	Non-English-speaking background
NLLIA	National Languages and Literacy Institute of Australia (later known as Language Australia)
NPL	National policy on languages (Australia)
OFSTED	Office for standards in education (England)
SFL	Systemic functional linguistics
SLA	Second language acquisition

TESOL	Teachers of English to speakers of other languages
UBC	University of British Columbia
VATME	Victorian Association of TESOL and Multicultural Education (Australia)
VCE	Victorian Certificate of Education (Australia)

Publisher's Acknowledgements

We are grateful to the following for permission to reproduce copyright material:

Figure 1.1 from Campbell, W.J. and McMeniman, M. (1985) *Bridging the Gap: Ideals and Realities Pertaining to Learning English as a Second Language* (ESL), published by Commonwealth Schools Commission, Commonwealth of Australia copyright reproduced by permission; Figures 2.2 and 2.3 from *Curriculum Standards Framework* (2000), copyright Board of Studies, reproduced with permission of the Board of Studies, Victoria, Australia; Figure 2.4 from Cleland, B. and Evans, R. (1988) *ESL Topic Books: Learning English Through Topics About Asia, Teachers Book*, reproduced with permission of Pearson Education, Australia; Figure 2.5 from *Language and Social Power: The Action Pack – Animals* compiled by N. Murray and K. Zammit, published by Metropolitan East Disadvantaged Schools Program, © NSW Department of School Education 1992, reprinted with the permission of the New South Wales Department of Education and Training (Australia).

While every effort has been made to trace the owners of copyright material, in a few cases this has proved impossible and we take this opportunity to offer our apologies to any copyright holders whose rights we have unwittingly infringed.

Introduction

This book is concerned with English as a Second Language (ESL) in school.[1] It is important to define the focus of our attention and the context in which the term ESL (or second language learning) is used. Our primary interest is in ESL for learners whose first language or mother tongue is a language other than English, who have to use English for social and learning purposes within the school or college setting. In a vast majority of cases these learners live in predominantly English-speaking countries such as Australia, Britain, Canada and the United States of America. In many cases these learners come from long-term settled resident ethnic minority communities; others are from newly settled immigrant families; yet others are temporary visitors to the mainstream schooling system. Examples of the latter group are the children of professionals who have been posted to another country for a period of two or three years and the children of diplomats on an overseas posting. These learners are at various stages of their first and second language development. However, they share *a common need to learn English and the content of the school curriculum at the same time.*

Given that many of our arguments touch on issues concerning second language medium education, some of this discussion will be of interest to educators working in settings where the medium of instruction and learning within the mainstream curriculum is the learners' second language. An example of this type of setting is an English-medium international school located, say, in Belgium or Thailand which is attended by students from a variety of language backgrounds. Another example would be a public schooling system which offers English-medium education to, at least some of, the local population who do not speak English as a first language or mother tongue. Hong Kong is an example of such a system.

ESL AND THE EDUCATION OF LANGUAGE MINORITIES IN ENGLISH-SPEAKING COUNTRIES

The presence of ESL learners in schools is sometimes seen as an accidental, peripheral happening, a temporary local inconvenience, or an interruption in the normal course of affairs. In fact, it is part of a global, large-scale, long-term change.

The main outlines of this change are sketched in by Kennedy (1993: ch. 2). The large-scale presence of immigrants in developed societies is a result of the world 'demographic explosion'. Future developments of these immigration patterns, strongly influenced by demographics, are likely to intensify rather than diminish. Between 1925 and 1976, the world population doubled from 2 billion to 4 billion, and is highly likely to double again by 2025. In the period between 1990 and 2025, the 1990 world population of 5.3 billion is predicted to increase to between 7.6 billion and 9.4 billion. Demographic growth, however, is unevenly distributed between developing and developed countries. About 95% of the growth from 1990 will occur in developing countries. By contrast, many developed nations will experience stagnant or even, as in most of Europe, negative growth. At the same time, their workforce is ageing, and fewer workers will have to support more elderly. Thus today 'contemporary migrations chiefly move from less developed societies toward Europe, North America and Australasia . . . offsetting the economic problems of negative population growth and an ageing work force in the developed countries' (Kennedy, 1993: 42). These migrations have been accompanied by social and political tensions: 'Although the laws of the host countries officially ban discrimination, a nativist prejudice against immigrant communities clearly exists' (Kennedy, 1993: 43).

These changes in immigration are having a strong impact on school populations. Yet many educational systems and institutions are failing to serve immigrant students and students from settled ethnic and linguistic minority communities. There are a variety of myths about the education of language minorities. There is the myth that language minorities will acquire an education and a second language easily and quickly simply by exposure; there is the alternative myth that all that language minorities need is a basic course in the second language; there is the myth that the education of language minorities can safely be isolated from the mainstream of education; and there is the myth that educational changes for the benefit of language minority students will happen automatically, or by the efforts of ESL or bilingual teachers acting without curriculum change, institutional support or professional development. Some of these myths arise from thinking of the education of language minorities on the traditional model of teaching a foreign language; others are based on an apparently liberal view of education which believes that, providing there is a supportive social environment and exposure to the target language, second language development will follow, irrespective of the students' language and social backgrounds. At the rhetorical level at any rate, few contemporary educational systems would wish to produce students unable to operate beyond their own language and culture. However, there tends to be a gap between broad social goals and actual educational practice. The general features of this discrepancy are rather similar, not only in England, Australia and Canada – the focus of our discussion – but also in the USA. Indeed, we can use the recent developments in the USA to highlight a number of key issues which we will take up in some detail in the subsequent chapters. The fact that we are able to refer to US experience as an illustrative example suggests that ESL as a discipline and as a profession in these English-speaking countries is grappling with major policy and practice issues.

A succinct statement of the American experience is given in August and Hakuta (1997: 13):

> A large and growing segment of the population of students in the United States comes from homes where English is not the primary language spoken. Many of these students live in poverty, their families often do not have a deep history of formal education, and many are not yet proficient in English. At the same time, schools, and more generally the educational system, are not adequately prepared to respond to the rapidly changing student demographics. Such conditions combine and probably interact to produce educational outcomes that demand attention. Consider the following statistics: Among persons between the ages of 16 and 24 in 1989, 42 per cent of those who reported difficulty with English had dropped out of high school, compared with 10.5 per cent of those who spoke only English.

'Approximately 9.9 million children and youth, or more than one in five, live in homes where a language other than English is spoken. This figure represents an increase of 22.4 per cent over the 8.1 million recorded for 1980' (Anstrom and Kindler, 1996). Typically more than one-third of these students have difficulty with spoken English. In 1996–97, the number of Limited English Proficient students enrolled in school was 3,452,073, an increase of 6.9 per cent over 1995–96 (Macías et al., 1998). In England, Australia and Canada, Limited English Proficient students are more usually referred to as English Language Learners.

> Although LEP students are spread across the country, they are concentrated in a relatively limited number of school districts . . . Los Angeles, New York and Chicago had the highest enrolment levels of LEP students in the country . . . the nation's 25 largest metropolitan areas accounted for approximately 20 per cent of all students but about 42 per cent of all LEP students. These large urban districts face significant challenges including large numbers of students living in poverty, lack of resources and funding, high dropout rates, and increasing violence and drug activity in their schools. (Anstrom and Kindler, 1996: 2–3)

In 1994, the Goals 2000: Educate America Act codified systemic education reforms aimed at helping all students to reach challenging academic and occupational standards. Key components of this reform include: (1) high standards for all students; (2) curricula and instruction tied to these standards;

(3) student assessments tied to the curricula; (4) professional development for teachers; and (5) parent and community involvement. These reforms were designed to respond to economic changes and globalisation and increase requirements for literacy and fluency.

> Now, as the US economy has shifted from an industrial base to one requiring workers to possess technological and analytical skills, schools are being asked to prepare all students to read and write at a sophisticated level, to think critically and apply their knowledge to solving real-world problems, to work collaboratively with others, and to become lifelong learners. A much higher level of English fluency and literacy is now essential, even for today's manufacturing jobs, than in the past. (McLeod, 1996: 2)

This movement towards setting high standards is accompanied by a general recognition that the system must be for all students, including ESL students. The reforms mandate both excellence and equity for ESL students. This recognition is backed by civil rights laws that stipulate that failure to take appropriate steps to educate ESL students constitutes a violation of equal educational opportunity.

Given this apparent coherent articulation in policy, it is a matter of some surprise that the record of recent reform in the USA shows that the education system has not taken significant account of this massive presence of ESL students.

> Large numbers of LEP children continue to receive instruction that is sub-standard to what English speakers receive. This amounts to a two-tiered system of education, with challenging curriculum for some and mediocrity for the rest. There is an urgent need to address the school failure of LEP students given current demographic trends. The US Census Bureau reports that the number of US residents who 'do not speak English very well' is growing at a very fast rate – 37.3 per cent during the 1980s. Fundamental changes are clearly in order, yet the mechanisms have been elusive . . . Often, this means that resources are dispersed, children's needs are only partially addressed, and no one is held fully accountable . . . the education of LEP students is not conceived as part of any larger mission. Programs to address their unique needs tend to remain ghettoized – if not physically, then in administrators' attitudes and practices . . . Systemic reform holds promise for improving instruction and learning for all students, including LEP students. But such an outcome is not a foregone conclusion. Thus far the reform movement has generally sidestepped the particular conditions, needs and strengths of LEP children. (August et al., 1994: 5–6)

The general features of this brief discussion of the USA can be summarised. English as a second language learners are poorly served by the educational system. Government policy, in actual practice, marginalises them by not giving adequate acknowledgement to their significant presence in urban schools, and not accepting sufficient responsibility for their educational welfare. Educational practices for ESL learners are ghetto-ised, and poorly coordinated with mainstream practices. Similarly, there is a lack of an educational vision that would see any common cause, or even relation, between the needs of these ESL learners and the needs of the wider educational system such as increased literacy and fluency.

The issues raised here are also being acknowledged in other social and language contexts. For instance, in the European Union context it is recognised that

> '[a]s traditional educational approaches are not always able to meet the challenges ... resulting from the demographic changes as well as the critical socio-economic situation, outcomes for minority ethnic pupils tend to lead to low levels of achievement and high levels of exclusion. (Eurocities, 1994: 4)

ESL AS A SOCIALLY CONSTRUCTED PRACTICE

At one level of analysis, the issues surrounding ESL and the education of linguistic minority students can be seen as a case of educational institutions failing as 'learning organisations'. Change challenges social institutions as 'learning organisations' to learn from change and transform themselves for the new reality. But often institutions fight to remain the same, responding with 'dynamic conservatism.' Some of the strategies of dynamic conservatism are: 'selective inattention', or ignoring the 'threatening' message of change; pre-emptive strikes, or launching a preventive attack to remove the messengers of change; 'containment' or 'compartmentalisation', which allows the change a limited scope of activity and keeps it bottled up; co-option, or absorbing the agent of change and defusing their energies; and finally, responding with the least change capable of neutralising the intrusion (see Schön, 1971; Senge, 1990).

At another level of analysis, the practical and theoretical difficulties faced by ESL can be seen as part of the never-ceasing shaping and forming process of discipline building. In everyday experience academic disciplines such as English, history and physics have a thing-like quality. This is particularly so when they appear on the school curriculum. The truth is, however, that they represent particular discourses and activities which have been negotiated and 'agreed' by the practitioners in the field and the educational authorities. This 'agreement', however, is often unstable and fragile. One of the most vivid examples of this impermanence is the ongoing debate in England concerning the questions of what is standard English and what should the subject English consist of within the National Curriculum. (For instance, see Bourne and Cameron, 1996; Williamson and Woodall, 1996).

ESL as a discipline, just like other disciplines, is defined by a particular conceptualisation of ideas and activities as articulated by its key stakeholders at any one time. Such conceptualisations are not necessarily arrived at through consensus; ESL, as part of wider public educational provision, is often shaped by ideological and political processes which determine educational policy. It is argued here that because ESL is in very close contact and interacts with social, cultural, political and economic developments in multiethnic and multicultural societies it is exceptionally 'unstable' and that it undergoes fundamental changes frequently. We do not regard ESL as existing in some social vacuum or some value-free zone, nor do we accept that the status quo is pre-ordained in any sense.

Thus, it is not enough to say that educational policies and institutions have to be restructured to deal with a multicultural, multilingual population, and, more widely, a multicultural, multilingual world. Or to say that educational institutions must become more effective 'learning communities', institutions which learn collectively as the world changes and which address those changes. In addition, educators must learn about how policies and institutions change – and fail to change – and how to support change, particularly change towards multiculturalism and multilingualism. This means that educators must go considerably beyond the traditional second language teaching assumptions that what is needed is for ESL learners to acquire some conversational skills and a basic acquaintance with the grammar of English, and must look beyond the goals of second language acquisition. As a minimum they have to think of the coordination of the language development goals of ESL learners with the language development goals of native speakers of English, and what that means for departments of Foreign and Community Languages and of English as a Mother Tongue. Further, they have to think about language as a medium of learning throughout the whole educational experience, and what that means for all subject areas. Moreover, they cannot assume a single uniform culture shared by all, but have immediately to acknowledge cultural questions and differences in the cultures of learning and teaching. In particular, they have to reject the assumption that the burden of learning rests solely on the individual learner and not on the institution and the wider system. Finally, if they are to support these far-reaching changes, they have to draw on their knowledge of communication, language, culture and individual learning and develop them as resources for their institution and their education system as a learning community.

There is no easy label for all of this. Restructuring institutions for diversity covers a wide range of issues. For us, the core themes are: language as a medium of learning, language socialisation as the learning of language and culture, learning by the institution and social group as well as learning by the individual, and policy and professional development.

We speak as critical advocates of ESL as part of a wider social response to educational equality and, as educators, we have to examine continuously the relationship between policy and practice, the differences between ideals and real-life outcomes, and the gap between rhetoric and reality. It is with this understanding in mind that we offer this study of three specific developments of ESL since the 1950s in Victoria (Australia), Vancouver (Canada) and England. In each case we will raise questions of changes which acknowledge the place of ESL students in the school and the wider context of the education system as a whole: changes in educational policy, in educational practices, and in educational research and theory.

NOTE

1. Over the past twenty years or so the term ESL has been used to refer to a broad field of language teaching and language learning. At times the terms EFL (English as a Foreign Language) and ESL are used synonymously; the more 'specialist' areas of EAP (English for Academic Purposes) and ESP (English for Specific Purposes) are sometimes regarded as a part of ESL. The term ELT (English Language Teaching) is sometimes used as a super-ordinate label for all non-mother tongue English language teaching. All these labels represent vast overlapping of areas of language teaching and different types of learners or learning situations. There is no doubt that pedagogically there is a degree of commonality between these 'internal' professional divisions.

Part I

AUSTRALIA

Chapter 1

ESL in Australian schools:
from the margins to the mainstream

Chris Davison

INTRODUCTION

ESL teaching in particular, and education in general, is as much a political as a pedagogic act, shaped by a complex mix of historical, social, economic, cultural, political and demographic forces. This chapter, therefore, will start with an overview of the Australian sociopolitical and educational context before examining changing models of ESL program provision in schools in the state of Victoria.[1] Chapter 2 will describe and evaluate current policy and practice in that state, including the key aspects of child ESL programming, curriculum and assessment, teacher qualifications and professional development and pedagogic practices. Chapter 3 will focus on current problems and issues in ESL curriculum development and implementation and Chapter 4 will explore unresolved policy and professional development issues.

THE AUSTRALIAN SOCIOPOLITICAL AND EDUCATIONAL CONTEXT

Australia is a large and geographically diverse country, a federation of eight states and territories, with a total population of nearly 18 million. This study will concentrate on one of the smaller but more populous southern states, Victoria, which has traditionally had a very high immigrant population and a strong interest in ESL education.

There are many similarities but also important differences between Victoria, England and Canada, both in education and in the wider sociopolitical climate.

Firstly, there are similarities in terms of educational structures. Like England and Canada, Australia provides for both state and private education with schooling usually divided into two distinct stages, primary, typically prep-year 6, and secondary or post-primary, years 7–12. Within some state education systems there are also semi-autonomous intensive language centres which historically have catered for recently arrived children from a language background other than English in their first six to twelve months in Australia.

However, although Australia also has a devolved education system, with each state having constitutional responsibility for the compulsory years of schooling, there is greater centralisation of educational provision.[2] Because the federal government is responsible for immigration, there is also a history of federal intervention in and funding of initiatives in the education of ethnic minority pupils, including initial ESL programme delivery.[3] The inevitable tensions created by this federal-state nexus have often been exploited by different advocacy groups.

Secondly, there are similarities between the three contexts in terms of educational influences and philosophies. Victorian teachers in general have been strongly influenced by the British 'language across the curriculum' movement of the late 1960s and 1970s (Barnes, 1976; Britton, 1970; Rosen and Rosen, 1973) and the Bullock Report (Bullock, 1975) as well as by locally grown whole language and natural learning approaches (Cambourne, 1986, 1988), although changes in actual classroom practice and teacher training have varied. 'Genre theory', based on systemic functional linguistics, has also been widely adopted in English and ESL classrooms and has led to a renewed focus on language 'teaching', not just language learning (Christie, 1987b). As in the USA and Canada (Brinton et al., 1989; Crandall, 1987; Mohan, 1986) there is also a great deal of interest in and experimentation with the integration of language and content teaching, stimulated by the development of communicative language teaching, in particular the early work of Widdowson (1978) and the immersion teaching experiences of Canadian bilingual programs (Cummins and Swain, 1986; Harley et al., 1987).

Like England, Victoria has also been caught up in the development of a common national curriculum and more explicit outcome-oriented assessment and reporting frameworks. National curriculum initiatives in Australia, as in England and Canada, have had to respond to a rapidly changing industrial landscape, with the demand for award restructuring and multiskilling. However, because Australia is a federation of states, there has been a greater need to negotiate national language policy and educational curricula, with each state asserting its right to adapt the national curriculum to its own needs. In all states there have been recent widespread changes to curriculum and assessment, exemplified in Victoria by the development of statewide Curriculum and Standard Frameworks in eight key learning areas and ESL as well as by continuous modifications to the Victorian Certificate of Education (VCE), which encompasses the final two years of schooling.

Finally, there are similar demographic forces at work. Australia, like Canada, is a land of immigrants with the indigenous population of Aboriginal and Torres Strait Islanders comprising less than 1 per cent of the population. However, states vary quite significantly in their demographic profile, with some states, such as Victoria, having a much larger proportion of LOTE background students than the national average. For example, according to the Victorian Department of School Education, in 1996 there were 125,315 children enrolled in the publicly funded school sector who were either born in a non-English speaking country or born in Australia with one or both parents born in a non-English speaking country (Department of Education (Victoria), 1997: 9). This definition does not include Koori (Aboriginal) students but does include children from language backgrounds other than English who have impairments or disabilities. Overall, LOTE background children comprise 24.2 per cent of the state school population. About 30 per cent of these students receive ESL support, mainly in the first three years of residence. Hence, it is clear that in Victoria there is a large proportion of students from language backgrounds other than English with many refugee and family reunion migrant children as well as children of business migrants.[4] The vast majority of migrants take out Australian citizenship. There is also a growing pool of 'second-generation' LOTE background children, many of whom appear to speak English at home but who may still require ESL support to develop their full academic potential.

The Victorian state education system, however, has not always been sympathetic to the needs of LOTE background children. There have been quite dramatic changes in ESL education over the last 30 years, from assimilation to integration to multiculturalism to 'mainstreaming', accompanied by corresponding shifts in the view of the ESL learner, the ESL program and the ESL teacher. These responses are themselves a direct reflection of shifting state and national agendas and ongoing tensions over the issue of how best to 'manage' Australia's increasing ethnic diversity.

ESL EDUCATION AS 'ASSIMILATION'

Until the late 1960s the response of the Victorian education system to the presence of large numbers of recently arrived immigrant children from LOTE backgrounds was, in fact, no response at all. It was assumed that such children had no 'special' distinguishing characteristics, other than their migrant status, and that they would become Australian through a natural process of acculturation. The official government policy was assimilation, which did not recognise the value of migrant culture, language and institutions. Under such a policy of assimilation blame for failure to adapt was borne solely by the individual. This was, however, not a unique policy decision. As Jakubowicz (1984: 10) points out, 'similar and closely related assumptions also dominated government attitudes to Aboriginal children – that their Aboriginal identification and cultural experience would disappear naturally if ignored'. For LOTE background children this hypothesis was apparently extended to their language learning experience. Although a national adult English language program, the Adult Migrant Education Program (AMEP), had been established as early as 1947, it seemed to be the commonly accepted belief in political and educational circles of the time that the children of immigrants would 'pick up' English very easily.

According to the Secretary of the Victorian Education Department, writing to the General Secretary, Victorian Teacher's Union, in October 1954, quoted in Martin (1978: 94):

> In general, it has been found that migrant children acquire a working knowledge of English in a comparatively short time, and if these children are given some attention by the class teacher, they create no serious problem. It is considered unwise to segregate migrant children . . . as contact with (Australian children) hastens the acquisition of the ability to speak English.

Where immigrant children were considered a 'problem', that problem was individual-psychological, never structural, and such problems were firmly lumped into the category of learning difficulties to be dealt with by the relevant clinical or remedial service: ESL, as a label, was not used. Many 'migrant' children were placed in grades well below their age-level and, as Martin (1978: 92) has pointed out:

> The school returns consistently revealed the assumptions that migrant education meant teaching English, that assimilation was the ultimate goal and that 'national groups' in community or school hindered assimilation and were therefore to be discouraged. There were also a number of references to problems . . . usually attributed to the fact that the native language was spoken in the home.

This situation remained virtually unchanged, despite a number of government surveys and reports until the establishment of the Child Migrant Education Program (CMEP – the counterpart of the AMEP) in 1971. Its appearance was the result of a gradual shift in Federal government attitude and policy towards LOTE background groups which both reflected and stimulated a much more subtle shift in the relationship between the Anglo-Australian majority and the various ethnic minorities. There were many complex reasons for this change. Martin (1978: 99) points out that:

> One set of influences that helped to produce changed perspectives in the (late) sixties came from the explosion of interest in education in general and from a shift in orientation among educators from a system-centred to a child-centred philosophy, with an attendant increase in school and teacher autonomy.

There may have been some genuine concern for the minority children's education chances. More cynically, Smolicz (1985: 83) suggests that this 'new enthusiasm for the welfare of migrants and their children' may have been prompted 'by a sudden fear that insufficient knowledge of English would undermine the cohesion of society'. Other influences suggested by Martin (1978) include the rising public controversy over the continuation of large-scale immigration which focused attention on government policies, especially in Victoria.

Whatever the reasons, a strong grassroots movement began to create a more generalised awareness of the educational 'problems' of children of LOTE background in the community. 'Migrant English' programs began to appear, in embryonic form, in schools and the widespread publicity given to them helped to create the momentum which led to the appointment of the first 'Co-ordinator and Adviser on Migrant Education' in Victoria in 1967.

At the same time, there was a growing interest in broadening the educational curriculum so that more emphasis was placed on the languages, history, geography, arts and cultures of European nations. The opinion of the 1965 Citizenship Convention, quoted in Harris (1979: 33), was that 'if more European content could be included in school curricula, then Australia would be able to promise prospective migrants that their children would have the opportunity to cultivate their own traditions and language.

The concept of 'migrant education' was shifting from almost exclusive attention on teaching English to adult migrants in the pure assimilationist era to a position which incorporated immigrant children, albeit on very restricted terms.

ESL EDUCATION AS 'INTEGRATION'

The establishment of the national CMEP reflected the emergence of a new government policy, later to be officially entitled 'integration', which explicitly recognised that migrants had an important cultural contribution to make and should not be expected to abandon their ethnic identity. As Cox (1976: 112–13) observed, the assumption was that by combining the best cultural components of each ethnic group present in a given social system a 'new superior society' would emerge in which no one would need to, or be compelled to, suppress or deny his or her values and behaviour patterns.

Wilton and Bosworth (1984: 26) point out that this change in policy was influenced by ideas from within Australia as well as from the USA.

> In its attitudes and policies to migration, domestic models for the inventing of Australia were borrowed no longer from England but instead from the United States. Migrant power was only one of a number of movements . . . which, from the 1950s, planted seeds that would blossom in the Vietnam years when it still seemed possible to create a world that was heterogeneous, prosperous and free.

One of the most significant catalysts for change, however, was the intervention of the federal government, which, despite its direct responsibility for immigration, had until now refused to acknowledge any need for 'special' or additional resources for the education of 'migrant' children.

When the CMEP was finally set up, it was envisioned purely as a short-term measure to in-service and employ teachers to work with migrant students to teach them English. It was assumed that once the 'backlog of remedial work' with children already in the education system was handled, there would be few demands on the program. The scope and intensity of the need was drastically underestimated, mainly because of the still very vague definition of the target group. According to Martin (1978: 112), 'official estimates appear to have taken 'migrant' to mean 'born overseas, other than in the United Kingdom'. It was anticipated that about one-third of all these migrant children would be in need of assistance with English language but, in fact, many children born in Australia of parents from non-English speaking countries were also grossly disadvantaged by unfamiliarity with English. In the early 1970s, however, this group had not even been considered and a very narrow definition of an ESL student was assumed.

Furthermore, the CMEP was seen purely as an adjunct or 'top-up' to the existing structures and curriculum of schools. It was still explicitly based on the definition of child migrant education as a problem of communication, located in the individual migrant child. As Martin (1978: 113) points out:

> A simple solution befitted this simple definition: change the migrant child by teaching him English – and no other changes would be needed.

These initial assumptions about the purpose and scope of the CMEP influenced the nature of the programs offered and more significantly, the recruitment and deployment of staff. In Victoria, teachers who wanted to work in 'migrant education' were forced to resign from the Education Department in order to apply for temporary positions in the CMEP. They had none of their colleagues' rights or privileges and were treated like visiting teachers, or glorified teacher aides. They were housed in special portables supplied by the federal government, usually on the muddiest perimeters of the school. Failing that, classes were accommodated in corridors, laundries or, legend has it, even broom cupboards.[5]

Students were withdrawn from mainstream classes to be given specialised English tuition for one or two periods per day. Obviously, this form of organisation had many disadvantages: not only did it often lead to stigmatisation of the migrant child but it also tended to alienate the ESL teacher even further from the school. The withdrawal system tended to shift the responsibility for the migrant child from the mainstream teacher and the school itself onto the shoulders of the ESL teachers who, more often than not, found themselves trying to cope with all the students' concerns, irrespective of whether they had anything to do with language. Furthermore, the actual physical isolation of the ESL teachers meant that they were even less able to cope with the task of preparing students for the linguistic demands of mainstream classes. They usually had little recognition from their peers and effective liaison was difficult.

The thrust of these first ESL programs was also undermined by the usually inadequate training given to specialist teachers. Teachers rarely had any knowledge of the languages spoken by their students and their in-service program, when offered, tended to rely on behaviourist theories of language learning which assumed significant interference between the first language and English and relied on the avoidance of error and a lock-step sequential approach to teaching through formal grammar and repetitive, rote drills. The few course materials that were developed by the CMEP reflected this view of language learning and there was a heavy dependence on the ubiquitous *Situational English* (Commonwealth Department of Education, 1967) which was first produced for the teaching of adults in the 1940s. There was virtually no attempt to relate the content of the ESL syllabus to the demands of the mainstream curriculum.

Thus, despite the high-flown rhetoric of integration, the model of migrant education promoted within the CMEP was still a deficit-model. Emphasis was placed on student difficulties or weaknesses and little recognition given to the skills, values and knowledge students brought to the classroom from their first language background. The status of the ESL teachers reflected their students' stigmatised position in the education system.

Gradually, however, during the 1970s, opinions and practices seemed to change, the result of a variety of factors. First, the expected levelling-off in demand for 'migrant English' classes did not eventuate as the CMEP '"flushed-out" children whose educational difficulties were being ignored or being accepted as irremediable or as a sign of backwardness' (Martin 1978: 113). At the same time, demographic changes caused by the much higher rates of migration at the end of the 1960s, compared with the early 1970s, meant that the great majority of children of migrant parents were Australian-born. Slowly, the definition of the minority once again began to change. More and more students of LOTE background began to be categorised as needing ESL assistance and increasing public awareness was focused on the differences between the so-called remedial and the migrant child (Knight, 1977). The term 'second-phase learner' began to be used as a label to describe students of non-English-speaking background born in Australia or having completed all their education in Australia but still requiring English language assistance (Aird and Lippmann, 1983; Tsolidis, 1985) Often students were not identified as such until they reached the middle years of secondary school where the linguistic demands of the mainstream curricula became much more complex and abstract, very different from the more concrete, everyday English of the primary school. Students were expected to analyse an argument, write an expository essay and interpret work of literature rooted in distant and often alien cultures. Their superficial mastery of the English language and its value system was suddenly and ruthlessly exposed.

Grassroots descriptions of this phenomenon abound in the literature of the period, reflecting widespread concern within the emerging ESL field. For example, Tsolidis (1985: 75) notes that:

> Students are often seen to be orally fluent but this is restricted to informal registers. They speak what could be termed 'survival' English. This camouflages their inability to use or cope with more subtle or complex written and oral language. They often lack complete competence in their mother tongue as well. Because of difficulties in both languages, they may miss out on acquiring certain concepts. Their inability to cope with classroom language can lead to motivation or behaviour problems. A negative self-image, reinforced by frequent categorisation as a remedial student compounds the problem.

However, even when the need of this group for ESL assistance was acknowledged, it was difficult to 'fix them up'. ESL resources were already stretched to the limit attempting to cater for recently arrived students in the initial stages of learning English. The most common form of ESL organisation, withdrawal, was ridiculously inappropriate, particularly in the many inner-city schools in which 90 per cent or more of the school population was from a non-English speaking background. As Tsolidis (1985: 3) observes:

> Unfortunately, it is common to see ESL teachers catering solely for new arrivals in classes of two or three while the majority of second-phase learners were neglected and a handful of the 'worst' are handed over to the remedial teacher ... (even) in schools which have succeeded in ... separating newly arrived migrant students from those needing remediation.

Clearly a very different kind of ESL program was needed – one that took into account the implications of the change in definition of a 'migrant' student. In both primary and secondary schools, there was 'more demand for language development courses for second phase learners and less for the kind of elementary teaching of English that formed the original thrust of the CMEP' (Martin, 1978: 120). 'Remedial', 'deficit' or segregating educational practices were beginning to be found wanting.

Within the broader educational and social context, radical changes in policy and practice also seemed to be occurring. There had been a number of inquiries and committees into the issue of the education of children of LOTE background and newly founded ethnic organisations such as the Australian Greek Welfare Society, and the Ethnic Communities' Councils facilitated debate and discussion to a degree that had not previously been possible. There was widespread dissatisfaction with the integration–interactionist model of ethnic relations, which most now saw as merely a variation on the basic theme of assimilation.

With 'integration' there had been some recognition of the 'migrant problem' which was an important advance on previous policy which had failed to acknowledge any problem or difficulty with language and culture. However, during the 1970s official policy 'inched' towards seeing the problem not merely as one for migrants alone, but as a concern for all Australians.

ESL EDUCATION AS 'MULTICULTURALISM'

By the late 1970s, 'multiculturalism' was the new catchcry, officially adopted by political parties on both sides of the fence. According to the Australian Ethnic Affairs Council (1977), its goal was:

> To create a society in which people of non-Anglo Australian origin are given the opportunity, as individuals or groups, to choose to preserve and develop their culture – their languages, traditions and arts – so that these can become living elements in the diverse culture of the total society.

In this new atmosphere of reform many questions were raised about the effectiveness and appropriacy of the CMEP and its ESL programs. The Department of Education (1975: 6) revealed that, apart from the CMEP, 'the usual school programs are designed for Australian children and make no concessions to the particular needs and backgrounds of migrant pupils'. In general, schools continued to operate in a 'narrow, assimilationist mould' and tried to make migrant children fit a predetermined pattern. The vast majority of migrant children were found to be impeded in their education by 'language difficulties'. The terms of reference of the inquiry and its recommendations reflected the great shift in the definition of child migrant education. The concern was now not merely with the teaching of English, but with bilingual education, the teaching of community languages and multicultural education for everyone.

In 1976 control of the CMEP passed to the Schools Commission who replaced the general support element with block grants to States to be used for 'Migrant and Multicultural Education' – not only for teaching English but for developing a variety of other programs for both ethnic and Australian children. The policy of the Commonwealth Schools Commission (1975: 125) was that:

> The multicultural reality of Australian Society needs to be reflected in school curricula, in staffing and in school organisation. While these changes are particularly important to undergird the self-esteem of migrant children they also have application for all Australian children growing up in a society which could be greatly enriched through a wider sharing in the variety of cultural heritages now present in it.

It is, however, significant that in initial descriptions of multicultural education 'cultural' was equated with ethnic and interpreted very narrowly. For example, the Schools Commission's Committee on Multicultural Education, set up in 1979 as a direct result of the Galbally (1978) review of post-arrival programs and services, adopted the most common, popular usage at that time, equating culture with a social group's 'heritage', that is, its traditions, history, language, arts and other aesthetic achievements, religion, customs and values. Such an interpretation of multicultural education led to a plethora of 'spaghetti-eating and basket-weaving' additions to the schools program which concentrated on the exotic and strange.

However they did meet the Commonwealth Schools Commission's goal (1981: 14–16) 'to promote diversity and choice while maintaining social cohesion'. Diversity and choice for the majority of children, but unfortunately no real change for the children of ethnic minorities. In fact, such programs often led to more stigmatisation and, worse, ignored the adaptive and evolutionary nature of a group's culture.

Given the dubious effectiveness and marginalisation of many aspects of multicultural education, it is interesting to look at the fate of ESL programs during the late 1970s and early 1980s. ESL provision was a child of an earlier era and thus there was suspicion as to its motives and philosophical affiliations. For a program that had never had much status or permanency, this was disastrous. Despite slight improvements to teaching conditions with the transfer of the general support element of the CMEP to the Victorian Education Department in 1978, ESL programs seemed to falter and lose direction. It was much clearer what should not be happening than what should be.

Beneath the full force of the multicultural rhetoric, ESL teachers became almost apologetic about teaching English and in many situations were accused of 'assimilationist' tendencies. Their confusion was due to a number of factors, including the lack of a clear definition of an ESL student, uncertainty over the content of an ESL program, pressures to adopt new modes of organisation, continuing low status and insecurity, an overwhelming sense of powerlessness and loss of identity.

Under multiculturalism the definition of an 'ESL student' had become so general that it encompassed whole schools. Second language acquisition research was still in its infancy, thus most definitions were politically inspired or based on intuition rather than on a critical systematic study of the linguistic and social characteristics of the learners. Thus teachers found themselves facing unresolved contradictions such as LOTE background students from similar socioeconomic groups who had lived in Australia all their lives, displaying dramatically different levels of proficiency in English, and students whose linguistic competence was clearly superior to their Anglo-Australian peers but whose 'ethnicity' gave them the right to extra assistance with English. This led to growing dissatisfaction with labels such as 'first-phase' and 'second-phase'.

ESL teachers were left with responsibility for enormous numbers of students without any real training in assessing language proficiency or learning difficulties within a sociopolitical context. Many ESL teachers felt lost without any idea of where to start working, particularly in schools with few recent arrivals.

A second problem emerged even in schools where the target group had been clearly defined. This problem revolved around the content of an ESL program. In the pre-multiculturalist era, the content of ESL was clear cut. ESL was an English language teaching program and English language meant grammar. Now, however, with a multicultural, multilingual framework being proposed, ESL teachers began to feel very guilty about teaching English, and due to changes in views about the nature of language and language learning, they felt even more guilty about teaching grammar. Suddenly *what* to teach in an ESL program became a major issue with as many questions as answers. The educational climate of choice and diversity and the isolated nature of the ESL program did not help teachers to reach a decision easily and eclecticism reigned supreme.

A third source of confusion was strong and competing opinions regarding the appropriate organisation of ESL classes. The advocates of 'multiculturalism' felt that bilingual education was the ideal, although it was neither appropriate nor practical in many ESL settings, even if it had been funded. Certainly, withdrawal classes were universally condemned as stigmatising ESL students and being a very inefficient use of teacher time, catering as they did to only a handful of students. Increasingly, ESL teachers were encouraged to act as resource people 'available to the whole staff, capable of assisting with planning language programs, modifying curriculum and upgrading the sensitivity to language of other teachers' (Martin, 1978: 125). However, little guidance was offered as to how this arrangement might occur, given the continuing low status and poor recognition of ESL in schools. As a result, ESL teachers felt guilty about clinging to traditional forms of organisation where, at least, they felt in control of the curriculum and the social dynamics of the classroom, but were uncertain how to change their modes of organisation and still survive. Those who experimented with support or team-teaching often felt relegated to the role of a teacher's aide and had trouble establishing or asserting any sense of identity. Campbell et al. (1984: 66) observe that:

> Many ESL teachers report resistance from their mainstream colleagues, who feel threatened by having another teacher in *their* classroom and resent having to give prior notice of the lessons which they plan to teach.

Continuing low status and insecurity also undermined the strength of ESL programs and policies. Unfortunately, multiculturalism, in reacting against the indifference and neglect of the assimilationist era, did little to raise the image of ESL in the eyes of teachers or educational authorities. ESL became rather a dirty word in many circles, which led to further stigmatisation of programs. In many cases, ESL actually competed with community language and multicultural education programs for scarce resources, time and attention. In Victoria between 1978 and 1985 the number of ESL programs in schools dropped dramatically as the Education Department and schools themselves took advantage of the relative powerlessness of ESL as a force on the multicultural platform. There was no career structure for ESL teachers and, unlike the early years of the CMEP, no clearly defined allocation in the school. Often continuation of the ESL program (and the position of the ESL teacher) depended on the teacher's ability to lobby the decision-making bodies in the school and compete for time with other pressure groups, including the teacher unions (who have been guilty on more than one occasion of sacrificing an ESL program in the pursuit of lower class sizes or reduced teaching hours). This tenuous existence was mirrored at the systems level by the distancing of ESL advisory and coordinating services such as Multicultural Education Services from mainstream curriculum agencies, such as the Curriculum Branch, and regional offices. Furthermore, such services were usually lumped together with other similar low status minority groups to make up, in Victoria, the Special Programs Branch.

In summary, then, despite many name changes and continual restructuring and reviewing of ESL programs during the multiculturalist period, very few gains were made, by either ESL teachers or their students. In the final analysis, multiculturalism, like the previous policies of integration and assimilation, meant that ESL provision remained marginalised, 'special' and, ultimately ineffective as the social relations between the ethnic minority groups it supported and the mainstream it served remained essentially unchanged. By the mid 1980s, there was a growing sense of disillusionment with the concept of multiculturalism; this, however, was not only among ESL teachers, but in the wider community.

On the one hand, there was widespread criticism of instant or benevolent multiculturalism (Callan, 1986: 77) as being a political tactic to get the 'ethnic' vote without threatening the Anglo-Australian hegemony and traditional class and power stratification. Jayasurija (1984: 23) argues:

> Multicultural policies and programs which stress the freedom to choose lifestyles . . . fail to respond to critical issues of migrants' life chances, these revolve around the question of overcoming structural inequalities and have to do with competition, power and conflict rather than consensus.

While schools had been firmly identified as 'loci of social power' within which wider social relations were created, contested, reinforced or transformed, government policies and programs were criticised for continually avoiding these issues. For example, Jayasurija (1984: 23) claimed that the Commonwealth's Multicultural Education Program consciously rejected problems of social disadvantage which affected educational performance and personal development, failing to support studies of racism in education or projects which aimed to contest the power structures in schools and the wider society. In Jakubowicz's words (1985: 4):

> The issues affecting immigrants and their children in the education system have too often been allowed to become engulfed by a concentration on issues of culture and language to the exclusion of structures and processes which prevent fair access and equitable outcomes.

On the other hand, there were increasing concerns that the Anglo-Australian majority were also being stereotyped. Barlow (1985: 184–5) argues against the view that to be born into mainstream Australian society is to be advantaged over more recent settlers, and claimed that racism could be engendered by policies which were seen to favour others at the expense of mainstream Australians and their families. Such comments assume some notion of mainstream which is itself problematic, but they underscore the complexity of the issue.

The shift of focus and policy, when it came, appeared under the banner of 'mainstreaming'.

ESL EDUCATION AS 'MAINSTREAMING'

'Mainstreaming' was a concept first advocated by those seeking 'to strengthen multiculturalism by bringing welfare, educational, and government servicing needs from the margins into the central concerns of core social institutions' (Castles et al., 1986: 2). It was part of a national move away from a focus on individual 'difference/deficit' towards a re-examination of the nature of societal structures.

The catchcry of 'mainstreaming' was quickly taken up in the ESL field as a way to give new identity and direction to ESL policy and practice and as a strategy for ensuring that the 'mainstream' take more responsibility for ESL learners. For example, in their review of the Commonwealth ESL Program,

Campbell and McMeniman (1985: 32) called for an active reform of 'main-stream' services, arguing that

> While some ethnic-specific services can be defended, the path ahead lies in reconceptualising so-called 'mainstream' programs so that they cater adequately for the needs of the total population. It should not be a question of 'NESB versus the rest', but of acknowledging that, having been brought into Australia, NESB persons are now 'us'.

However, it is critical to note that within the ESL field 'mainstreaming' was not seen as a watering-down of ESL provision or as the replacement of ESL specialists. According to Campbell and McMeniman (1985: 32), a 'mainstreamed' ESL program can involve 'direct' assistance where the ESL teacher works with the ESL students, and 'indirect' ESL assistance where the whole school is involved in teaching ESL students (see Figure 1.1).

Direct assistance

1. Tuition by ESL specialists:
   (a) program of systematic language development
   (b) subject-specific language and tasks

2. Tuition by bilingual teachers:
   (a) mother-tongue development and maintenance
   (b) subject-specific language and tasks
   (c) home-school liaison

3. Bilingual counselling:
   (a) personal
   (b) career

4. Special services:
   (a) intellectually handicapped
   (b) sight-impaired
   (c) hearing-impaired

5. Tuition by non-specialist teachers in subject-specific language and tasks

Indirect assistance

1. Within-classroom opportunities for receptive and productive use of English:
   (a) 'enforced' participation of NESB students by deliberate, teacher-allocated turns
   (b) 'responsive' teacher-talk: presentation of material visually; paraphrasing of difficult language; use of non-culture-specific examples: checking on quality of linguistic input, both teacher and peer; continual checking on NESB students
   (c) peer tutoring and placement of NESB students with good language models

2. Extra-classroom availability of opportunities to practise English:
   (a) library facilities with graded and bilingual reading material
   (b) excursions and extra-curricular activities
   (c) encouragement of Anglo-Australians to mix with NESB students

3. Overall school climate

Figure 1.1 The conceptualisation of mainstreaming (Campbell and McMeniman, 1985: 32)

The notion that the 'mainstream' itself was some monolithic identity was also being challenged and discredited. In education, concern over the increasing fragmentation and disparity in curriculum and the decline in 'common core' values led to a call for the development of a common curriculum (White and Hannan, 1986: 5), that is, access to common beliefs, knowledge, symbols and understandings. The particular responsibility of education was seen as making these common understandings accessible for all students in a way which enhances further development for both the person and the meanings. Diluted or soft options for some learners and curricula that were centred only on 'culturally relevant' themes, such as migration and ethnicity, were rejected. Such courses were perceived as failing to incorporate the knowledge and understandings of the mainstream which should not be regarded as the majority's own private domain but as the common possession of all citizens (Smolicz, 1985: 76). Exactly how to define these understandings was seen as problematic, but Golding (1987: 6) argues that:

> The selection of knowledge and understandings must be somehow representative of the range of knowledge and understandings that are valued by the people in Australia and not merely those deemed to be worthwhile by the dominant ethnic (or social) group.

Notions such as inclusivity are inextricably linked to developing knowledge and any curriculum must take into account qualitative distinctions between students of various ages and levels of schooling (White and Hannan, 1986: 28). This placed the emphasis in schooling on pedagogy, that is, developing methods of teaching, strategies for achieving access and success and the production of a school climate that enhances those aspects (White and Hannan, 1986: 5–6).

It was simple, powerful rhetoric, but very easily misunderstood. In reality, process and product became confused. Structural rather than curriculum issues were emphasised, leading to the near forcible integration of ESL students, teachers and programs into the generalist or mainstream program.

As ESL teachers worked more and more in the mainstream classroom, their primary concern became how to provide 'technical' assistance to the mainstream teacher. As Herriman (1991: 122) points out:

> Mainstream teachers need to know more about how language works in the classroom but they also need access to a stock of easily comprehensible strategies which will help them gain initial and then developing confidence in their ability to help their students become more proficient in English. They also need the opportunity to become acquainted with collaborative teaching methods which maximise teaching effectiveness in classes with mixed linguistic backgrounds.

By the end of the 1980s, the perception of the ESL teachers' primary role in many schools had changed irrevocably. Official documents stressed the need for 'promoting colleagues' awareness of the language demands of all aspects of the curriculum, and assisting in developing teaching strategies throughout the school to promote NESB students' language development' (Ministry of Education, 1987), thus many ESL teachers reoriented their work away from direct teaching and towards enhancing mainstream teaching knowledge and skills. In the process, the mainstream curriculum became the *de facto* ESL curriculum and ESL gradually came to be perceived as merely a question of methodology, not content in its own right and not affecting mainstream content.

Initially, then, 'mainstreaming' was a double-edged sword. It 'legitimated' ESL education, but at the same time endangered hard-won ESL-specific services and institutions designed to meet the particular needs of ESL students. At worst, it returned ESL education to assimilation.

After savage budget cuts in August 1986, it was also clear that the federal government was not adverse to using the rhetoric of minorities for its own ends. The proposed merger of the ethnic broadcasting service with the national broadcaster, the abolition of the Australian Institute of Multicultural Affairs (AIMA), the huge cuts to the general support ESL program and the discontinuation of the Multicultural Education and Professional Development program, among other moves, were all justified on the grounds of mainstreaming. According to the then federal Minister for Education (Ryan, 1986):

> The specific purpose programs (which include the ESL program) have been designed to encourage new and improved methods and directions in areas of educational need . . . Where these objectives have been achieved, the Commonwealth can withdraw; in some areas, the objectives of the programs can be integrated with its mainstream provisions of States and systems.

Despite a series of government reports (Campbell et al., 1984; Campbell & McMeniman, 1985) highlighting the serious under-resourcing of child ESL and documenting the very limited impact to date of ESL methodologies on mainstream subject teachers in schools of high migrant density, Ryan's words suggest that the mainstreaming of ESL was now a relatively simple step. It is little wonder that many members and supporters of the ethnic minority groups saw this version of mainstreaming as a thinly disguised cost-cutting exercise which reflected a growing backlash against ethnic minorities by the Anglo-Australian majority. As Castles (1986: 5) argued:

> There is a risk that the emerging ideology of mainstreaming is a façade for a retreat from the project of securing full social participation for people of non-English speaking background. As such, it would be a step backwards away from what has been positive in multiculturalism.

As an educational policy 'mainstreaming' affected not only ESL students but also Aboriginal children, the deaf and the differentially abled. Many critics suggested that in reinforcing the dominant ideology of equality of access to educational resources, it actually reproduced structured inequalities. For example, Branson and Miller (1993: 33) argue that 'mainstreaming' is a 'discriminatory practice':

> Its orientation towards the normalisation of the formerly segregated demands their assimilation into the educational and cultural environment, demanding of them as of the other students, 'that they have what it does not give . . . linguistic and cultural competence'.

However, the response of the Australian ESL field to 'mainstreaming' has been more pragmatic. The profession has resisted any attempts to undermine the provision of ESL-specific services, at the same time using the rhetoric of 'mainstreaming' to argue for widespread changes to school policies, curriculum, structures and attitudes. The tensions involved in this position have been crystallised in recent debates surrounding the development of national curriculum and reporting frameworks.

ESL AND THE NATIONAL CURRICULUM

In 1987, the Ministers of the various Australian states and territories, stimulated by a highly interventionist federal Labor government, developed an agreed set of National Goals for Schooling. This statement defined eight Key Learning Areas, including Language other than English and English, but not ESL.

The original intention of the National Curriculum developments (see Figure 1.2) was that ESL be incorporated within subject English and the language development of ESL students mapped on the National English Profile. However, as the work on developing the English profile and statements progressed, it became clear that ESL learners did not 'fit' the profile of English-speaking background learners' development, especially those learners entering the Australian school system after school age. Both quantitative and qualitative research studies (Meiers, 1994) found that there was a need for a separate ESL Profile.

The major problem with the English Profile was that it was not sufficiently sensitive to the fact that LOTE background learners may start at different points to the 'mainstream' norm and move through different stages to achieve the same outcomes as ESB learners. Thus, there was official support and funding for the development of two ESL profiles, the DEET/NLLIA funded ESL Band Scales (NLLIA, 1994) and the ESL Scales (Curriculum Corporation, 1995). The story of the origins of these two scales is itself a long and controversial one (McKay, 1994) but both represented a formal recognition nationally that there were aspects of ESL teaching and learning which were distinctive and which could not be encapsulated within a common English framework.

The development of such documents for the school context was a protracted undertaking, not just because there were so many ESL students entering Australian schools from a variety of backgrounds and at a variety of age levels, but because ESL programs in Australia were themselves so complex and varied. Thus in developing the ESL Band Scales (NLLIA, 1994), McKay (1994) proposed a framework with multiple entry points so that learners' development towards that of the ESB groups could be captured as well as their progress through the common stages of L1 and L2 English language and literacy development.

The ESL Band Scales were context-embedded (McKay, 1994) – that is, set within the mainstream learning context – and they attempted to reflect the learners' progress within the realities of the mainstream learning context. Stages or levels within context-embedded ESL scales are 'progressive cameos of typical progress of ESL learners within the context, moving towards upper levels of ability in English within the mainstream context'.

McKay (1994) argues that such recognition of the mainstream learning context is absolutely crucial. It determines the nature of ESL learners' language performance, determines how the performance is written down, and guides ESL teachers and mainstream teachers to observe the level of ESL learner ability as it is manifested in the real mainstream language context.

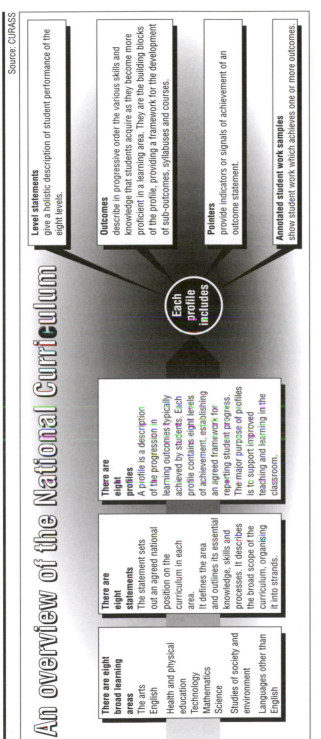

Figure 1.2 National Curriculum Developments 1993 (*The Age*, 11 May 1993, Melbourne)

Three scales at junior primary, middle/upper primary, and secondary broad age groups, each covering the four macro-skills, allow the mainstream learning context of each of the main broad age groups to be defined, and subsequently to be used to describe the ESL learning progress within each of them. The level descriptions in the ESL Band Scales include indications of what learners can do with contextual support (slower interlocutor speech, repetitions, illustrations in texts). The learners' likely differences in language performance in social and academic contexts are also highlighted. To assist teachers to make actual assessments of learners' performance over a number of tasks and in a number of contexts, exemplar assessment activities and observation guides were developed as part of the NLLIA project.

Based on such work, all states have now developed an adjunct ESL curriculum and reporting framework to accompany their various adaptations of, or alternatives to, the National Curriculum and Profile in English, although there is considerable variation between states (Breen et al., 1997). For example, the NLLIA materials, together with the ESL Scales, form the foundation of state-based ESL Companion to the Victorian Curriculum and Standards Framework (CSF) (Board of Studies, 1996, 2000) which will be described in more detail in the next chapter. However, despite a certain degree of success in including ESL in national and state curriculum and assessment frameworks, many critical conceptual issues remain unresolved, in particular the issue of the relationship between ESL and the other curriculum and reporting frameworks.

Recent alterations to the funding and structure of the Commonwealth's Child ESL Program as a result of a change of federal government in 1996 have meant that these critical issues have been overshadowed by a major concern with accountability and benchmarking in literacy more generally. In the current drive for educational reform, ESL is being reconstructed by the Commonwealth as a subset of literacy (Lo Bianco, 1998). Hence, it is more important than ever for the ESL field to articulate clearly and effectively the nature of its relationship to the mainstream curriculum. As Lo Bianco (1998: 1) argues:

> Central to ESL is the idea that the acquisition of a second language and the ability to participate fully in formal learning contexts cannot be left to osmotic processes and blind faith. Or, to put it more technically, that ESL learning cannot be left entirely to incidental, indirect, inductive or implicit acquisitional processes. Nor is there some natural or inevitable developmental progression such that targeted intervention (the famed six months of intensive initial instruction) will be sufficient to activate a subsequent automatic learning process. A sort of kick-start ESL. That is because ESL involves expert intervention at all stages of learning, as the student progresses (through individual pathways) from non English-speaking status towards full participation in learning. There is a need for explicit support at each stage of learning, as the growing complexity of domains and literacy practices of the curriculum unfolds. In ESL teaching there may often be a shift from deliberate focus on language to a sort of ESL-informed general teaching. Whatever practices are favoured in any case they all derive from the trained expertise of the ESL specialist.

CONCLUSIONS

In retrospect, mainstreaming, on the whole, has been a positive force in ESL education. There is now widespread agreement on many issues surrounding ESLness, including the definition of an ESL learner, an ESL program and an ESL teacher, although there is still tension between the philosophical base of the ESL field which emphasises diversity and complexity, and the demands of the 'mainstream' educational agenda for commonality, simplicity and homogeneity. This is particularly the case when ESL is subordinated to literacy. However, in Victoria in particular, a long history of collaborative activity between different stakeholders has led to strongly defined and fairly coherent ESL policy and practice – which will be described in more detail in Chapter 2.

NOTES

1. An example of how political as well as pedagogic factors are often critical in shaping definitions and reconceptualising programs is the issue of labels for 'ESL'. For example, Limited English Proficient (LEP), commonly used as a *synonym* for ESL in the USA, is perceived by Australian ESL practitioners to have extremely negative deficit connotations, particularly in the acronym's association with 'leper'. On the other hand, 'bilingual' or 'emergent bilingual', until recently the preferred term for ESL in England, is seen as blurring important pedagogic distinctions about the learner's English language needs. Home language use does not itself equate directly with ESL need, although 'bilingual' is a reminder of the critical importance of the first language.
2. For example, there is no real equivalent in most Australian states to Local School Boards or Local Education Authorities. Power, control and funding of schools at the state level is still held centrally, despite token gestures towards greater devolution of decision-making, e.g. as in Victoria's Schools of the Future Program.
3. There are parallels between the Australian situation and the English situation with its Section 11 (recently renamed Ethnicity Minority Achievement Grant) grant-aided projects and 'tagged' Section 11 teachers, which are funded centrally but administered locally. Canadian school boards have long lobbied the federal government for similar funding arrangements based on the same rationale (see Flaherty and Woods, 1992), albeit with little success.
4. The term 'migrant' is the more common term used to designate an immigrant in Australia.
5. The 'broom cupboard' story probably arose as a metaphor for all those ESL teachers and students who were in fact allocated no room for teaching at all, relying on finding unoccupied classrooms or corners of the school and forced to keep essential (Commonwealth-funded) resources in a storage cupboard.

Chapter 2

Current policies, programs and practices in school ESL

Chris Davison

INTRODUCTION

In the previous chapter, it was argued that Australia, like other English-speaking immigrant countries, has witnessed rather dramatic changes in ESL education over the last decade – a reflection of shifts in government policy from assimilation to multiculturalism to mainstreaming. In retrospect, the latter half of the 1980s and early 1990s was marked by a relatively favourable climate for the development of long-term ESL policy and practice. The release of the National Policy on Languages (NPL) (Lo Bianco, 1987), the establishment of the National Languages and Literacy Institute of Australia (NLLIA, now known as Language Australia) and the release of the Australian Language and Literacy Policy (DEET, 1991) kept the spotlight on ESL issues, although not always for the same reasons (Moore, 1995). There was significant government funding of research into child ESL and literacy issues and the development of a strong research culture through the establishment of federally funded Child Literacy and ESL Research Networks in every state. These policy and structural developments promoted the development of a strong and vigorous professional dialogue between language and literacy specialists. There was a major critique of 'natural learning' and whole language approaches which renewed interest in the role of language in learning and generated a greater concern for more explicit language development (Christie et al., 1991). This period was also marked by an intense debate over the role and content of the ESL program, especially its relationship to the mainstream (Davison, 1993a; Ferguson, 1991) and the promulgation of a series of policy statements on ESL in almost every state and territory.

In Victoria, this activity resulted in the establishment of significant policy guidelines (Board of Studies, 1996; Ministry of Education, 1987, 1988) on various aspects of mainstreaming ESL, particularly in relation to program provision, teacher qualifications and professional development and curriculum and assessment policy, which have all had a direct effect on the nature of pedagogic practice. These specific areas of child ESL policy and associated practice will now be explored in more detail.[1]

CURRENT PROGRAM PROVISION

In Victoria, there is now broad policy agreement as to the most appropriate goals for an ESL program. These goals are explicitly articulated in many recent national and state curriculum documents, including *The ESL Companion to the English Curriculum and Standards Framework* (Board of Studies, 1996: 5) which states:

> The broad goals of ESL programs are to develop in students:
>
> - a level of competency and confidence in using English that allows them, over time, to fully participate in both social and school-based contexts
> - continuing conceptual development while developing English language skills
> - an understanding of the learning styles and expectations of the Australian school system

Such statements emphasise that the central concern of ESL teaching in Victoria is English language development, but that ESL also aims to enhance subject matter learning and induct ESL learners into both the culture of the school and the broader Australian community. Thus, as in North America and in England, an ESL teacher's concerns are more than just linguistic.

This reflects the relatively early recognition in Victoria that to wait for English language learning to be 'complete' before assisting ESL students with learning and development in subject areas would be discriminatory, as subject area learning would be severely disrupted. This is especially true when bilingual programs are not a program option. At the same time, the adoption of 'communicative' approaches to ESL teaching emphasised the value of utilising relevant, interesting and intrinsically worthwhile subject matter as a basis for language development. Consequently, some sort of concurrent learning of both ESL and subject matter, involving the integration of ESL and content objectives, has been widely advocated and adopted in Victoria since the late 1970s.

The mainstreaming of ESL program provision necessarily involves such ESL and content integration, but the two developments have very different historical origins and philosophical orientations, thus should not be conflated. Language and content integration is essentially a curriculum movement, of equal interest to all language teachers, whereas mainstreaming is an ideology which aims to redress perceived social inequities, thus emphasises structural issues. In Victoria, the ESL profession has strongly resisted any reductionist tendencies, arguing that in a mainstream environment, ESL programming is necessarily complex. It involves not one but many separate but interrelated decisions about curriculum focus, first language input, modes of delivery, learner groupings and teacher roles. Such a multifaceted and flexible conceptualisation of 'mainstreaming' is presented in Figure 2.1 overleaf (Davison, 1993b), a view of programming widely promoted by the ESL profession and implicitly reflected in current policy.

In this conceptualisation of ESL programming, ESL need is seen to determine curriculum focus, and curriculum focus shapes structural and

Figure 2.1 Mainstreaming: programming choices

Underlying principles: whole school planning and responsibility policy, structural and attitudinal support within multicultural framework, different choices to suit different needs at different times, focus on language development, not just language use

ESL need (e.g. as identified by ESL CSF)	High	Medium	Low
Curriculum focus	Language (integrated with content)	Language/content	Content (integrated with language)
Role of L1 L1 Maintenance orientation (continuing systematic L1 development)	L1-medium content classes/ESL with L1 support	L1-medium content classes L1 as LOTE ESL with L1 support	L1 and L2-medium content classes L1 as LOTE
L1 to L2 Transitional orientation (L1 development until 'coping' in L2)	L1-medium content classes/ESL with L1 support	Some L1-medium content classes ESL with L1 support	L1 perspective
L2 Support orientation (L1 used as incidental support for L2 learning)	L2-medium classes with L1 support	L2-medium classes with L1 support	L1 perspective
Timetabling options	Intensive classes; Similar needs ESL classes with some mainstream classes (parallel and adjunct classes, electives, self-access, focused groupings, 'sheltered instruction')	Mainstream multiethnic classes with some similar needs ESL classes (electives, self-access, focused groupings)	Mainstream multiethnic classes with flexible groupings; Mainstream multiethnic classes

(*cont'd*)

ESL need (e.g. as identified by ESL CSF)	High	Medium	Low
Student groupings	Similar ESL proficiency age/grade level L1 background	Similar ESL proficiency age/grade level L1 background L1/L2 groupings	Age/grade level L1/L2 groupings
Teacher roles[1] ESL teacher	Direct ESL teaching	Collaborative teaching/ direct ESL teaching; Team teaching	Collaborative teaching/ support teaching in content classes; Resource for content area
Content teacher	Resource for ESL area	Collaborative teaching/ support teaching in ESL classes; Team teaching	Collaborative teaching/ direct content teaching; Direct content teaching

[1] Collaborative teaching is defined as a situation in which an ESL teacher and a content teacher cooperate in some way in the planning, implementing and evaluating of a curriculum. Collaborative teaching may or may not include team and/or support teaching, although the the reverse should always be true. Team teaching is defined as a mode of teaching in which the ESL and content teacher have 'equal responsibility for all students in that program, and for the planning and teaching of that program. Teaching may occur separately but in a highly integrated way or it may be done jointly' (Ministry of Education, 1988: 16); ESL support teaching is defined as when 'the ESL teacher assists the class or subject teachers' in mainstream multiethnic classes (Ministry of Education, 1988: 16).

organisational decisions such as learner/teacher deployment and timetabling options. This is a reversal of the initial simplistic interpretation of mainstreaming in Australian ESL. Individual school practices do still vary greatly, depending on their level of awareness and commitment to ESL issues, but official ESL policy in Victoria, unlike England, highlights choices in curriculum focus and program options, albeit choices which are always constrained and limited by the availability of teaching resources.

Curriculum focus is defined in Davison's (1993b) framework as a choice in emphasis varying along a continuum from content (or subject matter) to language. However, even a curriculum focus at the language 'end' of the continuum is strongly related to the requirements of the mainstream curriculum – in an 'ESL in the mainstream' policy context, such a relationship is perceived as essential and inevitable. There would be no curriculum in a Victorian school setting which does not integrate ESL and 'mainstream' content in some systematic way, although their interpretations of key terms such as language, content and integration may vary considerably, a major issue which will be explored in Chapter 3.

The needs of ESL students, as described in and reported by the ESL Curriculum and Standards framework or its predecessors, are at different stages of ESL development, hence different but integrated modes of delivery will be required at different stages of schooling. Generally older learners will require more direct ESL assistance than younger learners, but the language, literacy, sociocultural and educational knowledge, attitudes and experiences that ESL learners bring to the classroom may vary significantly, even when their goals and aspirations are the same (Aird and Lippmann, 1983; Campbell and McMeniman, 1985; McKay and Scarino, 1991). In terms of classroom/school organisation, this conceptualisation of an ESL program assumes an enormous variety of groupings and varying class sizes, depending on the needs of *all* students. It also implies a range of teaching arrangements, including bilingual teaching and cross-age tutoring as well as small-group conferences and team-teaching.

The Australian ESL profession has consistently argued for a definition of 'mainstreaming' which allows for ESL-specific programs, that is, direct ESL instruction. It is assumed that almost all ESL learners will require regular and intensive small group work with a qualified and experienced ESL specialist at some stage of their learning in order to ensure both access to the common curriculum and the systematic development of the English language. This may be through an introductory period in an intensive language centre integrated into a school, or it may be through timetabled, parallel or elective classes or through flexible groupings within the mainstream classroom. However, the choice of the most appropriate delivery of the curriculum should be guided by the needs of the individual learners, not by rigid ideology.

For example, a recently arrived Somali pre-literate refugee cannot be treated in the same way as a Hong Kong-born student who has studied EFL since primary school and has had successful and uninterrupted L1 literacy development and schooling in Hong Kong. The latter may be able to build on his or her solid foundations in both English language and other content areas with ESL support in the mainstream multiethnic classroom, through individualised or parallel work, use of ESB 'models' and judicious use of pair-work which extends participants in different ways. In Victoria, such a student would also be likely to undertake five hours of common study English in a similar needs class rather than in a larger 'mainstream' English class. In contrast, the Somali student will probably need a far more extensive period of adjustment to formal education and specialised instruction in ESL and literacy as well as intensive instruction in mainstream content areas, especially Mathematics. It is far more effective in terms of student outcomes and resources to conduct this program in a specialist but integrated environment, such as in an intensive language centre within a secondary school. Gradually, over a period of years, such students would choose to transfer into a mainstream multiethnic classroom with ESL support, usually at different stages for different subject areas.

It is important to note that these kinds of flexible groupings are not defined as 'withdrawal'. If you are not yet ready to enter a class, you cannot be withdrawn from it. Rather, such students are seen as being enrolled in intensive, parallel or similar needs classes which are more appropriate to their particular needs. None of these arrangements is compulsory or permanent. Thus, for example, in Victoria, you see quite wide variation between regions and schools as to their preferred modes of ESL delivery depending on their student profile and resources. As you would anticipate, there is also more team teaching in primary schools than in secondary schools and more involvement in intensive language centres/schools by secondary than by primary students, due to the differences in learning and teaching context.

This is not to suggest that all programming delivery issues in ESL have been resolved. It is worth drawing attention to a noticeable gap in program types in Victoria – that is, maintenance, or even transitional, bilingual programs. As can be seen from the data on types of ESL programs (Department of Education, 1997), there are some bilingual ESL programs in the primary sector but none in the secondary sector, although there were a number of successful transitional programs in the mid-1980s in secondary language centres.

In the educational arena, the rationale for bilingual instruction for ESL students is well known and accepted, but in practice this is restricted to the incidental use of the first language (L1) to support learning through English (L2) and development of the first language through separate Language other than English (LOTE) programs. There is also public funding of 'ethnic' teacher aides, interpreting and translating services, multilingual materials and media and after-hours 'ethnic' schools. However, unlike the USA, the Australian ESL situation has been marked by rapid change in migration and settlement patterns with no one dominant minority language group. This creates major resourcing problems, especially in the area of teacher training and materials development. These problems can be overcome, given the necessary political will and community support, but so far this option has not been well developed in Australian ESL. For example, the Australian Language and Literacy Policy (DEET, 1991), in its discussion of modes of delivery of

ESL, talks only about bilingual instruction, but allocates no specific funding to such programs – which is yet another instance of the frequent gap between rhetoric and reality.

This leads us to the question of the role and responsibilities of the ESL teacher in a mainstreamed ESL program. In Victoria, mainstreaming does not mean the end of specialist ESL teachers but rather a redefinition of their role and responsibilities. This redefinition was first officially promulgated in guidelines for *The Teaching of English as a Second Language* (Ministry of Education, 1987: 15–16), which divide the ESL teacher's role into two separate but interrelated components – cross-curricular support and direct instruction – and established the school responsibilities in relation to this. The policy highlighted the vital role of specialist ESL teachers in relation to teaching, the assessment of student needs and the provision of advice to other teachers within schools. At both the whole school level and at the classroom level, the ESL teacher is expected to be involved in and inform the planning, implementation and evaluation of all the key learning areas (Ministry of Education, 1988; Board of Studies, 1996). Such policy statements have also been critical in establishing an agreed definition of an ESL teacher and their qualifications and training.

However, such developments do not happen without supportive administrative structures and policies at the school level and a positive, collaborative teaching and learning environment (Davison, 1992), thus current Victorian ESL policy documents and guidelines stress the importance of the ESL teacher being on the important decision-making bodies within the school and emphasise the shared responsibility for ESL students. In practice there is still a relatively common perception that ESL teachers are the group in the school responsible for ESL students, and that marginalisation is still a concern in some contexts.

In summary, then, in current Victorian policy there is broad agreement as to the definition of a 'mainstreamed' ESL program, characterised by distinctive but variable curriculum focus, flexible teacher and learner groupings and organisational models and specialist ESL teachers. It is based upon strongly defined policies and practice in teacher accreditation and professional development for both ESL and content area teachers. These will now be described.

TEACHER QUALIFICATIONS AND PROFESSIONAL DEVELOPMENT

In the last decade or so in Australia, there has been an unprecedented focus on teacher education in general and language and literacy teacher education in particular. The Quality of Education Review Committee (Karmel, 1985), the Joint Review of Teacher Education (1986), the In-Service Teacher Education Project (DEET, 1988) and Teaching Counts (Beazley, 1992) have all emphasised the need for greater professionalisation of the teaching force and more effective pre-service and in-service education to meet rapidly changing educational demands. In the child language and literacy field there has been a comprehensive review of the pre-service preparation of English and ESL teachers (Christie et al., 1991) reinforced by a Special Follow-Up Conference on Literacy organised by DEET in Canberra in May 1992. The Australian Language and Literacy Council also conducted a review of both adult and child language and literacy teacher preparation and professional development programs (ALLC, 1995).

These reviews have consistently highlighted the need for all teachers to be aware of the sociocultural, linguistic and educational differences, as well as similarities, between learners and emphasise the ability to incorporate linguistic objectives systematically into curricula content and to use appropriate methodology. Such knowledge is encapsulated in recommendations for generalist teacher education by Derewianka and Hammond (1991: 55) who propose that all teachers should have:

> an understanding of the process of first and second language development, including an understanding of the factors which will affect second language development

> - a knowledge of how to adjust classroom practices (curriculum, methodology, materials, organisation, etc.) to cater for the needs of NESB students
> - an awareness of the characteristics of NESB learners
> - an understanding of the implications of bilingualism and role of bilingual education
> - an awareness of the nature of and significance of attitudinal and affective factors in language learning
> - a knowledge of strategies for coping with new arrivals in the mainstream classroom when ESL specialist assistance is not available
> - familiarity with the principles of multiculturalism
> - an understanding of how the role of the ESL teacher complements their own role and the range of organisational models available.

In Victoria, there is now a high level of awareness of the need to prepare all teachers to deal with linguistic and cultural diversity, although much still needs to be done in terms of in-servicing teacher educators and in providing greater depth of coverage of TESOL issues in general teacher education. A recent trend in at least some of the universities (including the University of Melbourne) has been to introduce two-year post-graduate degrees for initial teacher training, which has led to greater consideration of language and literacy issues in the pre-service training of all teachers. However, the relative autonomy of universities, reduced public funding for education generally and the move towards teacher competencies have meant that there is still a significant gap between rhetoric and reality.

With regard to the qualifications of ESL specialists, two national conferences on TESOL in the early 1980s set ground-breaking recommendations for the field. In Victoria, these were reinforced by a State Conference on Teacher Education for ESL, Community Languages and Bilingual Education (May 1985), the recommendations of which were enacted into policy by all the major ESL providers, both child and adult. Influential state sector networks such as the Joint Education Systems and Tertiary Institutions TESOL (JESTI) Forum in

Victoria maintain a 'watchdog' role over the standards of TESOL teachers and facilitate productive dialogue between employers and teacher educators.

In all Australian states, current policy requires ESL specialists to have an ESL 'method' as well as general teaching qualifications to teach in the TESOL field, with a one-year post-graduate specialist diploma becoming the 'industry norm'. In Victoria teachers wishing to specialise in ESL must have completed studies in language and language acquisition, TESOL methodology and curriculum design, policy and programming, and the historical, institutional, political and sociocultural context of Australian TESOL. A teaching practice component is required in all specialist TESOL programs, involving a minimum of 22 days supervised TESOL teaching and the opportunity to link theory and practice through peer observation, modelling and critical reflection.

However, again, this policy has not always been consistently enforced, particularly when local schools have been urged to take increasing responsiblity for staff appointments. For example, in recent years there has been a steady decline in the number of ESL qualified teachers appointed to ESL-tagged positions in both primary and secondary schools. Provision of appropriate incentives and leave has been made to allow these teachers to obtain such qualifications and there is an ongoing commitment to such improvement of standards, although the trend towards greater school autonomy in staffing will continue to make it more difficult to ensure that policy is translated into practice.

Another emerging problem is the move to replace existing teacher accreditation mechanisms with a competency-based system. The response of the ESL profession to this potential threat to established standards has been cautious support and pre-emptive action. For example, a national statement of TESOL teacher competencies has been developed by the Association of Teachers of English to Speakers of Other Languages (ATESOL) (NSW), for the Australian Council of TESOL Associations. However there remain deep-seated problems around the issue of competencies which will be taken up in more detail in Chapter 4.

At the in-service level, there is also strong policy and structural support for mainstreaming ESL provision. Practising teachers can access the publicly funded ESL in the Mainstream professional development which was developed in 1987 with Commonwealth funding and has been very successful in raising all teachers' awareness of ESL needs and strategies (Kay, 1991). Its aims (Education Department of South Australia, 1991: 3–4) are:

- To develop teachers' understandings of the language needs of (LOTE background) students and ways of meeting their needs.
- To develop awareness of materials and teaching approaches which take account of the diverse cultural backgrounds and experiences of students in all classes.
- To further develop the collaborative working relationships between classroom/subject teachers and ESL teachers in their schools.
- To increase teachers' awareness of the need for ESL programs.

It is a ten-week course of 20–30 hours contact conducted by a teacher-tutor, with set reading requirements for each unit and between-unit activities. It is deliberately structured to ensure the commitment of the whole school to the in-service activity and the active participation of administrators as well as content or generalist classroom teachers. Usually three staff from each school, one ESL and two mainstream teachers attend together, but such is its current momentum that in Victoria, where it has been offered since 1992, the entire staff of some schools have completed the course. Over 6,000 people nationally have completed the full program (South Australian Teaching and Curriculum Centre, 1995).

However, there is some concern that the high profile and short-term gains achieved by the ESL in the Mainstream course have perhaps obscured some significant limitations in its orientation and structure which are only now beginning to emerge. This issue will be taken up further in Chapter 4.

CURRICULUM AND ASSESSMENT FRAMEWORKS

The development of common curriculum and assessment frameworks in all key learning areas has been a major area of policy development in the last five years, but this has not been without controversy. In Victoria there was a struggle first to ensure that ESL as a distinct curriculum area was included in this process, then to ensure that the policy documents produced were relatively congruent with current practice. It is a measure of the degree of cooperation between key stakeholders in ESL education in Victoria that to a large extent these efforts have been successful.

The English Curriculum and Standards Framework (CSF) (Board of Studies, 1996, 2000) is the current key curriculum and assessment policy document used in planning, implementing and evaluating ESL curriculum outcomes, irrespective of whether learners are in a mainstream multiethnic classroom or separate ESL classes. In its conceptualisation of the goals and content of an ESL curriculum it builds on previous work in the field, in particular on the ESL Scales (Curriculum Corporation, 1995) and on the ESL Framework of Stages (McKay and Scarino, 1991) which has been used as the framework for the last four or five years to develop Victorian curriculum materials for both primary and secondary contexts.

The Curriculum and Standards Framework (CSF) ESL Companion to the English CSF is based on the assumption that there is a need 'to control English language input, and systematically and explicitly teach English language skills to ESL students before the outcomes of the English CSF will be appropriate for them' (Board of Studies, 1996: 1). It provides both an overview of the broad overlapping stages of ESL development for the Years P–10 and 'a benchmark of what might be expected of ESL learners given optimum learning conditions' (Board of Studies 1996: 2) (Figure 2.2 overleaf). Each stage is divided into three strands: listening and speaking, reading and writing. Each mode is further subdivided into four sub-strands: communication; contextual understanding; linguistic structures and features; and (communication and learning) strategies. The description of each stage comprises two key elements: a detailed statement of the curriculum

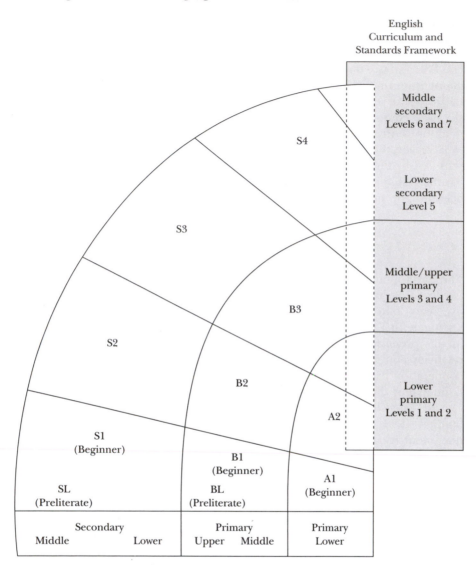

Figure 2.2 Stages of the ESL companion to the English CSF

focus appropriate to that stage and a list of expected learning outcomes, expressed as action statements or competencies. Each outcome is accompanied by a series of performance indicators (see sample, Figure 2.3). (Only extracts of the 'Curriculum Standards Framework' have been included and students and teachers should consult the whole document which can be found at www.bos.vic.edu.au/csf.) The overall framework allows for different pathways for ESL students at different levels of schooling, with different levels of English language proficiency and with different first language literacy or educational experiences. It also allows for variable rates of development. The

Figure 2.3 Sample from CSF ESL companion and performance indicators S2 Speaking and listening in Board of Studies (2000) pp. 138–41.

Curriculum Focus

Communication

Teachers help students build upon their basic understanding of spoken English to communicate for a widening range of social and academic purposes. Teachers set tasks that draw on the students' developing knowledge of the vocabulary and language structures of English as well as their understanding of word stress, rhythm and intonation. These tasks contain some degree of unpredictability to challenge students to become more independent users of English. For example, in structured activities, students may be supported to listen for a range of purposes to spoken texts which may involve a change of topic or lack chronological order. In pair or group work activities or through role modelling, students are provided with the English to use when negotiating or clarifying meaning. Students are given a range of activities, where they listen to, question, clarify and report back to the teacher or to other students. Teachers set tasks where students listen to, give and follow instructions, play games, and follow classroom procedures.

Aspects of language

Contextual understanding

Through appropriate classroom activities, such as role-plays, short dialogues and structured listening tasks, teachers help students to develop their awareness of how contextual factors influence the ways English is used and interpreted. Teachers help students extract selected information from accessible spoken or visual texts, for instance teacher instructions, taped dialogues or videos, or accessible CD-ROM materials on topics from across the curriculum. Contextual cues, including visual support, and spoken features, such as stress and intonation are also focused on to assist students to understand. Teachers support students as they learn to use formulaic expressions and subject-specific vocabulary appropriate to the context.

Linguistic structures and features

Teachers guide students through speaking and listening activities that help them build on and extend the use of their existing vocabulary and structures. Teachers highlight examples of how stress, rhythm and intonation are used to convey and also interpret information in spoken texts. Teachers introduce students to both familiar and unfamiliar language in context as they engage with a greater range of spoken texts from a subject-based curriculum. Students' understanding of subject-based texts is extended through content material which reflects more complex relationships, placing greater demands on the students as they deal with changes in location, events and characters. Teachers support students to take longer turns in interactive activities through the use of simple conjunctions as well as simple formulaic expressions.

Strategies

In the classroom context, teachers support the use of creative utterances by providing students with activities requiring them to draw on all their available resources in different ways to respond to or deliver messages. Students are encouraged to use the opportunity of pair and group work for exploratory talk with their peers instead of relying only on teacher guidance. Through activities such as pair or group work, teachers help students develop communicative strategies, for example, asking for clarification, basic paraphrasing and circumlocution. Students learn to use their existing language structures to make longer utterances.

Figure 2.3   (*cont'd*)

Learning Outcomes & Indicators

At Secondary: Stage S2 the student is able to:

Communication

S2.1   **Interact in routine social or subject-based activities using mainly creative**
ESSLS201   **utterances and handling a degree of unpredictability.**

> *This is evident when the student is able to:*

- extract specific information from short spoken or visual texts, using guide questions from the teacher
- comprehend the gist of a range of simple instructions, descriptions, explanations
- interact in English with peers in pair or group work activities in familiar contexts
- use modelled language to recount the steps in a classroom activity
- express intended meanings without relying on negotiation of meaning by the listener, e.g. give reasons for unfinished homework or absences from class
- express simple opinions, describe feelings, e.g. 'I feel sorry for him because . . .'
- give a short classroom talk on a familiar topic.

Aspects of language
Contexual understanding

S2.2   **Use appropriate English in familiar classroom situations, demonstrating an**
ESSLS202   **awareness that English changes according to purpose and audience.**

> *This is evident when the student is able to:*

- use simple, modelled language appropriately in familiar contexts to give instructions, describe, explain
- show an understanding of when to use common polite forms, e.g. 'Excuse me Miss', 'Would you like one?'

Linguistic structures and features

S2.3   **Use and respond to the structures and features of spoken English, in most**
ESSLS203   **familiar and some unfamiliar classroom situations.**

> *This is evident when the student is able to:*

- use pronouns, and a limited range of conjunctions, e.g. *so, then, but, also, because,* to link ideas, e.g. She waited for Alex at the station *but* he didn't come
- pause appropriately to make extended utterances more intelligible
- use stress to emphasise key words in sentences, e.g. Birds don't have *fur* they have *feathers*
- distinguish, with guidance, different intonation patterns, e.g. for questions, statements, lists etc.

Strategies

S2.4   **Use a repertoire of communication strategies to negotiate communication in English**
ESSLS204 **and to support interaction.**

> *This is evident when, for example, the student is able to:*

- deduce the meaning of some unknown words from context cues
- repeat sentences, modelling aspects of the rhythm, intonation and pronunciation of the other speaker
- initiate and maintain exchanges, e.g. using simple conversational openers, turn taking, leave taking
- make direct appeals for assistance, e.g. 'How do you say this in English?'
- make some extended utterances by experimenting with known features or vocabulary to express new meanings
- use eye contact appropriately in a short classroom talk.

actual methods of assessment and choice of resources and teaching activities are decided by the teacher (although there is detailed Course Advice for different ESL teaching contexts). It is also assumed that the teacher has the skills to plan, implement and evaluate appropriate integrated ESL and content curriculum for each specific ESL program.

The CSF has been generally very well received within the educational community, and ESL teachers in particular see it as critically important in affirming and legitimating their specialist knowledge and responsibilities. However, there remain a number of concerns with the CSF, including its reliability as a reporting tool and the reductionist and fragmented quality of its descriptions, an inevitable characteristic of competency-based curriculum. One problem more particular to the ESL field is the way in which the framework maps on to the key learning area of English, thus suggesting that ESL is a subset of English and ESL learners moving towards some unmarked cultural and linguistic norm. Within the ESL profession, many would prefer it to be conceptualised in curriculum terms as a Language other than English (LOTE), like Italian or Chinese, at the same time being integrated into and influencing all other key learning areas. There is ESL advice embedded within the Course Advice for each key learning area, but this is not seen as sufficient. On the other hand, the close relationship between English and ESL is obvious and desirable. This debate has once again foregrounded the complex issue of the definition of ESL as a distinct area of curriculum activity, which will be explored in Chapters 3 and 4.

At the senior levels of schooling, similar issues of relationship and overlap have arisen. In a recent review of the Victorian Certificate of Education (VCE), which covers the final two years of school, there is a common and compulsory English study for all students, irrespective of language background or competence. Substantial course advice and professional development support are provided on how to cater for ESL students across the curriculum; all external exams in English are set by a panel consisting of 50 per cent ESL-qualified teachers; and all papers completed by ESL students are marked by ESL-qualified examiners according to modified criteria. Exams in other subjects are all vetted by ESL-qualified specialists. More time is given to ESL students to complete examination requirements, bilingual dictionaries are allowed and the number of texts studied is reduced.

However, in curriculum terms, at the senior level ESL is still perceived as something that needs to be taken into account in planning and assessment, not as an objective in its own right. In other words, the content curriculum, rather than the learners' stage of ESL acquisition, drives the language choices. In a recent review of VCE English, it was argued that there needed to be a complementary focus on teaching ESL in the context of other curricular content, not just the reverse (Board of Studies, 1995). A commitment was given to establish an accredited course which gives recognition to the second language learning achievements of ESL students, similar to the situation in many Australian universities where ESL is a part of standard award-bearing courses in modern languages.

The nature of ESL as a curriculum area has also been problematised in the development of the CSF by the demands that only non-technical (i.e. non-linguistic) language be used in its curriculum descriptions and indicators of standards. This also reveals a lack of understanding or acceptance of ESL as a 'content' area; the same demand would not be made of Mathematics or Science. Many linguistic concepts and ideas can only be expressed using technical language, and the CSF, like all other curriculum documents, requires appropriate professional development in order to be used effectively. It also requires appropriate implementational frameworks showing how curriculum can be developed for different contexts at different stages of ESL development. It is this area of curriculum that is least theorised and conceptualised, although there is much good practice. We will return to the issue of curriculum focus in Chapter 3, but first we will examine some examples of actual grassroots practice in curriculum integration.

PEDAGOGIC PRACTICE

Current classroom practice in Australian child ESL education has been shaped and influenced by a number of factors, including recent trends in both mother tongue and English as a Foreign Language education. Teachers often draw on a great diversity of methods and approaches in their day-to-day teaching, although some common characteristics of such teaching have been defined (Ferguson, 1991; Derewianka and Hammond, 1991).

Some quite elaborated and explicit teaching approaches that involve the specific organisation of language, subject matter and teaching procedures have also been developed, most notably the 'topic approach' and the 'genre-based approach', both of which have also been accompanied by a wealth of teaching materials. The topic approach is not widely known outside Australia, and although genre-based pedagogy has received widespread international publicity, it is not necessarily well understood.

The topic approach (Cleland and Evans, 1984, 1985, 1988) was developed by ESL teachers in order to meet the needs of adolescent students from LOTE backgrounds who were completing short-term intensive English courses prior to entry or return to study in mainstream secondary schools in Victoria. It is used widely within intensive language centres and ESL programs within Victoria as well as less frequently inter-state. Elements have been adapted and incorporated into mainstream classroom practices, although not in any systematic way. Three textbooks (including both student and teacher books) have been published and two videos produced. In addition, many teacher-produced materials using the approach have been developed and published in local journals or through institutions.

Cleland and Evans (1984: 4) state that their approach evolved from classroom practice but not in a theoretical 'vacuum':

> We have applied, extended and modified various notions about the nature of language until our own interpretation has emerged. We have crystallised the

notions about language teaching that we believe are of the utmost importance in teaching and learning about language into four key statements. These statements reinforce the view that language is meaning centred.

These statements assume that language competence 'is based upon the learner's knowledge of linguistic rules and his (sic) ability to use this knowledge for effective communication', teaching should be subordinated to learning, meaningful language comes from personal experience and language learning is a problem-solving process. The notions that they drew on came from the work of Barnes and Britton on the role of language, particularly talk, in learning (Barnes, 1976; Britton, 1970), Gattegno's 'Silent Way' approach to language teaching (Gattegno, 1972, 1976) and Widdowson's arguments that attention to both language use in making meaning and language form is important in learning to communicate in another language (Widdowson, 1978).

The topic approach consists of four key stages, described and exemplified in detailed teachers' notes and explanations of the approach, and in recommended teaching strategies and activities (Cleland and Evans, 1984, 1985, 1988) (Figure 2.4 overleaf).

In the first stage, 'the visual stage', a visual is used to present the topic, and students use exploratory talk to develop their understanding. Terminology is modelled and practised. Students construct spoken and written sentences about the topic. In the second stage, 'building a reading passage', statements about the visual are assessed as true or false by the students. These are then joined, sequenced and organised into paragraphs to form a tightly written piece that describes the topic as presented in the visual. In the third stage, 'analysing and extending reading passage', a variety of written exercises explicitly focus students' attention on the features of language in a reading passage. A second, more complex passage may also be presented for comparison with the first. In the final stage, 'creating a passage', the students produce their own piece of writing, based on the informational and conceptual content of the topic, and hopefully utilising features of language encountered in the topic.

This approach can be used to develop topics of varying linguistic and conceptual complexity. The specific details and structure of the activities in the different stages of each topic can be varied according to the nature of the topic and the specific circumstances of particular groups of students, and there can be variation in the nature of the exercises and activities.

Williams (1995: 44) describes the implementation of the topic approach:

> Students encounter and come to understand (or revise) a topic which is then used as a meaningful context for new language input, practice of language in terms of both expressing the students' understanding of the topic and in terms of manipulation of specific features and aspects of the language. It is encountered and developed in such a way that different amounts of previous knowledge of the topic amongst the students can be exploited and accommodated. The manner of presentation, involving students attempting to provide explanations based on their interpretation of a visual, is such that it could be revision for some students, or it could be the introduction of the subject matter of the topic

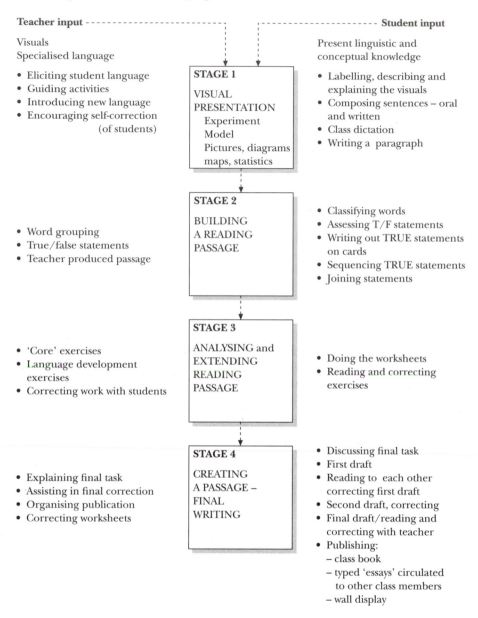

Teacher input - **Student input**

Visuals
Specialised language

- Eliciting student language
- Guiding activities
- Introducing new language
- Encouraging self-correction
  (of students)

Present linguistic and
conceptual knowledge

- Labelling, describing and
  explaining the visuals
- Composing sentences – oral
  and written
- Class dictation
- Writing a paragraph

STAGE 1

VISUAL
PRESENTATION
  Experiment
  Model
  Pictures, diagrams
  maps, statistics

STAGE 2

BUILDING
A READING
PASSAGE

- Word grouping
- True/false statements
- Teacher produced passage

- Classifying words
- Assessing T/F statements
- Writing out TRUE statements
  on cards
- Sequencing TRUE statements
- Joining statements

STAGE 3

ANALYSING and
EXTENDING
READING
PASSAGE

- 'Core' exercises
- Language development
  exercises
- Correcting work with students

- Doing the worksheets
- Reading and correcting
  exercises

STAGE 4

CREATING
A PASSAGE –
FINAL
WRITING

- Explaining final task
- Assisting in final correction
- Organising publication
- Correcting worksheets

- Discussing final task
- First draft
- Reading to each other
  correcting first draft
- Second draft, correcting
- Final draft/reading and
  correcting with teacher
- Publishing:
  – class book
  – typed 'essays' circulated
    to other class members
  – wall display

Figure 2.4   The topic framework (Cleland and Evans, 1988: 2)

to other students for the very first time. The topic is constructed in such a
way as to include information and concepts considered essential to the topic in
terms of its subject matter, while not expanding beyond a core area, so a topic
on the history of Chinese domination of Vietnam in the first millennium AD
will focus on the political themes of invasion, rebellion and independence,
rather than the cultural consequences. Language is introduced at the levels of

vocabulary (both phonology and orthography can be a focus), sentence structure, the structure of texts and style of discourse, with an emphasis on formal, academic styles of writing. The diverse language elements are encountered in differing ways. Some features are encountered only in an experiential manner, as students use English to make and understand meaning and complete tasks. Other features are dealt with in a clearly analytical manner involving explicit discussion of specific features.

The topic approach is an example of practice explicitly developed to meet the demands of the Victorian ESL classroom. On the other hand, the genre-based approach was originally developed within English mother tongue education in metropolitan Sydney but has been widely adapted for ESL contexts. There is now a range of classroom materials and guidelines for teachers (Callaghan and Knapp, 1989; Christie et al., 1992; Derewianka, 1991; Love, 1996; Rothery and Stenglin, 1994), exemplifying the approach, its theoretical underpinnings have been discussed in many academic articles and books (Christie, 1987a, 1987c; Hammond, 1987; Martin, 1984: 25, 1985, 1986; Martin et al., 1997; Rothery, 1984) and its applications in teacher education explored in detail (Christie et al., 1991). It has also been the subject of a great deal of spirited critique (Freedman and Medway, 1994; Reid, 1987).

The notion of genre, 'a staged, goal-oriented purposeful activity in which the speaker/writer engages as a member of the culture' (1984: 25), is theoretically grounded in the extension and adaptation of systemic functional linguistics (Halliday, 1985; Halliday and Hasan, 1985). The label 'genre theory' is used both to refer to this theory and to talk about its application to learning and teaching. In its explicit articulation of the function or purpose of a genre and its linguistic form, genre theory been valuable in highlighting features of the social context which shape linguistic texts. It also provides a systematic framework for talking about text level features and grammatical patterns. As Hammond et al. (1992: 51) argue:

> The theoretical basis of systemic linguistics which assumes language is essentially a social process, provides a systematic basis for exploring how cultural and social differences are realised in speaking and writing, in ways that are impossible with theories such as psycholinguistic and schema theory, which presume language is essentially an individual activity.

Genre pedagogy varies from context to context and continues to evolve but the core elements are encapsulated in a recently revised model (Rothery and Stenglin, 1994). This consists of a cycle of three key stages which can be entered at any point, deconstruction (formerly conceptualised as modelling) in which examples of the particular genre are analysed and discussed in order to understand why and how they are organised to make effective meaning, joint construction of a text by teacher and students, followed by independent construction (Figure 2.5). In addition, critical elements which influence all stages are the setting of context and the building up of knowledge about the field or topic. Derewianka and Hammond (1991: 52) describe the application of genre theory to a topic on mammals:

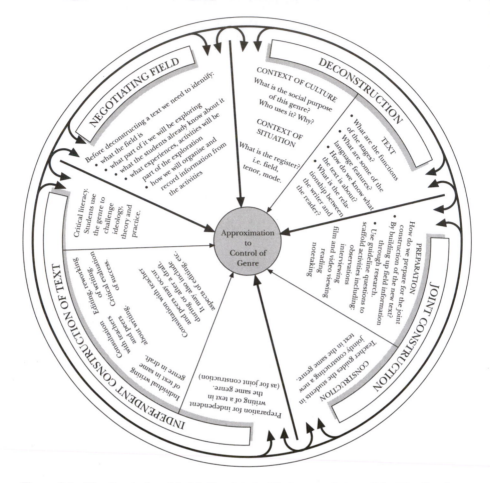

Figure 2.5 The Curriculum Model. Reprinted with the permission of the New South Wales Department of Education and Training (Australia)

(Firstly) it is important that there be ample input about mammals from the teacher, from other 'experts', from videos, reference books, as well as opportunities for first-hand observations, comparisons, classifications and discussion. It is through the oral interaction and discussion of information gathered from various sources that ESL students develop and control the vocabulary and language patterns that enable them to talk about mammals. At this point the emphasis is very much on communicative interaction, in order to build control of the language necessary for studying the topic . . . the ESL teacher is likely to draw on activities that typically would be part of any ESL program. As well the teacher may include lessons that focus on particular aspects of vocabulary and grammar. . . . As the students move towards writing about the topic it is important that they also have access to information about how to shape and organise the text. . . . Thus it is essential that ESL students are provided with models of the texts that they will need to write and opportunities for shared construction of texts with teacher and other students before they are expected to write independently.

Such a pedagogy, through its explicit modelling and analysis of the schematic structure and distinctive linguistic patterning of particular genres, can help ESL students to deal with the demands of the content curriculum and, at the same time, build up their academic language skills.

More recent adaptations of genre theory have begun to incorporate aspects of critical literacy into the pedagogical framework. However, many in the field would argue that as the theory provides a mechanism to make the structure and functions of the powerful genres explicit, genre theory has always had the capacity to promote critical literacy. As Threadgold (1988: 100) observes:

> To teach genres, discourses and stories is inevitably to make 'visible' the social construction and transmission of ideologies, power relationships and social identities.

However, genre theorists themselves have pointed out that there is a danger in some interpretations of genre theory that discourse structures will be oversimplified to become a series of rigid formulas (Hammond et al., 1992), an issue which will be raised again in Chapter 3.

Both the topic approach and genre theory are valuable and effective resources for teachers but they also raise certain problem areas for classroom practice. For example, both approaches are pitched at the unit of work level which means that they provide no systematic way of linking units of work. Although both stress the importance of embedding language-related analysis and practice in meaningful contexts, there is some tension in the relationship they set up between language and content. Both advocate explicit teaching about language features but the implications of this for the balance between form and meaning are left unexplored. Finally, both approaches have been criticised for assimilationist assumptions and a lack of a critical perspective. These issues parallel some of the concerns that have been raised in relation to the CSF, and will be taken up in Chapters 3 and 4.

CONCLUSIONS

The push to mainstream ESL in Victoria over the last decade has stimulated some innovative concepts, policies and practices in ESL programming, curriculum and assessment and professional development support as well as many examples of 'ESL in the mainstream' learning and teaching. However, there remain significant unresolved problems both in theory and in practice which constrain, even undermine, the current effectiveness of ESL education.

One of the most critical concerns revolves around the issue of the relationship of ESL teaching to the mainstream content area curriculum. The ESL profession has promoted a particular role and type of curriculum activity, but the actual integration of language and content teaching in Australia is relatively untheorised and implicit, and models of practice are not theoretically linked. Specific problems relating to the identification, selection and sequencing of curriculum elements have been buried beneath the far more powerful and pressing political problem of 'mainstreaming' or are assumed to have been resolved in the development of broad curriculum frameworks.

Another key concern relates to the relationship between policy and practice, exemplified by the widespread concern to monitor and evaluate the actual impact of changes in the conceptualisation and delivery of ESL education on students, teachers and schools, and to ensure that evolving policy addresses the real problems at the chalkface. As in Canada and England, TESOL is an emergent profession which has had a very unsettled and short history and faces an even more precarious future. There is always concern over gaps between rhetoric and reality, a constant struggle to balance competing priorities and a fragile, even threatened sense of self exemplified in the continual need to define and hold the field together and educate the 'other', whether the other be subject teachers, administrators or policy-makers. As a field, Australian ESL has often been accused of conforming to the old cliché of wanting 'to have its cake and eat it, too'. There is some truth in this in current policy and practice: the claim to be both methodology and 'content', both service and subject area, both in the mainstream yet separate, both English yet not English, both conforming yet critical. It could be argued that this has led to some fundamental contradictions in ESL professional orientations and practices which beg resolution. The situation is exacerbated by the continually changing nature of the sociopolitical and institutional context in which the ESL field is located and the wider power struggles in education over the nature of professional expertise and over control of the educational agenda.

These two major concerns will be explored in more detail in the next two chapters in order to resolve, or at least articulate and clarify the issues and suggest future directions.

NOTE

1. I am particularly indebted to my colleague, Alan Williams, for comments and contributions to this chapter.

Chapter 3

Integrating language and content: unresolved issues

Chris Davison and Alan Williams

INTRODUCTION

In the previous chapter, it was argued that Australia, like other English-speaking immigrant countries, has witnessed rather intense debate over the role and content of the ESL program, especially its relationship to the mainstream. There has been strong policy support for the concept of an integrated language and content curriculum. However, despite, or even because of, the very public development of national and state ESL curriculum and reporting frameworks, less attention has been paid to the issue of how actually to develop and implement such an integrated language and content curriculum in a 'mainstreamed' ESL environment. In Victoria various models and approaches to integration have been developed for use at the level of the lesson or unit of work, while, at the same time, the Curriculum and Standards Framework (CSF) has established guidelines for schools as to the broad curriculum focus at different stages of ESL development and the key learning outcomes to be expected. However, there is a gap in curriculum planning and development at the intermediary level – at the level of curriculum or syllabus design.

We believe that this gap creates a vacuum in both theory and practice which has the potential to undermine the effectiveness of a 'mainstreamed' ESL program. It leaves unresolved inherent contradictions and tensions in language and content integration. This chapter will explore this issue in more detail in order to clarify the actual nature of the perceived problem and suggest areas for further research, policy development and professional support. First, however, we will look at the rationale for, and the definition of, language and content integration.

LANGUAGE AND CONTENT INTEGRATION: RATIONALE

English-speaking countries with high ESL populations have been influenced by similar theoretical work on language and content integration, but they have selected and adapted different perspectives to suit their own purposes.

Australia, like England and Canada, has had a long history of different forms of 'concurrent learning' or integrated language and content-based teaching in ESL, stimulated by the early work of Widdowson (1978). Particular insights into language and content issues have also been derived from research into the Canadian French immersion programs (Lightbown and Spada, 1990; Swain, 1985) and from the 'language across the curriculum' movement in schools that began in the early 1970s and has continued to evolve in different ways over the last 20 years (Barnes, 1976; Britton, 1970, 1975, 1979; Bullock, 1975; Lightbown and Spada, 1990; Marland, 1977). This has led to the development of a variety of different models of locally developed language and content curriculum integration in Australia, including the action-sequence approach (Corbel, 1986) and the topic approach (Cleland and Evans, 1984, 1985, 1988). As well, pedagogical extensions of genre theory (Martin, 1986; Martin et al., 1987; Rothery, 1984; Christie, 1987a, 1987b; Cope and Kalantzis, 1993; Derewianka and Hammond, 1991) have been widely used in ESL programs since the early to mid-1980s. A common rationale has developed for such approaches, despite their different theoretical origins and orientations.

Williams (1995) suggests that this common rationale for language and content integration is derived from four main arguments widely promulgated in the literature.

The first argument relates to the time that ESL students take to acquire language proficiency to match their English-speaking peers in academic achievement. There are no large-scale Australian studies of this issue as the lack of any standardised testing in schools in the last 20 years has made the collection of such data difficult. However, anecdotal evidence (and official ESL policy) supports the findings of North American research which suggests that, depending on a number of factors, it can take between five and ten years for students to match their English-speaking peers in achievement in subject matter learning (Collier, 1987, 1989, 1995; Cummins, 1996). The provision of concurrent instruction in both subject matter and language is advocated as a means of speeding up this process, an argument that appears straightforward and unproblematic.

The second argument relates to the assumed distinction between language proficiency in social contexts, and proficiency in academic domains. This is frequently cited as indicating the need for teaching approaches that explicitly address the language of academic domains. The distinction that Cummins (1980) makes between 'Basic Interpersonal Communication Skills' (BICS), which relate to language use in day-to-day familiar contexts, with an orientation to social interaction, and 'Cognitive Academic Language Proficiency' (CALP), which are language skills related to language used in formal situations and academic study, is frequently mentioned in the literature (Brinton et al., 1989; Cantoni-Harvey, 1987; Chamot & O'Malley, 1992, 1994; Crandall, 1987; Crandall et al., 1987) and has been very influential in Australian TESOL. Claims that ESL students need particular help with CALP are common. The distinction and claim are usually treated as unproblematic, despite Cummins's subsequent revision of the distinction (which he came to see as an oversimplification) and debate about the relationship between such dichotomies and deficit theory (Adamson, 1993). In some discussions, this dichotomy is extended to the notion of social proficiency providing a threshold level of proficiency for the development of academic language skills (Cantoni-Harvey 1987) – a view that has become highly problematic in view of Cummins's rejection of a dichotomy between BICS and CALP, in favour of two intersecting axes, one indicating the level of contextual support and the other the level of cognitive demands involved in particular instances of language use (Cummins, 1993). The invocation of a distinction between 'social' and 'academic', while appealing to teachers who often perceive relatively speedy progress in the ability of ESL students to use English effectively in social interaction, but not in academic domains, is problematic because of the lack of clarity in determining the precise nature of the distinction between these entities.

Related to the claim of a distinctive variety of academic language is the sub-argument that attention to the nature of tasks and patterns of interaction in an academic context is a significant factor in the success or failure of students. This view holds that language instruction alone is not sufficient to enable such students to succeed in mainstream studies (Adamson, 1993; Richards & Hurley, 1990; Saville-Troike, 1984). Such a view has been used to argue that ESL students need support in accessing key subject matter, some type of modelling of valued patterns of behaviour, as well as provision of language support (see, for example, Crandall, 1987).

A third justification for an integrated language and content curriculum is its claimed consistency with current 'communicative' trends in language teaching that emphasise the meaningful use of language in appropriate contexts in the language classroom (Crandall, 1987; Cantoni-Harvey, 1987; Brinton et al., 1989; Snow et al., 1989). The subject matter of academic learning is adopted as a meaningful basis for the selection of language for teaching and the means of integrating various language features and skills to be taught. However, it does need to be pointed out that this justification is simply a claim of consistency with the prevailing paradigm in language teaching, which itself may be problematic.

The fourth argument presented to support an integrated language and content curriculum is that it is 'efficient' in providing concurrent learning in two areas. Research evidence is invoked which suggests that such a curriculum is a means of enhancing language learning while not interfering with subject matter learning (Brinton et al., 1989; Crandall, 1987; Wesche, 1993). Similar results from immersion education programs are cited to support this claim. Some writers quote research findings that indicate that content delivered through a second language improves second language proficiency and delivers content knowledge and skills just as efficiently as Ll instruction (Brinton et al., 1989; Wesche, 1993), while others cite anecdotal reports of increased motivation by students in their learning (Brinton et al., 1989; Crandall, 1987).

Many of these arguments are essentially intuitive, and there is a very limited research base to support these claims, despite their widespread face validity with ESL teachers. Thus, it is essential that a rigorous definition of an integrated language and content curriculum and its related methodology can be provided, so that both can be subjected to scrutiny and evaluation. However, in the ESL literature, conflicting and even confused definitions of language and content integration need to be first disentangled.

INTEGRATED LANGUAGE AND CONTENT CURRICULUM: PROBLEMS OF DEFINITION

Definitions of language and content integration in the ESL literature are complicated by the diverse theoretical origins and orientations of the field. Attempts to clarify particular concepts are also rendered problematic by the breadth of key terms such as language, content and integration. For example, the work of Brinton and colleagues (1989: 2) focuses on 'the integration of particular content with language-teaching aims'; Crandall (1987: 1) also speaks of 'integrating language instruction with subject matter instruction . . .'. Snow et al. (1989: 201) describe 'a model of language education that integrates language and content instruction'. However, the way in which such approaches are defined would seem to depend absolutely on the interpretation of these key terms and their relationship. The difficulties of definition have increased as the theoretical understandings about what is being learnt and taught have been explored and elaborated.

In the ESL field, language has traditionally been interpreted to mean 'communicative competence' (Bachman, 1990; Canale and Swain, 1980; Hymes, 1972; Savignon, 1991) and content as the meanings that are made, that is, what is communicated. However, attempts to identify and describe what such communicative ability involves have led to increasingly complex identification of its components. Early attempts to define this notion added competence in the sociolinguistic rules that govern the use of language ('sociolinguistic competence') as well as the rules that govern the structure of the language ('grammatical competence') (Hymes, 1972). These were elaborated by Canale and Swain (1980), who identified 'strategic competence' (the ability to participate successfully in, and to help to shape, interactions), as an additional crucial element in communicative language ability. Canale and Swain further broadened the elements that contribute to communicative language ability by arguing that the general knowledge of individuals, and their understanding of the nature of discourse, impinged on their ability to use language effectively. Bachman (1990) provides a similar yet more elaborated model, which sees communicative language ability as an interaction between a range of factors – the general knowledge of the individual, the language knowledge of the individual, appropriate psycho-physiological mechanisms and the context of the situation. In this model language knowledge is broken down into over a dozen factors within grammatical and pragmatic knowledge. While these theoretical views are becoming more specific in identifying the elements that comprise linguistic competence, the interactions between these elements are still expressed in generalities and they are still restricted to individual/psychological views of the language learner.

'Communicatively oriented' approaches to language curricula have tended to take situations of language use as the key elements in a language curriculum, in order to provide some meaning-based unit around which a wide variety of factors, both linguistic and non-linguistic in nature, can be integrated. A number of such bases have been proposed, including functions and notions (Wilkins, 1976), tasks[1] (Long and Crookes, 1992; Prabhu, 1987), activities (Scarino et al., 1988) and situations and topics (Krahnke, 1987). In addition, there have been claims that language syllabus should continue to be influenced by language forms, which draw either on a limited range of identifiable progressions and stages (Pienemann, 1989), or on frequency of use of vocabulary items and collocations drawn from an extensive corpus of samples of real life language use in a lexically based syllabus (Nation, 1991; Willis, 1991).

'Integration' is a significant dilemma for proponents of such a view of language, but their debates essentially revolve around the issue of the balance between focus on form and focus on meaning. While for many it is a matter of degree – the issue being what relative balance of each should be provided in particular teaching contexts (Stern, 1992) – debate about whether any focus on language as form should be included in language teaching is spirited (for a recent exchange on this issue see Krashen (1993) and Pienemann and Lightbown (1993)).

Howatt (1984) has identified a 'strong' form of communicative teaching, which holds that students should only be involved in making meanings in classrooms, with no focus on language form. This can be contrasted with a 'weak' form of communicative language teaching, which holds that while genuine dealing with content or meaning is an essential part of language classrooms, a suitably contextualised focus on language form should be included in teaching, and that contextualised language practice is not only appropriate, but necessary (Long, 1985; Long and Crookes, 1992). Integration is thus defined as a psycholinguistic issue by these writers, a matter of internal linguistic and cognitive processing.

On the other hand, there are significant critiques of the very notion of language as 'communicative competence' and its separation of language and content. For example, Bernstein (1996: 56) argues that such a view of language assumes 'an in-built procedural democracy, an in-built creativity, an in-built virtuous self-regulation . . . a celebration of what we are in contrast to what we have become'. He suggests that the 'idealism of competence' has abstracted the individual from the analysis of the distribution of power and principles of control which selectively specialise modes of acquisition and realisation. Such a view of the integral relationship between language and content also underpins the systemic functional linguistic framework shaping Australian genre theory. For example, Halliday (1978) would argue that the uses of language are inseparable from its social functions, with language defined in terms of its meaning potential, as a set of linguistic choices to be made. Mohan (1986: 1), working within a language socialisation framework, draws on this Hallidayan notion of language to explicitly challenge the separation of language and content (also see Chapter 6, this volume):

> A language is a system that relates what is being talked about (content) and the means used to talk about it (expression). Linguistic content is inseparable from linguistic expression.

Kramsch (1993: 4) also argues against 'dubious dichotomies', claiming that all students acquire content as they learn the new forms of the language, although 'much of this content is not verbalised, it is the unspoken ideological substratum of the educational system, the community, the peer group, the family'.

This view of language problematises the very notion of 'integration' in the narrow psycholinguistic sense, in that you cannot integrate something which is already integrated. However, a key requirement of language socialisation is participation in social or collective activities with others, in situations which require or demand particularised cognitive and linguistic skills. Integration is still an issue but in Vygotskian terms, in order to support the effective language socialisation of the learner (see Mohan, Chapter 6 and Leung, Chapter 11, this volume for further discussion). From this perspective, the issue of language and content integration is seen as a different set of relationships, sociocultural rather than psycholinguistic, socially constructed and ideological rather than universal or autonomous.

Examined from this perspective there is a second, very different, interpretation of the terms language and content in ESL education, that is, as labels for different fields of curriculum activity and professional and/or institutional allegiances or affiliations. For example, ESL teachers (significantly, not 'content' teachers) commonly use these terms to define what they see as critical differences between ESL and other school subject areas in their curriculum concerns. This sharp distinction, or classification, in Bernstein's (1990) terms, can also be seen as a significant political statement, an expression of different disciplinary membership. As Lemke (1995: 1) reminds us:

> The textual, in the broad sense of all the meanings we make, whether in words or by deeds, is deeply political. Our meanings shape and are shaped by our social relationships, both as individuals and as members of social groups. These social relationships bind us into communities, cultures and subcultures. The meanings we make define not only our selves, they also define our communities ... (and) the relationships between communities ... all of which are quintessentially political relationships.

The interesting thing about this interpretation of language and content is that what is considered language and what is content is always shifting and changing, and may be contested or co-opted by different disciplinary communities, especially if definitions of language or content in the earlier sense of the term change. An example of such contestation is the recent collapse of the traditional boundary between language and literature which

Widdowson (1975) argues is one of disciplinary not intellectual, content, but which serves to maintain certain academic, political and economic power structures.

In practice, ESL teachers draw on both uses of the terms language and content to describe curriculum focus. For some with a strong psycholinguistic orientation, focus will be interpreted relatively narrowly as an emphasis on form or meaning, whereas for those with a stronger sociological orientation, the issue may be more one of alignment, that is, the extent to which a curriculum activity is more oriented towards ESL or content area concerns. Both interpretations are needed for effective practice.

We will return to some of these problems later but for the moment it is probably more productive for our present purposes to define integrated language and content teaching as a heuristic label for a diverse group of curriculum approaches which share a concern with facilitating language learning, broadly defined, through varied but systematic linking of particular subject matter and language in the context of learning activities. The issue then becomes one of classifying or mapping these diverse processes in order to be able to show the range of possibilities in integrated language and content teaching and the various factors which impact on curriculum decisions. This will be addressed in the next section.

LANGUAGE AND CONTENT INTEGRATION: TOWARDS A DESCRIPTIVE FRAMEWORK

There are very few attempts in the literature on language and content integration to describe, rather than prescribe, different approaches.

One exception is Brinton et al.'s (1989) classification which is well known and widely used in North America. In advocating language and content teaching, Brinton et al. identify three different types of integration: theme- or topic-based instruction, adjunct courses and sheltered instruction. However, at a theoretical level, this categorisation has the problem of incorporating two different entities in the labels being proposed, and therefore leads to problems in classifying different types of practice. While 'adjunct' and 'sheltered' refer to forms of program organisation, 'topics or themes' refers to units of syllabus within a course. Given the current conceptualisation of mainstreaming in Australia and the unresolved issues at the level of practice, there has been a concern to develop greater discrimination in definitional categories and modes of analysis.

Davison (1993b) has proposed a comprehensive framework that enables a description of the focus of teaching at the level of program, syllabus, unit of work, lesson or, conceivably, to activities within a lesson (although this is not explicitly explored in her framework). Unlike Brinton et al. (1989), this framework clearly distinguishes between curriculum focus, theoretical model or approach, teaching materials, likely organisational arrangements and teacher roles (Figure 3.1 overleaf).

Figure 3.1   Approaches to integrated language and content teaching

Curriculum focus	Theoretical model/ approach[1]	Teaching materials	Curriculum function (e.g. syllabus, unit, lesson, activity)	Program type/student groupings	Teacher roles
Language teaching	Pre-communicative approaches	e.g. Learning English in Australia (CSC, 1976)	Language syllabus	ESL intensive or similar needs classes[2]	Direct ESL instruction, no content influence
'Contextualised' language teaching	Early 'weak' communicative approaches[3]	e.g. Cambridge course materials	Language syllabus with contextualisation		
	Situational approaches, e.g. Action Sequence approach (Corbel, 1986)	e.g. Using the System (Corbel, 1986)	Language syllabus with content dimension		
	Functional-notional approaches (e.g. Wilkins, 1976)	e.g. English in Focus (Allen and Widdowson, 1978)	Language syllabus loosely linked to content syllabus	(ESP/EAP-oriented classes)	Direct ESL instruction
	Genre-based approaches, e.g. Genre Theory (Rothery, 1984; Martin, 1986; Christie, 1987c; Derewianka, 1991)	e.g. DSP materials (Callaghan & Knapp, 1989; Christie et al., 1992)	Units of work/ 'de facto' language syllabus built around content syllabus		
	Topic approaches, e.g. Topic Approach (Cleland and Evans, 1984)	e.g. Teaching English through Topics (Cleland and Evans, 1984, 1985, 1988)	Units of work/ 'de facto' language syllabus presenting as content syllabus		(Content teacher as resource)
'Simultaneous' integrated language and content teaching	Intuitive practices?			Mainstream class with some similar needs ESL classes	Collaborative teaching and/or ESL support/team teaching[4]
	Genre-based approaches, e.g. Genre Theory (Rothery, 1984; Martin, 1986; Christie, 1987c; Derewianka, 1991)	e.g. Rothery & Stenglin, 1994; Love, 1996	Partial language-based 'syllabus' embedded in content syllabus	Mainstream class or ESL adjunct/ parallel classes[5]	
	Activity-based approaches, e.g. CALLA (Chamot & O'Malley, 1992, 1994)		Language-based units of work in content syllabus	Mainstream class or ESL adjunct/ parallel classes	

Figure 3.1   (*cont'd*)

Curriculum focus	Theoretical model/ approach[1]	Teaching materials	Curriculum function (e.g. syllabus, unit, lesson, activity)	Program type/student groupings	Teacher roles
'Language-conscious' content teaching		e.g. Science Exercises (O'Toole, 1989)	Language-based adjunct units of work embedded in content syllabus	Mainstream class with ESL perspective or sheltered instruction[6]	ESL teacher as resource
	'Language Across the Curriculum' approaches, e.g. Barnes, 1976; Britton, 1979	e.g. Marland, 1977	Language-conscious activities embedded in content syllabus	Mainstream class with language awareness	
Content teaching	'Immersion', e.g. Natural Learning (Cambourne, 1988) 'Submersion'[7]		'Language-rich' content syllabus, 'language-poor' content syllabus	Mainstream class Mainstream class	No ESL influence

NB: All vertical lines represent more or less parallel continua although in practice teachers may alter the 'mix'.
[1] This descriptive framework focuses on the content of what is taught, rather than how it is taught, i.e. the methodology, although it is recognised that it is not always possible or desirable to separate these two aspects of curriculum.
[2] ESL intensive or similar needs classes refer to classes in which there are only ESL students (Ministry of Education, 1987).
[3] 'Weak' communicative approaches recognise that dealing with content or meaning is an essential part of language learning but assume that this is best accomplished in language teaching by adopting a suitably contextualised focus on language form (Howatt, 1984).
[4] Collaborative teaching is defined as a situation in which an ESL teacher and a content teacher cooperate in some way in the planning, implementing and evaluating of a curriculum. Collaborative teaching may or may not include team and/or support teaching, although the the reverse should always be true. Team teaching is defined as a mode of teaching in which the ESL and content teacher have 'equal responsibility for all students in that program, and for the planning and teaching of that program. Teaching may occur separately but in a highly integrated way or it may be done jointly' (Ministry of Education, 1988: 16); ESL support teaching is defined as when 'the ESL teacher assists the class or subject teachers' in mainstream multiethnic classes (Ministry of Education, 1988: 16).
[5] Adjunct classes are defined as ESL classes which reinforce and complement the curriculum of the mainstream class and which are usually taught by an ESL teacher (Brinton et al., 1989). Parallel classes have a similar function but replace the content class. A more accurate descriptor would be to define them as 'intersecting' with the mainstream class at some future time.
[6] Sheltered instruction refers to similar needs ESL classes which are given content-area instruction by a content specialist, i.e. such classes have a content not language objective (Brinton et al., 1989).
[7] 'Submersion' refers to the situation in which ESL students are taught in English without first language or ESL support.

This framework is congruent with that presented in the previous chapter (Figure 2.1) in that curriculum focus is seen as a choice in emphasis which varies along a continuum from content (or subject matter) to language, broadly defined. Curriculum function is seen as the way in which a particular focus is generally realised in terms of practice. Decisions about the modes of delivery, physical grouping and location of pupils and the role of teachers is perceived to be a separate although obviously related decision.

An important distinction is made in this framework between different types of content- and language-based curricula. The term 'content-based language teaching' is rejected as conflating a number of different models and approaches with different emphases. Instead, language and content integration is seen as a cline ranging from 'contextualised' language teaching to 'language-conscious' content teaching. Curriculum focus is defined according to the varied significance, depth of treatment and internal coherence of the language and content elements of the curriculum. For example, an approach which used content, in either sense of the term, simply as a vehicle for language-teaching purposes, would be placed towards the language end of the continuum. In the same way, any approach which embeds some language objectives into a content syllabus or which is focused on the teaching of particular subject matter as an end in itself, but in language-sensitive ways, would be placed towards the content end of the curriculum. Thus, it is possible for an 'ESL' curriculum to be more content than language oriented or vice-versa, depending on the actual weighting of the different curriculum elements.

Existing approaches to language and content integration can be mapped on to this framework, although such mapping necessarily involves interpretation. Some of these approaches have been explicitly described (Widdowson, 1978; Corbel, 1986; Chamot and O'Malley, 1992; Cleland and Evans, 1984; Snow et al., 1989; Rothery, 1984; Krashen and Terrel, 1983), while others are presented as a statement of principles, sample materials and/or descriptions of model lessons (Crandall, 1987; Cantoni-Harvey, 1987; Brinton et al., 1989; Adamson, 1993), or as published materials (Cleland and Evans, 1984, 1985, 1988; Johnston and Johnston, 1990a–1990d).[2] These approaches have also been implemented at a number of different levels: in an individual lesson, as a sequence of lessons or unit of work or, much more rarely, at the syllabus or whole course level.

For example, at the content-end of the continuum, there are a collection of materials which have been developed to guide classroom practices and procedures in integrating language and content. There are a number of common features to these materials, including the use of visuals or real items to establish or present subject matter and language that are either authentic or closely replicate the features that would be encountered in mainstream classrooms in that subject area. There is also a similar set of principles for the sequencing of learning activities that are either explicitly stated or implied in the way that different materials or approaches are organised, with a strong initial focus on meaning, a move from experiential to expository learning, and from practical to theoretical content, with talking seen as an essential precursor to writing.

Examples from North America of such materials are provided in contributions by such authors as Crandall (1987) and Short et al. (1989). These approaches involve teachers in identifying the key linguistic features of elements of subject matter, either within a specific lesson, a unit of work or an entire syllabus. Teaching strategies and student activities – which are based on 'hands on' activities, tasks and student observations, and the use of real objects and appropriate visuals – are then devised. They include science experiments, cooking activities, or making observations of charts, visuals or realia and hypothesising about these. They incorporate language-based activities involving the use and practice of pertinent language features and other appropriate language and study skills. Weighting of such activities with either a language focus or a subject matter focus can be decided by the teacher, depending on the nature of the class (language class or subject matter class), or on priorities related to the needs of the students. Other writers have provided similar possibilities for the implementation of integrated language and content teaching in school ESL programs (Cantoni-Harvey, 1987; Enright and McCloskey, 1988). These, like the other approaches described above, are usually based on units of work at the level of a topic or theme from a particular subject area. Typically they have been developed for use with ESL students, although some language across the curriculum materials and methodologies would also fit this classification in focus, if not in intent.

Similar material, but at the other end of the continuum, has been developed primarily for use in English for Specific Purposes (ESP) courses, derived from and building on early work in the functional–notional tradition and exemplified by the English in Focus series of teaching materials (Allen and Widdowson, 1974). Although very similar in nature to the above materials, the focus is on language functions and features across often very diverse and fragmented content areas, hence the view of these materials as being language rather than content focused. Typically they are aimed at an older and tertiary-educated cohort who are assumed to have 'done' the content, needing only to acquire the new language.

While these practices and materials may lend themselves to adaptation, they are limited in articulating principles that should guide the selection of subject matter, language and the relative attention and focus that should be provided to different aspects of each, with comments often being couched in statements such as 'meet these students' needs' (Cantoni-Harvey, 1987: 22). There is a wealth of Australian material which also fits this classification but because of the eclectic and essentially untheorised nature of all this type of material, it will not be examined here.

Some more elaborated and theorised approaches to language and content integration which involve the specific organisation of language, subject matter and teaching procedures have also been developed, most notably the CALLA framework (Chamot & O'Malley, 1992, 1994; Christie, 1987a). Their approach seems to belong more at the content-based end of the continuum because they essentially adopt a model of curriculum integration in which the content choices drive the language choices. However, unlike the teaching materials already described, neither CALLA nor the Knowledge Framework (Mohan, 1986, and Chapter 6 this volume) have been widely adopted in Australia, perhaps because the 'home grown' varieties of integrated language and content teaching attempt to meet similar needs.

The mapping of genre theory onto this descriptive framework is a little more problematic in that genre theory has been deployed for both ESL and content-area teaching in quite different ways. For example, it has been adopted as a model for a unit of work in a specific content area in order to teach report writing in a science classroom or to show students how to position an argument about the greenhouse effect in senior secondary English. That is, in a mainstream classroom, the language to be taught has been grounded in and derived from the content curriculum. However, there are also an increasing number of ESL courses which adopt a graded genre-based syllabus, although it is almost always mixed with other elements. In this syllabus there will still be a strong content dimension, but selection and sequencing will be based on language criteria and may even use content from a number of different but related fields.

In summary, then, it can be argued that there are a range of different definitions and approaches to integrating language and content teaching but that it is possible to develop a descriptive framework which maps some of the important distinctions between different approaches. This mapping is essential to develop a common language to talk about language and content teaching. We would suggest that Davison's (1993b) framework is useful in this respect. It provides for a continuum between mainstream teaching of subject matter and language teaching, although it does not attempt to provide any systematic advice as to the contexts in which language forms are encountered, used and studied. Such a continuum allows for varying degrees of balance between each of these elements, and for varying 'settings' within a particular unit, course or even lesson. The use of such criteria allows for classification of curriculum function at different levels, at the level of activity, lesson, unit of work, syllabus, course, program or even policy.

The framework is particularly useful for highlighting gaps in provision and for problematising the nature of an ESL curriculum. For example, it is significant that there seem to be no comprehensive models or even teaching materials which can be placed at the centre of the language and content continuum. This may be due to the inherent theoretical complexity of attempting to map two or more curricula onto each other. As Leung points out in this volume, 'one of the difficulties for teachers in a mainstream situation, is that there does not seem to be any principled way of organising the language teaching input'. Hence, most models of language and content teaching used in the mainstream classroom use a unit of work as the principal organising feature which provides a common focus for ESL and content teaching. However, in determining the selection and sequencing of activities, priority is usually given to meeting the demands of the content curriculum. The long-term effects on ESL development (and on ESL teacher effectiveness) of such a curriculum focus have yet to be researched or evaluated in any systematic way. The gap in curriculum type may also be due to a more practical reason – that is, any effective syllabus that balances language and content demands simultaneously in the same teaching context would be so context-specific that it would be hard to envisage commercial materials being 'readily adaptable'. However, it is an important gap in terms of the theory of integrated language and content teaching which needs to be addressed.

Another way in which the framework may be used is to highlight an imbalance in ESL provision. For example, if all the 'ESL' teaching in a particular institution is at one end of the continuum or another, this may become a source of debate or conflict. An example of such debate over the appropriate curriculum balance for ESL students was mentioned in Chapter 2 – that is, the 'positioning' of ESL in the Victorian Certificate of Education (VCE).

Davison's framework, then, provides great flexibility for the analysis and description of different courses, classroom practices and learning materials, and has the potential to provide a common point of reference for diverse practices in a range of different circumstances. However, the question of what constitutes curriculum focus is a significant theoretical problem that is not addressed and requires further exploration. The description also does not capture the process of curriculum design – in particular, the selection and sequencing of curriculum elements. It also assumes that language and content are the only two variables to consider in developing an integrated language and content curriculum. This dichotomy itself needs to be problematised. In fact, investigation of the definition and description of integrated language and content teaching appears to raise rather more problems than it resolves. Yet it is important to explore such theoretical issues as they have very practical consequences, showing us ways in which integrated language and content teaching must necessarily be constrained or ways in which it needs to be further developed. The next section will briefly outline these problems as we see them.

Problems with language and content integration

Approaches to integrated language and content teaching share common beliefs about the preparation of ESL students for academic success and are concerned to provide students with encounters with significant content and the language and language use associated with this content. However, they are still imprecise about how they see these entities and how they go about integrating them effectively. This is because they have yet to develop an internal dialogue and debate, which would have the effect of forcing a more careful articulation of the assumptions and arguments of different perspectives.

The focus of this section has been to move towards such dialogue, and in doing we have identified two main theoretical problems in relation to planning an integrated language and content curriculum: the selection and sequencing of language and content and the scope of the curriculum.[3]

The selection and sequencing of curriculum elements

As understandings of the full complexities of language use are elaborated and the relationship between language and content explored, the identification of principles that will provide a clear basis for the selection and sequencing of an integrated language and content curriculum seems to become more difficult, rather than less. For example, a number of definitions of language and content integration assume a 'content-driven' language curriculum with the selection and sequencing of language elements determined by the mainstream content or subject matter (Wesche, 1993; Crandall and Tucker, 1989; Short et al., 1989). However, such definitions exclude some practices widely described in integrated language and content teaching, such as theme- or topic-based courses (Brinton et al., 1989) in which the selection or sequencing of material for certain types of courses results in a progression of themes or topics from diverse and unconnected subject areas. Williams (1995) has proposed that one way of dealing with this problem of definition is to extend the distinction that Howatt (1984) has made between 'strong' and 'weak' forms in communicative language teaching. That is, the view that subject matter is the sole factor in determining what language is to be learned, and in what order, may be described as a 'strong' form of integrated language and content teaching. This can be contrasted with a 'weak' version in which linguistic factors contribute to such decision-making. The 'weak' version allows for more input from a language curriculum, with subject matter as an integrating unit.

However, we would challenge the long-term effectiveness of any 'strong' version of integrated language and content teaching. We would suggest that although content can be a basis for the organisation of language and cultural elements at the level of the unit of work, mainstream subject content alone, no matter how accessible or interesting, is not sufficient to provide a properly developed ESL curriculum. There are a number of problems with the concept of the 'content-driven' curriculum in ESL education which need elaboration.

Firstly, there is a problem of curriculum coverage. All 'strong' versions of integrated content and language teaching hold that content must determine the language curriculum because particular disciplines, or even areas within disciplines, generate very different discourse. However, most models and materials for integrated language and content teaching privilege certain content areas, in particular, Science and Social Studies (Cantoni-Harvey, 1987; Crandall, 1987; Chamot & O'Malley, 1994; Cleland and Evans, 1984). This seems contradictory in that if specific content generates specific language, the whole curriculum needs to be covered. Yet it is obvious that there is insufficient time and resources to support such coverage; without it, ESL education is reduced to submersion. It is also possible that there may be unnecessary (from a language point of view) overlap or redundancy in language use across curriculum areas, that is, the 'natural' language that arises out of particular subject matter is likely (but not necessarily) to be useful for ESL development.

Secondly, there is an assumption that the content curriculum of the school provides an adequate basis for language developments.[4] Even if all curriculum areas are covered, as in French immersion education, there are strong arguments that this is not the case. Comprehensible input of subject content does not necessarily appear to enhance linguistic output and morphosyntactic features such as articles, which are grammatically significant but not necessary for actual communication, may never actually be acquired. It is also assumed that students can gain access to and participate in mainstream content interactions, a view which ignores the significant role of sociopsychological and intergroup factors in ESL learning. The implications are that a content curriculum, no matter how effective or interesting, does not necessarily lead to comprehensive language development.

Thirdly, it could be argued that a mainstream curriculum will not generate appropriate opportunities for ESL students to develop 'social' language proficiency. This reversal of the argument that the teaching of 'academic language' is necessary because the teaching of 'social' language does not provide an adequate basis for such language use (Cantoni-Harvey, 1987; Chamot and O'Malley, 1992; Cleland and Evans, 1984). In fact, we would suggest that many advocates of integrated language and content teaching seriously underestimate or ignore the complexities and sophistication required of language use in non-academic contexts. It is possible that this misconception has been further exacerbated by wide acceptance in the ESL field of Cummins's (1980) early conceptualisation of BICS and CALP, which viewed socially, oriented language proficiency as representing a more basic level of proficiency acquired prior to 'academic' language.

If mainstream curriculum content cannot be used as the sole determiner of language elements, then there needs to be reference to a broader ESL curriculum, such as the ESL companion to the Victorian English Curriculum and Standards Framework, which provides guidelines for ESL learning and teaching at different levels, ages and stages of schooling. Subject matter can be a component of such a curriculum, but cannot replace it. However, this in itself does not solve the problem of selection and sequencing, as Victorian experience has shown.

In Victoria there is wide acceptance that an ESL curriculum based on language alone appears inadequate in view of contemporary understandings of the nature of ESL learning, while a curriculum which is based on mainstream content can fail to develop fully the linguistic skills of the students for whom it was intended. However, if learning is based around a series of units of work, as suggested, there is enormous difficulty in arranging the units so that the selection and sequencing of all elements is evenly balanced in relation to both content and language. If an ESL curriculum is restricted to a single subject area, then, in view of the discussion above, it is likely that the coverage of language will be inadequate. Therefore, an integrated ESL curriculum needs to cover a range of subject areas. However, if curriculum elements can be sequenced to form some meaningful progression in terms of language development, then the curriculum is likely to provide less coherence or create incoherence in terms of the development of content.

Davison (1992) has suggested that too little attention to the coherence of the subject matter in an ESL curriculum can lead to what she dubs 'Flat Earth theories' – that is, a strong focus on language has not been balanced by sufficient attention to the teaching of content so that the knowledge of the subject matter is fragmented or fatally flawed, because fundamental concepts underpinning certain content are not established in the process of language contextualisation. On the other hand, too little attention to the coherence of the language components in an integrated curriculum may result in either 'Hole language', that is, a situation where language development is marked by significant gaps (because the subject matter did not create a context or need for that language), or 'Life Cycle of the Cabbage Tree Moth-itis',[5] in which language is 'trapped' in specific content and students so that students fail to develop 'communicative capacity' (Widdowson, 1983), that is, the ability to transfer language skills across contexts.

In response we would argue that balance in an ESL curriculum can be achieved in other ways, for example, by systematically varying the curriculum focus within a unit or course or by choosing a mix of approaches from different ends of the language-content curriculum for different areas of the ESL program. A diachronic rather than synchronic perspective on curriculum planning must be taken.

However, although there are descriptions of a number of different models or approaches to the integration of language and content at the level of a unit of work or lesson, there are no real descriptions of how to integrate the different curriculum elements over a longer time period. An exception is Snow et al. (1989), who provide a view of the key elements involved in the planning and organisation of integrated language and content instruction and offer advice as to how the interaction between the aims and knowledge of teachers of language and teachers of subject matter can be viewed and used to inform the planning of teaching. This interaction informs the identification of learners' needs, including their linguistic needs. A distinction is made between language obligatory to particular subject matter (language that must be used in dealing with a particular set of meanings) and language that is compatible with certain subject matter (that is, it can be taught and practised meaningfully in that context, even though its use may not be obligatory, as other language options are available). This is a useful distinction for teachers in planning how they might be able to integrate elements of language into particular content.

However, while this model provides an overview of the elements involved in planning integrated teaching, it has limitations of both a practical and theoretical nature. It provides no guidance for prioritising or resolving competing or conflicting requirements, for time constraints mean that the complete demands of both the ESL and the content curricula cannot be fully realised in most teaching situations. The model also assumes an interaction of two specialists, which will not always be the case as ESL teachers in intensive language-teaching programs may not have access to specialist subject matter teachers, and content teachers in schools often have little or no access to an ESL specialist; where the ESL specialist is working alone, the subject-based content is likely to suffer and vice versa. Thus this model is limited to identifying the elements of integrated teaching, rather than providing some guidelines as to how integrated teaching might be done.

Another possibility for the development of guidelines for the selection and sequencing at the syllabus level is to extrapolate from or extend existing models or approaches to integration. For example, although Cleland and Evans have not proposed a specific syllabus or sequence of topics, they do provide some guiding principles (Cleland and Evans, 1984, 1985, 1988) that relate to the areas of subject matter in which they have developed topics, and suggest the way in which topics may be sequenced. They propose that topic-based work should be taught concurrently with other facets of language, such as 'literary English' and spoken English, although their approach does not embrace a sufficient range of either language or subject matter to cover the full curriculum. Topics should be selected on the basis of factors such as the school curriculum priorities or current issues, the students' linguistic and conceptual knowledge, interest in and knowledge of the topic and the availability of teaching resources and equipment (Cleland and Evans, 1984: 6).

In relation to the sequencing of topics, they suggest aiming for a 'spiral' effect so that specific language elements – which they designate as 'grammar' and 'function' – are encountered and re-encountered in different topics. They claim that this effect has been achieved in their books (although if teachers are to select topics according to the criteria stated above, there is nothing in these criteria to guarantee achievement of this effect). In fact, within each of the Topic Books topics are sequenced from less complex to more complex on a mixture of linguistic and conceptual grounds. For example, in the book about Australia, the first topic is political geography involving identification and description in the Simple Present tense, the last is 'The Franklin Dam', which refers to an environmental battle over a dam that was never built, demanding speculation and hypothesis about events in the past which did not occur, involving grammatical structures such as the Past Conditional. On the other hand, although there is a broad thematic grouping of topics according to content in the Topic Books, there is little developmental sequence, a fact which has made them relatively unpopular with content teachers. However, teachers are explicitly advised that:

> We *do not* recommend starting at Topic 1 and working through to Topic 20. The teacher should pick the topics that are best suited to the language level and needs of the students. (Ibid.: 7, emphasis in original)

The nature of such language levels is not specified or elaborated, although the tone of Cleland and Evans's discussion implies a basis in functional and grammatical proficiency. Teachers using the approach also report that they select topics in order to provide a sequence of study skills that build from the present capabilities to what is expected in mainstream schooling.

Because it requires considerable time for the treatment of topics in class, it is best suited to intensive ESL contexts which provide considerable blocks of teaching time. Thus, while principles for the selection and sequencing of topics are provided, these are not very specific and require teachers to use their own insights and intuitions in decision-making. This implies that teachers will need to have an explicit awareness of the linguistic and conceptual dimensions of what they are doing as they select and sequence curriculum elements, although they may not pass on that consciousness explicitly to their students.[6] All ESL teachers (and ideally all content teachers) need to be able to identify language features that occur frequently in core areas of the curriculum and be able to articulate and plan for differential weighting of different linguistic elements based on particular insights from second language acquisition research as to what may be teachable (or more or less so in certain contexts or situations).[7] 'Core' areas of the curriculum include those which provide conceptual foundations, or which have been identified as critical to academic success. However, this notion of academic success leads us to an even more deep-seated theoretical problem with language and content integration – the validity or scope of its dual curriculum focus.

The scope of the curriculum focus

The problems of selection and sequencing explored above presume that the scope of the curriculum focus is self-evident. However, researchers interested in what may best be described as the cultural dimension of schooling lead us to question the belief that simply integrating language and content effectively will ensure success for ESL students in schools. This cultural dimension is interpreted relatively narrowly as an additional component of proficiency (Adamson, 1993; Richards and Hurley, 1990; Saville-Troike, 1984) or, more broadly, depending on one's view of language and language learning.

For example, at the narrow end of the continuum, Richards and Hurley (1990) argue that academic success requires 'student functional proficiency' (Tikunoff, 1985), incorporating interactional strategies, understandings of the nature of classroom tasks and the ability to meet various cognitive demands (Richards and Hurley, 1990: 146–7). 'Interactional strategies' include the ability to understand and use the social rules of the classroom, including turn taking, rules of movement and ways of demonstrating knowledge. 'Task demands' include an understanding of the nature of learning activities in classrooms, and expectations of other classroom participants in relation to them. 'Cognitive demands' include the ability to assimilate new information and concepts, and are related to prior experience and the nature of existing schemata.

While Richards and Hurley (1990: 157) approvingly report the curriculum approaches of Chamot and O'Malley, and Mohan and Crandall, they make the point that these and other content-based approaches deal mainly with the cognitive dimension and do not address the more culturally bound aspects of proficiency.

Adamson's (1993) concept of 'academic competence' explores similar territory, and includes three dimensions – background knowledge and school routines (what Adamson dubs 'scripts for school'), study skills and strategies (including metacognitive strategies, cognitive strategies and social-affective strategies) and academic language proficiency. Adamson adopts Spolsky's (1989) 'Preference Model' of language proficiency, which posits that different aspects of proficiency will be more significant than others in different academic contexts.

Richards and Hurley's and Adamson's consideration of the non-linguistic or cultural aspects of school experience go beyond the aspects of content and language usually considered in the literature on integrating language and content teaching, although these aspects certainly interact with both language and content. However, Kramsch (1993: 8) goes further, arguing against the 'entrenched' dichotomy of language and culture, the view that 'cultural elements' are something added on, mere information conveyed by language, not a feature of language itself. She proposes that if language is seen as social practice, culture becomes the very core of language teaching:

> Cultural awareness must then be viewed both as enabling language proficiency and as being the outcome of reflection on language proficiency.

This notion of cultural awareness has been extended by critical theorists working in ESL education (Janks and Paton, 1990; Paikeday, 1985; Peirce, 1995; Pennycook, 1990). Such theorists seek to develop in ESL students and teachers a greater understanding of the socially and culturally constructed nature of language and content, and the ability to challenge the deeply embedded assumptions of the 'mainstream'. Although critical theorists are themselves subject to vigorous critique, they have foregrounded the 'cultural politics' of ESL curriculum, and in the process raised many new questions about the nature and purpose of ESL education.

CONCLUSIONS

This analysis suggests that subject matter can form a coherent basis for the integration of a variety of linguistic elements at the level of a relatively short unit of work, but that this does not provide a complete basis for the selection of what is to be taught and leads to more questions than answers as to the sequencing of learning. None of the approaches or models of content and language integration discussed above has provided a principled basis for the selection and sequencing of units that will give rise to a coherent pattern of development of all aspects of subject matter, language and skills and the cultural dimensions relevant to schooling. Teacher intuitions are required to provide this. There is also a need for more comprehensive theory building and research to both capture the diversity of practice and explore and articulate a principled basis for different approaches to language and content integration which take account of different teaching contexts, and accommodate different theories of language and language learning. This would contribute to a clearer and more informed basis for practice.

This analysis has also revealed that current practices are generally focused on the orientation of ESL students to a 'mainstream' which appears to be taken as given and treated uncritically. This foregrounds some fundamental but generally implicit contradictions in the role and purpose of ESL education – issues that will be taken up in more detail in Chapter 4.

NOTES

1. The notion of task will be discussed in a variety of contexts. For a detailed discussion see Chapter 11.
2. As the Knowledge Framework (Mohan, 1986) is discussed in detail in later chapters, it is not included in the discussion here (see Chapter 6, for instance).
3. Clearly, there are also major problems in curriculum implementation, including problems in establishing collaborative relationships between ESL and content teachers, initiating and managing school-based curriculum review and change, and changing teachers' attitudes and practices (see Chapter 4). However, this chapter focuses first on conceptual issues in the belief that implementation will be impossible without an understanding of the theoretical nature of the curriculum task.
4. There is also an assumption that the school curriculum provides an adequate basis for ESL students' *content* development – a very questionable assumption given the very different educational backgrounds and experiences of most ESL students and the culturally bound nature of any content teaching. This latter issue will be taken up in more detail in Chapter 4.
5. The label is derived from a common phenomenon associated with inexperienced teachers who rely too heavily on a 'syllabus' of narrowly developed Topics (Cleland and Evans, 1984) and, as a consequence, get hung up on teaching vocabulary and 'content' in phrase book style.
6. As alluded to earlier in this chapter, the notion of explicitness in relation to teaching has multiple interpretations, depending on one's view of language and language learning; thus those that do argue for exposing students to a more explicit treatment of language often do so for very different reasons. For example, genre theorists would argue for a more 'visible pedagogy' (Bernstein, 1990) and more explicit teaching of the linguistic features of 'powerful genres' (Cope and Kalantzis, 1993) for sociopolitical and ideological reasons, whereas second language acquisition researchers would be more preoccupied with the psycholinguistic role of explicit instruction, and focus on form in improving 'learnability' (Long, 1985; Doughty, 1991; Pienemann and Johnston, 1987; Pienemann and Lightbown, 1993; Krashen, 1993). It is beyond the scope of this chapter to explore this issue further but we would argue that curriculum decisions as to what should be encountered explicitly and what can be left for experiential treatment do need to be informed. Stern's (1992) notion of a continuum between analytic and experiential treatment of language by teachers in planning, and between a learner's explicit and implicit encounters with specific language features is a useful framing device.
7. However, the greater the number of elements under consideration, the more difficult it is to find clear-cut criteria by which to select and sequence and there is a limit to just how much teachers (as well as students) can consciously deal with, although how this limit is ascertained and the extent to which it may be variable has not been explored.

Chapter 4

Identity and ideology: the problem of defining and defending ESL-ness

Chris Davison

INTRODUCTION

In Chapter 3 the relationship between ESL and the 'mainstream' was explored from a curriculum perspective, which revealed that there were still a number of unresolved issues to do with the scope, selection and sequencing of various curriculum elements. The chapter concluded with a brief discussion of the cultural orientation of integrated language and content teaching, and suggested that a more critical perspective would also reveal some fundamental but generally implicit contradictions in the nature, role and purpose of ESL education which may have a significant impact on policy and practice.

I would argue that in Victoria, such contradictions have occurred in spite of, or perhaps even because of, explicit policy guidelines regarding ESL (Ministry of Education, 1987, 1988; Board of Studies, 1996), and reveal that even at the theoretical level there is still considerable clarification and communication required as to the nature of ESL. The shifting and competing views of the ESL learner, the ESL teacher and the ESL program outlined in Chapter 1 are still with us as we start the new millennium. We may be no closer to a final reconciliation but more self-reflexivity and awareness of some of the problems may lead to greater understanding and even control of the process.

This chapter[1] will first establish the actual nature of this concern over the nature and purpose of ESL education by taking three different and real problems in the 'life' of students and teachers, and critique them through the eyes of a different player in the field. In doing so, the inherent tensions in the nature of ESL may be more explicitly revealed. The response of the ESL profession to these tensions can then be evaluated and some new directions for investigation and action suggested.

PROBLEMS OF IDENTITY

Problem 1: Defining the ESL student[2]

The location is a large outer metropolitan secondary school in a relatively affluent area of Melbourne. There are many recently arrived LOTE background students, mainly from Hong Kong, Malaysia, Singapore, Thailand and Taiwan and the middle East, as well as a significant number of Australian-born children of Italian and Greek migrants. In the final two years of schooling, there are 90 (out of 320) students who are 'tagged' as ESL students for the purposes of assessment and reporting.[3] Three teachers and a student working in the senior school were interviewed about their definitions of ESL-ness. Listen to extracts of their responses and ask yourself 'In what way are they constructing the identity of an ESL student?'

Extract 1

INTERVIEWER: Do you think you're an ESL student or a mainstream student?
STUDENT: How about in between?
INTERVIEWER: Why do you say that?
STUDENT: Well, like I'm capable of doing English but my standard is not as good as the mainstream people, but I think my standard is a bit higher than a normal ESL student, so I guess it's really in between.

Extract 2

TEACHER A: I know this girl personally who has just arrived from Hong Kong and she has gone to a school at . . . who does not have an ESL program and who is designated not ESL because she is a competent speaker but . . . then there is one boy, Wu, for example, who is exactly like Connie. He has been shunted between ESL and mainstream over this last four years. He's now in Year 10. He is not a particularly bright kid. He has got all the problems of structure, the grammar, the lot, but he is a mainstream student, so we keep saying if you're mainstream go to mainstream, but mainstream teachers scream and say he can't perform, he can't discuss Romeo and Juliet, he doesn't know what is going on, he comes back to ESL. So there is this constant back and forth because of this concern with 'is he' or 'isn't he' an ESL student? As I said, I have tended not to worry about it, if we can help him just bring him across, but he is still in English mainstream except that he is now getting ESL support. His problem . . . first of all he has a problem understanding what the whole thing is because he has problems with vocabulary, he has problems in articulating what points he wants to make, he doesn't have the structure and he learns very very slowly. He is not a bright kid . . . you can teach him the vocab but he can't apply it. So you keep giving him structures, he doesn't understand the concept. He came here when he was very young, he was probably in grade 5.

Extract 3

TEACHER B: Peter, who's been here since he was about an 8 year old so he's been here ten years, he's certainly not eligible for ESL under the rules, and yet at the same time, there is clear evidence in his writing of the same sort of problems with regard to tense and new verb usage in particular, other aspects as well, but Peter's not as bad in other respects, but the problem with verbs is just so evident in every one of them. Perhaps Vince, not so much with Vince . . . he writes pretty fluently but others in the group, particularly Connie, Mark, who's just outside the limit, he has heaps of problems with his writing as well.

Extract 4

TEACHER C: . . . the Malaysian students, who have very good knowledge of English, I've had students in my classes from Malaysia, and they don't really need to be (designated ESL) but they are because the system allows them to be.

Commentary

As can be seen, what comes through in all the comments about 'ESL-ness' is the view of an ESL student as somehow a deficit or 'incomplete' mainstream student, the view that 'ESL-ness' stops once you have achieved mainstream linguistic norms. The key difference between an ESL and an ESB student is seen as the level of their English language proficiency, their control of 'structures', their grasp of 'vocabulary', their ability to participate, and succeed, in a mainstream class. As Toohey (1992: 88) does in British Columbia, it is interesting to compare such grassroots constructions of ESL-ness with those of giftedness, which also assume that a certain student cohort may not be achieving the level of academic success expected of them but which see this as a problem located in the school and in society, a failure to develop the 'possibly hidden' special talents of such students, thus undermining their potential contribution to society. ESL students, no matter how favourably portrayed in current Australian curriculum documents, are still positioned in relation to 'native-speaker' norms; they are still assumed to be on a continuum of conformity between non-ESB-ness and ESB-ness; thus it is their 'lack' (of English) which is always stressed, not their previous educational achievements, their 'previous cultural or creative endeavours' (Toohey, 1992: 88), their possession of bi- or multilingualism/multiculturalism. This deficit construction is still clearly exemplified in the CSF which maps ESL development onto English, and in policy guidelines which continue to talk about ESL 'problems' or 'difficulties'.

The ESL profession has major problems with this situation. On the one hand, there are legitimate and real 'difficulties' associated with learning in and through a language which is not your mother tongue. To deny these difficulties would be to reverse the major achievement of ESL education in Australia over the last 15 years: official recognition that such difficulties do exist and must be addressed. On the other hand, evidence abounds in the literature on bilingualism of the cognitive, affective and educational benefits of learning two languages (Cummins, 1996). In Australian language policy documents, it is usual to quote such evidence, but it appears to remain at the level of rhetoric. Very little positive construction of bi- or multilingualism comes though in current definitions of ESL-ness that operate at the chalkface.

Problem 2: Defining the ESL teacher[4]

The location is a large inner-city girls' secondary school with a long-established ESL program. About 80 per cent of the students are from a LOTE background, mainly Greek, Lebanese, Turkish, Vietnamese and Italian, and most are 'second-phase' ESL learners. In response to state government policy and student need, the major thrust of the ESL programme is support and team teaching in the mainstream classroom. The following anecdote is based on one of the situations that arose at this school (Doyle and Reinhardt, 1992: 38). Look at the extract and ask yourself: 'How is the speaker constructing an ESL teacher (and the ESL teaching task)?'

> You are an ESL teacher . . . You have studied a bit of history but not much and a long time ago. Suddenly you find yourself obliged to team teach (in History) . . . You find out . . . what is programmed for the junior classes and do a bit of reading – not in the uni library – remember you only have to know as much as the kids. All you have to do is devise ways to get this material across to the kids in such a way that they will be learning and using language in the process of learning History. Once you have devised a couple of strategies . . . approach the (teacher) with some concrete suggestions for the class concerned which are tailored to meet the needs of the junior program. Result – she is impressed with your preparation and likes some of your ideas and is willing to try them. When one of them goes like a dream you offer to plan the next unit in consultation with her of course, although she is very busy with three unit Ancient history and may not have much time to spare. Do not be put off by this apparent lack of interest. The kids love the Barrier game and the role plays of the Sumerians were quite impressive – suddenly Margaret is talking about Year 8 next year. Your activities are not only language rich they are fun . . . You could make yourself invaluable to this faculty and with the head on your side the other teachers may take you more seriously.

Commentary

This construction of an ESL teacher, which is still dominant in grassroots documentation of 'mainstreaming', is marked by two very distinct features. Firstly, and perhaps more obviously, one is struck by the almost furtive approach adopted towards collaboration, the expectation that the ESL teacher will have to work hard and live by his or her wits to achieve acceptance. There is no sense in which the school or the History Faculty shares responsibility for the successful development of ESL support, it is all the initiative of the ESL teacher. Despite this, the 'battle' is over the nature of the content curriculum, its accessibility and language-richness. There is little sense of a joint curriculum, no negotiation of the most appropriate selection or sequencing of content topics and the nature of their treatment so that students can achieve predetermined language as well as content goals. This basic assumption that any language learning is good needs to be seriously questioned in the light of the discussion in Chapter 3.

This anecdote also exposes a misunderstanding and a misuse of scarce ESL resources. The ESL teacher is construed as a technician who will help to make History more accessible, if he or she is allowed in and if the results meet with the History teacher's approval. ESL 'expertise' appears to lie in the activities selected, the methodology rather than the language 'content'. Following Jones and Moore (1993: 388), this could be seen as a move from a cultural to a technical mode of control over ESL expertise and from a professional to a technician model for the role and status of the practitioner:

> By decontextualising 'skills' and abstracting them from their constitutive cultural practices, these reductive procedures construct partial, disembedded representations of the complex social interactions (involved in ESL teaching) . . . A set of operations to be implemented and followed as instructed. Its practitioners have no automatic access to its theoretical base or means of critical examination.

This view of the role and purpose of the ESL teacher is almost universal among content teachers and is still widely entrenched within the ESL field, reinforced by the dominance of 'communicative' approaches to language teaching and the emphasis on activity or task-based learning.

The same contradictions and conflicts in the identity of the ESL teacher are found at the system level, for example, in the orientation of the ESL in the Mainstream in-service course (see Chapter 2). Although widely endorsed as an effective professional development activity, the course projects an image of ESL expertise as residing in methodology or strategies, rather than in curriculum content (curriculum being discussed only in relation to cultural-inclusiveness). In other words, the course either assumes a prior, shared understanding of ESL curricular goals or does not consider them to be significant. Paradoxically, the focus on 'how' rather than 'what' is both a major strength and weakness of the course. It is a strength because it makes the course very practical and attractive to teachers and gives them hands-on skills and techniques. On the other hand, the lack of attention to the underlying principles of ESL, its 'disciplinary content', and the very different, even conflicting cultural and belief systems of ESL and subject area teachers may lead to teachers recontextualising, distorting or transforming many of the techniques or strategies actually targeted in the course.[5] This weakness is exacerbated by the widespread assumption that ESL teachers need no guidance in developing collaborative relations, other than a sympathetic and supportive school environment and cooperative partners. A crucial challenge for professional development programs such as 'ESL in the Mainstream' is to make the epistemological features of ESL teaching an explicit focus of discourse and to talk about conflict, not just collaboration, socialising both language and content teachers into a critical perspective on their practices.

Problem 3: Defining the ESL program

The location is a large primary school on the rural fringes of south-eastern Melbourne. The school has been rapidly expanding in population and a swath of brown portables line the school's perimeter and almost obscure its smart red exterior. The area is within commuting distance of Melbourne industries and its cheap housing and open skies have attracted large numbers of recently arrived immigrants, radically altering the school's traditional ESB demographic profile. The teachers are struggling to cope with many newly arrived migrant children with little or no previous schooling in their country of origin. There are also significant numbers of Australian-born children who have learned some English at kindergarten but whose home environment is still strongly LOTE background. The school has just been given a 0.5 ESL allocation and has to establish an ESL program. The school has decided to devote a Professional Development day to this task. They are inviting an ESL consultant[6] in to act as a catalyst and respondent to their discussion. Look at one small group interaction on this day and ask yourself 'How are they constructing the nature of an ESL program?'

TEACHER A: I think that if we develop a program which focuses on the language required to deal with the themes in the mainstream classroom it will be a start . . . for example, we could teach the kids more vocab 'cos that's their really weak point and two teachers in the class will make things easier . . .

PRINCIPAL: (*aside*) We'd have to get a trained teacher though . . . or maybe Angela would be interested . . . her parents are Italian, aren't they?

CONSULTANT: You'd need to be a little systematic about your language program though . . . for example, you could organise it around text types or genres . . . Procedural, Recount . . . you know . . .

TEACHER B: We could maybe add a theme or two . . . you know . . . Tet . . . Festivals . . . bring in the parents a bit more . . .

TEACHER C: The difficulty will be in planning . . . it's so time-consuming already maybe the ESL teacher could just . . . we could just give them our curriculum and they could you know adapt it take it from there . . . ?

CONSULTANT: But if you are doing the same thing . . . then it makes it easier . . . the ESL teacher can do more work with the ones who need it on the specific language features . . . like with a Procedural text, the imperative or the layout of instructions for an experiment . . .

Commentary

In this extract the role of the ESL program is constructed by the teachers as a preparation for, and reinforcement of, the mainstream content curriculum. Little or no consideration is given to the need to construct an ESL curriculum which takes as its starting point the ESL learners.[7] Orientation to other cultural and linguistic aspects of schooling is largely implicit and limited in scope. Again, ESL-ness is viewed as a problem rather than a resource, the Principal's aside in particular revealing very little understanding of the complexity of the language learning task.

In terms of curricular content, two suggestions are made: to adopt 'genres' as a common focal point for an integrated curriculum, and to add more culturally relevant elements to the existing content curriculum. These ideas and their effect on the construction of the ESL program will be discussed in turn.

The suggestion of a genre-based pedagogy does offer a potentially valuable strategy for both language and content integration and cultural awareness. For example, the theoretical basis of genre theory in systemic functional linguistics links texts with their social and cultural context, and this connection can be used to highlight the cultural relativity and social function of both spoken and written texts. As Derewianka and Hammond (1991: 51) demonstrate:

> (Genre theory) provides a systematic way of exploring how cultural differences are realised ... cultural differences are often not obvious but are of great importance in how the ESL learner is 'heard' in the new culture. Through an emphasis on the social function of texts, this theoretical base also deals with who produces texts in the broader community, why they say or write them, in what context areas they are likely to be located and how the overall function of the text relates to its organisation and development.

The emphasis in genre theory on first building students' field knowledge could be the basis for culturally-based reflection, but, as the extract above demonstrates, many teachers, consciously or unconsciously, adopt a more assimilationist stance, a more reproductive approach which treats mainstream content practices as 'natural' and necessary. Where prior knowledge is discussed, it tends to be as a foundation for further input by teachers (reflecting the mainstream curriculum) rather than as a point of reflection or recognition of differences in the way that knowledge may (or may not) be structured and valued by different cultures. Genre pedagogy needs to be even more explicit about incorporating such a cultural orientation, to present genres as dynamic and fluid, as culturally constructed, not as presumed truths. This would have the potential to raise the self-awareness and self-confidence of students through an explicit affirmation of their cultural backgrounds, at the same time making students more aware of options, alternatives, and possibly the expectations of many in the educational system.

Secondly, the suggestion to incorporate more 'multicultural themes' into the curriculum is a positive step and may raise all students' awareness of different cultural backgrounds, but again there is no questioning of main-stream educational practice. Such treatment of culture reflects the penultim-ate level of multicultural education ('respect') described by Nieto (1996), and has affirmative aspects of the highest level ('affirmation, solidarity and critique'), but lacks any explicit critique. There also seems to be little aware-ness among the teachers of the cultural-constructedness of classroom pro-cesses and tasks (Adamson, 1993). This aspect of culture also needs to be taken into account in curriculum decision-making.

Meta-commentary

All three of these 'slices of life' show the serious dilemma confronting ESL teachers. As Williams (1995: 104) points out:

> The preparation of ESL students for success in the mainstream inevitably involves orienting them to the norms of the mainstream. Empowering students within their social context means that they need to be assisted to function within the cultural and social patterns and discourses that reflect power, credibility and influence within that social context. Not to teach toward this sort of success would be an extreme form of exclusion and discrimination, and would lead to extensive material and social disadvantage for students from NESB. It is also likely that it would be directly contrary to the wishes of ESL students, their families and their cultural communities.

Nevertheless, Williams (1995) argues that it would be a return to assimila-tion for ESL teaching to focus exclusively on assisting students to conform to mainstream expectations and 'become like' the dominant group(s). Instead, he argues for ESL practices which are directed towards access to and par-ticipation in the mainstream, yet which enable ESL students to be critically aware of their own background and the nature of their own cultural frame-work and its relationship to the mainstream.

He affirms the work of Benesch (1993) and Ho (1993) in North America, who are concerned that unreflective approaches to ESL lead to assimilationist practice. For example, Ho (1993) has argued that from a critical theory per-spective, communicative language teaching, and by implication, integrated language and content teaching, serve to replicate existing conditions, rather than allowing students to address their particular needs, and in so doing, transform the social environment in which their learning takes place (Ho, 1993: 41). Such a perspective is a new development in discussion of integrated language and content teaching, and suggests that its social impact requires further consideration, and that discussion of the 'best' ways to go about integrated language and content teaching need to be cognisant of the social environment in which they take place. A coherent theory of integrated lan-guage and content teaching would need to address this area.

On the other hand, Benesch (1993: 713–14) claims that it is a self-defeating exercise to study the demands of mainstream courses and try to make them accessible to ESL students, as it is these very demands which restrict the participation of ESL students. She concludes that:

The politics of pragmatism leads to a neglect of more inclusive and democratic practices, such as negotiating the curriculum and collaborative learning because they are rarely practised in non-ESL classes.

However, this comment reveals a certain paradox in that the very techniques Benesch and many other educators perceive as enhancing ESL participation are themselves socially and culturally constructed and lead to a bias towards and a privileging of certain pedagogic practices as the new cultural norms.[8] This is not an isolated perspective. Similar concerns have been expressed in relation to teacher education, for example, Hawkins and Irujo (1993: 13) comment on the conflict in trying to empower students to become the creators of their own knowledge yet imposing particular learning styles and value systems on them, thereby 'creating an imperialism of our own views'.

According to Williams (1995), it is a dilemma that may be insoluble but it is a dilemma in which the alternatives can be articulated and their implications examined. We can leave it to the individual or group to choose or, if choice is impossible (Peirce, 1995), adopt an approach based on linguistic or cultural considerations. However, Williams argues that each of these alternatives implies certain values, which cannot be separated from the mainstream's view of linguistic and cultural minorities, nor from those groups' views of the mainstream and themselves, and how teachers of ESL may be perceived within these relations.

NEW CHALLENGES FOR THE ESL PROFESSION: BEYOND A PRAGMATIC RESPONSE

ESL is widely perceived to be an emerging profession, and, like other emerging professions, is developing haphazardly from two different directions: education down and practice up. Its response to these kinds of everyday conflicts and competing claims to identity has generally been very pragmatic. However, as Williams (1995) points out, a claim to a pragmatic orientation is likely to mean that the political and social impact of teaching is inexplicit and unexplored, and can readily mask a social conservatism. From a 'top-down' view ESL appears far from socially conservative. However high-profile political activity may mask uncertainty and confusion at the chalkface, and rhetoric can get way ahead of reality. The last 30 years has seen Australian ESL practitioners channel much energy and expertise into two main activities: the essentially political task of developing and promoting ESL as a profession and the much more complex pedagogic task of trying to define, articulate and 'operationalise' what it means to 'be' an ESL student, an ESL teacher, an ESL program.

However, in most areas of its activity the ESL field has not been in control of its own agenda and has not even understood the larger sociopolitical and economic forces influencing and shaping its work (Moore, 1996). Unfortunately, the times when education professionals could control or even influence education are long over, if they ever existed.[9] This raises the question of what the ESL field can do, in the present climate, to resolve the tension between their different roles and identities, and to better align reality and rhetoric, practice and policy.

I would argue that one thing the TESOL profession can do is to develop a better understanding of how entities such as ESL and mainstream, language, content and culture, are constructed and how they change, issues which have not thus far featured strongly on the TESOL agenda. ESL practitioners also need a better understanding of the nature of identity-formation and development within the education profession itself in order to establish a stronger sense of their own and their 'mainstream' colleagues' professional identity and professional development needs. In particular, the TESOL field needs to ask itself how subject areas and subject teachers, including ESL, come to be constructed as distinctive institutional specialisms and how they are socially distributed. Jones and Moore (1993: 395–6) argue that different bodies of expertise are themselves classified, ranked and ordered, and individuals and groups differentially located and positioned in relation to a hierarchy of expertise. They suggest that:

> A significant dimension of the activity of key expert systems (policy, management and administration) can be seen as primarily to do with regulating such positioning. This raises issues of power and ideology. Hence, a critical concern must be with the agencies regulating expertise itself.

The remainder of the chapter will take a more critical look at the nature of professionalism and professional development and suggest some possible ways to support and enhance the implementation of 'good' ESL policy in Victoria.[10]

DEFINING AND REDEFINING PROFESSIONALISM

One of the most important characteristics of a profession is seen to be its ownership of a very specialised and relatively complex body of knowledge. According to Jones and Moore (1993: 391):

> Traditionally . . . (membership) is gained by a lengthy process of socialisation into the professional community in which individuals acquire not only the knowledge and skills of the group (its particular expertise) but also its distinctive cultural ethos and character. The procedures, rules and criteria by which professional judgements are made tend to remain implicit and obscure to non-members. In this sense, expertise appears esoteric in character.[11]

All the research literature on teacher knowledge and teacher change suggests that teachers develop their professional knowledge from practice up, rather than education down. For example, Yaxley (1991: 87) suggests that teachers come to know about classrooms and teaching through 'personally constructed meanings'. Cumming (1989: 46–7) sees such personalised theories as being shaped by and shaping classroom instruction:

> The kinds of practical knowledge which teachers use in teaching appear to exist largely in very personalised terms, based on unique experiences, individual conceptions, and their interactions with local contexts. It tends to have a personal significance which differs from prescribed models of educational theory.

Calderhead (1991) refers to this kind of specialised teacher knowledge as pedagogic content knowledge. Such views of teachers' professional knowledge emphasise the importance of theories or beliefs that grow out of and are changed by practice. Yet practice can never be constructed as simply pedagogic, to do with the act of teaching. It is always political and value-laden in the broadest sense. As Pennington (1989: 96) observes:

> Classroom behaviour will inevitably reflect . . . (teachers') underlying attitudes towards the students, towards themselves and towards the entire educational enterprise.

Teacher practice, inside and outside the classroom, is shaped both by the external context, that is, the institutional, sociocultural and political practices of the society in which the teacher operates, and by the complex interactions between learners and between teachers and learners.[12] Thus, in any construct of professional knowledge, theoretical and pedagogic knowledge interact with and are influenced by other sorts of implicit or explicit contextual knowledge, including institutional, sociocultural and political knowledge. Together these epistemologies or 'knowledges' could be perceived to form teachers' professional knowledge and are both reflected in and shaped by practice (Figure 4.1).

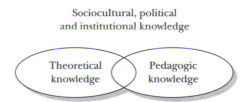

Figure 4.1   The conceptualisation of professional knowledge

This raises the issue of the nature of professional 'development'. Pennington (1989: 97) suggests that developing attitudes or personal theories is more important than, and has to precede, the introduction of teaching techniques and resources. However, we are not 'empty vessels' when we enter the teaching world. We already hold many unexamined and strong beliefs about the nature and scope of our task.

Many researchers suggest that, for teachers, development occurs when there is a reappraisal of these values, beliefs and attitudes as well as teaching practices, and an attempt to reconcile inconsistencies and develop greater coherence and applicability (Burns, 1992; Connors, 1991; Walker and Evers, 1984; Yaxley, 1991). The concern for more consistency seems to be based on an assumption that diversity of practices and beliefs is problematic and a sign

of the need for development. However, there is a contradictory possibility –
that uncertainty and unresolved conflicts in teaching are inevitable. As Hawkins
and Irujo (1993: 13) comment:

> We have been struck ... by the efforts of our colleagues to wrestle with the
> conflicts that arise when a field experiences a major theoretical shift ... We
> have begun to view issues and problems as inherent tensions, rather than as
> questions to which we must ultimately find answers ...

It could be argued that an awareness of such tensions is more likely to be
a sign of an enhanced professional than an indication of someone in need of
'professional development'. Moore (1992: 3), in rethinking the role of eclecticism in language and literacy teacher education, also argues for greater
openness and diversity in thinking about teacher development:

> Theories, principles and practices can be/are in open contestation; ideologies
> and embedded assumptions may also be in conflict ... each relates to the other,
> impacts on the other ... (it is) not a closed system ... ways of thinking are
> open to change and development, (they are) rarely entirely consistent with one
> another ... the power of each level rests in part on the degree of its openness
> and in part on its relationship to other levels.

In fact, in Figure 4.2 I would argue that 'development' is gained more in the
awareness of the inconsistencies or friction between different values, beliefs,
principles, theories and practices than in the neat resolution of such inconsistencies. Yet such a view reveals an apparently inherent conflict between
developing a sense of professional identity and professional development. As
Hawkins and Irujo (1993: 13) point out in relation to TESOL:

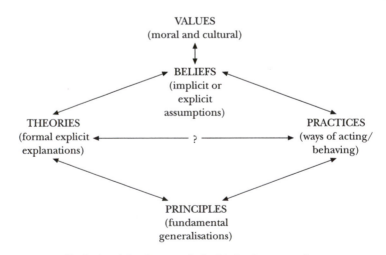

Professional development is the friction between values,
beliefs, principles, theories and practices.

Figure 4.2   The conceptualisation of professional development (teacher's perspective)

We are trying to create a sense of community in our (teacher) learners. A stable community, however, inhibits change. If we are successful in building a strong community, do we then lose the ability to change when necessary?

The answer to this question depends very much on the way in which change is presented to teachers. Change is almost always accompanied by professional development, but change cannot be equated with development. The term 'development' suggests evolution, enhancement, improvement, progress – but not all models of 'professional development' are perceived to have these characteristics. The next section seeks to define and evaluate different models of professional development according to their capacity to develop 'professionalism'. In doing so, I hope to offer the beginnings of a critique of one of the major modes of 'regulating expertise' and suggest some possible alternatives to current practice.

DEFINING AND REDEFINING PROFESSIONAL DEVELOPMENT

Eraut (1986) distinguishes four different paradigms of professional development: defect, growth, change and problem-solving. It could be argued that these models parallel Zeichner's (1983: 6) classification of beliefs about learning to teach: the behaviourist paradigm, the personalistic or growth paradigm, the craft or apprenticeship approach and the inquiry-oriented paradigm. The models assume particular views of the nature of professional knowledge and the function of professional development and each is associated with particular professional development strategies (and models of curriculum and program development).

Eraut (1986) sees one approach to professional development as redressing defect, focusing upon teacher obsolescence or inefficiency. Such professional development seems to be essentially product oriented with professional knowledge being externally constructed and given to the teacher. This model is commonly associated with lists of skills and competencies. It stresses teacher performance and accountability. Professional development is 'delivered' to the teacher through packages of lectures and workshops and there is usually little, if any, negotiation in content selection with teachers.

The problem with the deficit model is that it generally fails to recognise that teacher competence is a construct and not something that can be observed directly from quantifiable outputs (Nance and Fawns, 1993) which may lead to professional development practices which are static and unresponsive to different contexts and changing teacher needs. Emphasising top-down delivery can also breed an overly dependent 'workforce'.

Although this model may be politically popular, it lacks pedagogic flexibility and credibility. As Wajnryb (1992: 36) argues in relation to ESL teacher education:

In passing on the invented wheel – in the form of 'pat solutions' without the struggle to invent – we are perhaps generating more problems than we set out to remedy as we are denying others the excitement to construct their own knowledge and perpetuating the notion of dependence on outside agencies as the sources and mediators of change.

The second model of professional development identified by Eraut (1986) is growth, which views the practitioner as a self-motivated and reflective teacher seeking fulfilment through self-improvement. This model sees professional knowledge as almost entirely experiential and internally developed. It emphasises self-evaluation and teacher-selected content. It is associated with unstructured teacher discussion groups, collaborative workplace professional development and individual reading. This process of growth in competence and maturity is seen as a direct contrast to 'off the job education and training' (Costello, 1991: 131).

The growth model was the dominant paradigm in professional development and classroom practice in the 1980s, especially in Victoria. The problem with the growth model is that it can lead to a lack of uniformity in content or 'standards' across a profession and result in wide discrepancies in classroom practice. There is also a problem in developing appropriate public accountability mechanisms, the lack of which can undermine professional credibility. So, although the growth model may meet local pedagogic concerns, it is too open-ended and inward-looking to have political viability in the current educational climate.

Eraut's (1986) third model of professional development is that of change, the dominant model of development in contemporary Victorian education. This model recognises the need for educational systems to anticipate or be receptive of current changes in society (Connors, 1991: 6). The change model sees the system and/or the profession as constructing the professional knowledge rather than the individual teacher. According to Eraut (1986: 733) 'such changes will not necessarily be recognised, understood, or desired by all teachers but they will have to come to terms with them'. The assumption is that the teacher will fit the change, rather than vice versa. The model is linked with program evaluation in which teacher performance and development are seen as part of an overarching agenda. Teacher development and school development are intertwined (Fullan, 1991).

This model is associated with professional development delivery as structural change, for example, through the introduction of curriculum frameworks and common assessment procedures by the system. The teacher becomes an 'apprentice' to the structures and through models and exemplar is 'developed'.

Connors (1991: 58) points out that this model assumes three general outcomes of effective professional development for the teacher: changes in teachers' beliefs and attitudes, changes in teachers' instructional practices and changes in teachers' content knowledge. However, he also highlights the importance of understanding the teachers' perspective on change. In his study of teacher development (Connors, 1987), he found that teachers wanted to know about current developments in their field but they also rated highly learning things which they could readily adapt into their present practices. They viewed changes that would lead to major changes in their teaching practices negatively but were happy to develop knowledge, skills and strategies that would enable them to initiate changes.

This is a subtle yet important distinction. Although the change paradigm is politically very attractive, it is more remote from the classroom – this is its Achilles heel. The fact that the nature, timing and rate of change is driven by the system rather than by the teacher, means that as a model of professional development it can get 'too far ahead' of teachers and lose its purpose and relevance for them. Collins (1991: 17) argues that in such a situation: 'The teacher will simply decouple the classroom from the engine of political rhetoric.'

Eraut's (1986) fourth model of professional development is the problem-solving paradigm, associated with inquiry-oriented beliefs about learning to teach. This model assumes that the act and the context of teaching are complex and problematic but that solutions are best worked out by teachers in their own classrooms and workplaces. As Connors (1991: 56) emphasises in regard to teachers:

> Because of their knowledge of the school and its pupils, teachers are in the best position to identify the problems and solve many of them, assisted by their colleagues in the school. However, at times external consultants may be called in to work with school staff in solving the problem. Teacher development in this paradigm is achieved through active involvement in the problem-solving process.

This model of professional development appears to have elements in common with the growth model but teachers are more analytical and more focused in identifying their professional development goals. The model constructs professional knowledge as experientially based but there is much more explicitness about the nature of that knowledge and the processes of its development and a recognition of the value-saturated nature of teaching.

Critical reflection is the central strategy associated with the problem-solving paradigm, although the term has become somewhat of a cliché. For example, Schön (1987) focuses on 'coaching' whereby the student and 'coach' work together to solve a problem, and in the process the teacher's knowledge and reflective processes become explicit. Other interpretations use the term more in the sense of developing a critical awareness of the causes and consequences of classroom practice. For example, Burns (1992: 64) argues that:

> One of the useful roles for teacher education may be to find ways in which teachers can articulate and reflect upon what beliefs motivate the interactions they set in train in the classrooms.

Calderhead (1991: 3) highlights the common aims of most interpretations of reflective practice but also raises a number of problems with the approach, including: the difficulty in describing development; the uneasy relationship between personal knowledge and curricular knowledge with the inevitable privileging of the latter; the contradictions between the need to develop particular areas of knowledge, skill and attitudes and the aim of encouraging autonomy and professional responsibility within a professional set of obligations; the need to reconcile a focus on reflection with demands for teacher assessment; and the problems of individual differences in beliefs and learning practices. These concerns are also echoed by Hawkins and Irujo (1993: 13), who observe with regard to teacher education:

> Don't we have to control certain processes in order to allow our students to take control of themselves? How can we 'get' them to take responsibility for their own learning without forcing them to accept our view of the learning process? How do we ensure teachers acquire certain knowledge and skills while still allowing them to construct their own knowledge?

These comments highlight the weaknesses of a problem-solving model of professional development which ignores its institutional, sociocultural and political context.

Using Zeichner's (1983) terminology, all these models of professional development could be described as value positions. However, it would be wrong to suggest that these models are discrete types. Different approaches might also be needed at different stages of teaching. Fenstermacher and Berliner (1985) and Zimpher (1988) point out that teachers' needs vary over time and they may require different kinds of support and resources at different stages of their professional development, for example, induction, consolidation and so on. To adapt Fielding's (1983) terms, as the teacher begins to move towards becoming a novice professional, more 'apprenticeship-like' approaches may be needed, but as the novice professional moves into the client-centred stage and starts to be more analytical and critical, more reflective approaches may be appropriate.

The Australian TESOL experience shows that critical factors such as teacher stress, lack of collegiality leadership, and the scale and pace of change may also influence the effectiveness of professional development.

Teacher stress is associated with changing external demands, poor working conditions, constant disruption and time pressures and lack of control by teachers over their own job definition. This can be a particular issue when teachers are ESL teachers yet do not feel properly qualified or used. Stressed teachers do not have the energy to take risks, to try out new ideas, to accept the inevitable, if temporary, incompetence that accompanies experimentation. They adopt self-protection strategies rather then open themselves up to change. It could be argued that ESL in schools is often guilty of institutionalised practices which wear out rather than sustain those at the chalkface. Research on teacher development shows that teachers must be acknowledged as competent professionals (Logan and Sachs, 1988) and given both support in the personal risk-taking that professional development demands (Fullan, 1991) and a sense of control over the process. A significant 'success' factor in

Victorian TESOL has been the development of official policy and structural support for ESL practice and the development of agreed teacher qualifications and standards, but teacher stress is still a major factor inhibiting effective professional development and ESL policy implementation.

The second major factor inhibiting effective professional development is lack of opportunities for professional collaboration. Although professional development sponsored by outside agencies is important, for effective 'ESL in the Mainstream' the most crucial is that built into the school itself, part of the normal cycle of school evaluation and renewal (Goodlad, 1983, 1984; Joyce, 1986). Informed by a strong ESL policy framework, teachers need to be encouraged to observe colleagues, exchange feedback with colleagues, consult and reflect with colleagues and plan and evaluate together (Anastos and Arcowitz, 1987; Eisner, 1988; Little, 1984). Friendly and supportive professional relationships also contribute to the institutional climate and to teacher satisfaction. Hence, ESL teachers also need access to mentor figures and leaders in the field to whom they can turn for guidance and support (Ingvarson & MacKenzie, 1988). The nature of ESL teaching is such that teachers are often divided and isolated, even from others who face the same pedagogic challenges. Many teachers who have more skills and experience are seconded into research or curriculum development, or are promoted out of the classroom. Lack of secure career paths and the absence of any 'leading teacher' class in ESL exacerbate this trend. In Australia, institutional structures such as Language Australia and professional associations such as the Australian Council of TESOL Associations, which support this kind of collegiality and 'mentoring', have been vital. The contribution of such a collaborative ESL professional culture to achievements in Australian ESL education cannot be overestimated.

The final factor inhibiting professional development and change is that most critical one of all – time. Research shows again and again that developing new knowledge and skills and integrating new skills into practice takes a lot of time (Goodlad 1984; Fullan 1991; Joyce 1986). The Commonwealth report *Teachers' Learning* (DEET, 1988: 38) also emphasises that any changes to established practices need time:

> (For) Training and development programs (that) require changes in practice which are significantly different from those which are current, a period of three to five years is necessary.

Collins (1991: 19) argues 'it takes a lot of courage and support through months of feeling clumsy . . . a long practice time' before a fundamental breakthrough point is reached when teachers understand why this works better (Fullan and Hargreaves, 1992) and integrate the approach or idea into their own personal theory of teaching (Little, 1984). To be somewhat simplistic about it, this emphasises the importance of not confusing input with intake, intake with uptake and uptake with 'take-on'.

I would argue that the scale and rate of change in Australian education, exacerbated by pressure to meet political rather than professional timelines, has been a particular and obvious stumbling block to successful implementation of ESL education at all levels. Occasionally, too, the ESL profession has been carried away by the engine of its own rhetoric, creating an imperialism of views, and in the process leaving both its practitioners and content area teachers behind.

At the risk of being portrayed as an arch-pragmatist, this leads me to propose an alternative model of professional development – one in which the system or school or teacher negotiates the selection of content in professional development and presents its solutions as problems to teachers. This model would highlight the importance of focused, guided collaboration and professional dialogue. In this model, input is absolutely critical and the presence of mentor/supervisor/expert who can help to guide and direct the nature of the input and framing of discussion is essential. Visits to other schools, classroom observations, reading professional journals, participation in research projects and involvement in professional associations are also all vehicles for input.

In this model professional knowledge is seen as being jointly constructed and both experiential and theory-driven. Professional development and change take place through being confronted with and having to articulate different ways of doing and seeing the same thing, through conflict and critique, not just collaboration (or co-option), friction not just reflection. In the process, ESL teachers would be forced to articulate their own professional understandings and critique those of others, including the ESL profession, and, in so doing, would be better prepared for both the pedagogic and practical demands of working in a 'mainstreamed' ESL program. It would also enable grassroots needs, experiences and reactions to feed into ongoing policy development in a far more systematic way and return to teachers a greater sense of control over educational change.[13]

CONCLUSIONS

The development of coherent and effective ESL programs in Australian schools has been a long and ongoing struggle, but a struggle which has resulted in some major achievements. To better support our students, ourselves and our colleagues, attention now needs to turn to the task of consolidating and contextualising the rhetoric of much recent policy, developing and disseminating many more models of curriculum implementation and cultivating the habit of strong and vigorous critique. As the discussion above has demonstrated, attention also needs to be given to promoting a better understanding of professional development and system-level change in order to ensure that 'good' policy and practice is developed and implemented at all levels. In so doing, those at the chalkface – students and teachers, activists and followers – will be better prepared for the future whether that be the ongoing development of ESL in the Mainstream, or another right angle into the unknown.

NOTES

1. I am particularly indebted to my colleagues, Alan Williams and Sophie Arkoudis, for comments and contributions to this chapter.
2. These extracts are drawn from a study by the author which examines the language learning experiences of Cantonese-speaking background students in one major component of senior secondary English.
3. For official purposes in Australia there has been a long history of defining ESL learners using length of residence in an English-speaking country as almost the sole criterion. In the VCE an 'ESL' designation can only be applied to a LOTE background student who has been in Australia and/or in an English medium school less than seven years, irrespective of his or her actual English language level or need for ESL support. This reduces the possible 'ESL' cohort from about 40 per cent of the total school population to about 4 per cent.
4. This extract is taken from an article by Doyle and Reinhardt (1992), based on their experiences of team teaching in this school.
5. See Arkoudis (1995) for actual examples of such distortion and an examination of the enculturated pedagogical beliefs of mathematics, science and ESL teachers.
6. ESL consultants, along with other highly experienced specialist support teachers, used to be located in School Support Centres scattered across each school region. However, under the Schools of the Future Program, schools themselves have been given direct funding to use as they wish for professional development, thus many schools now have to recruit private consultants, raising major concerns as to the quality and continuity of advice and support.
7. This extract predates the release of the ESL Companion to the English CSF. It is hoped that the wide adoption of that document in schools will draw much greater attention to the problems of assessing ESL needs only in relation to the content curriculum.
8. In fact, in Victoria, progressive pedagogics such as curriculum negotiation, process writing, whole language, natural learning and cooperative learning have been dominant in schools since the early to mid-1980s. Although they appear to be more inclusive, their 'invisibility (Bernstein, 1990) and focus on student-led learning and participation have in fact created perhaps even more barriers for many ESL learners than more traditional teaching approaches.
9. See Jones and Moore (1993) and Lingard et al. (1993) for discussions of the current 'educational' context, and the shift of control from educational professionals to bureaucrats, from a cultural mode to a technical mode of production.
10. I take the position that 'good' policy is developed from top-down and bottom-up, that is, there needs to an awareness not only of the existing needs and constraints of the chalkface but also an understanding of the range of theoretical possibilities. Therefore, 'good' policy is not so much a product but an ongoing two-way process requiring multiple contextualisation.
11. Jones and Moore (1993: 391) argue that this may change as the humanistic-liberal model of professionalism is replaced by the competency mode. A significant feature of competency (compared with liberalism) is that it requires the production of formal specification of 'skills' or 'competencies' (such as the Australian TESOL Teacher Competences (Hogan, 1994)). Access and control can then be exercised through the regulation of outputs (performance indicators, etc.) rather than through inputs (knowledge and cultural attributes acquired through professional socialisation). This reduces the amount of time required to 'train' new members

in the depth of general, theoretical knowledge they require and weakens the significance of the distinctive occupational culture. An example of such weakening in England is the downgrading of university-based teacher training and the suggestions of alternative models of entry such as licensed and articled teachers.

12. In fact, Nance and Fawns (1993: 163) posit a strong developmental relationship between emerging subject and pedagogic knowledge and this kind of contextual understanding, arguing that teacher competence can only exist where the right combination of skills and knowledge, on the one hand, and contextual understanding on the other, co-exist.

13. Unfortunately the critical foundations of this mode and its joint ownership mean that it is unlikely to find great acceptance in the educational bureaucracy, but one lives in hope!

Part II

CANADA

Chapter 5

ESL in British Columbia

Mary Ashworth

IMMIGRATION

The first arrivals in Canada were the aboriginals who walked over the land bridge between the west coast of Russia and the Aleutian Islands. They were named 'Indians' by the first white men to arrive on the Atlantic Coast because they believed that they were in India. Now they are referred to as 'First Nations' people' in recognition of their early arrival in North America.

Since the mid-sixteenth century onwards, immigrants from all over the world have been arriving in Canada; first in Atlantic and eastern Canada and then in the west, either overland or by sea. Because British Columbia lies on the Pacific Rim, it has received more Asian immigrants than any other province. This resulted in the early years of this century in riots in Vancouver, and in discrimination both in school and out of school.

For example, in 1901 the Victoria School Board heard a petition from the residents of the Rock Bay District who asked that all Chinese children at Rock Bay School should be withdrawn or at least placed in separate rooms within the building. One trustee immediately called for the Chinese children to be put in a separate school. But Trustee Belyea spoke up. 'I would like to point out, Mr Chairman, that Chinese children, under our existing law, have the same right to a free education as children of any other race, and we, as the elected trustees, have no power and no right to take action on this petition' and the petition failed. In September 1922, however, the board faced a similar petition and this time agreed on a policy of total segregation. All Chinese children in all the schools in Victoria were directed to three schools set aside exclusively for them – the excuse being that their poor English hampered the other children, yet many of the Chinese youngsters had been born in Canada, spoke fluent English and were at or near the top of their classes. The parents of the Chinese children withdrew them from the segregated schools and the boycott began. The story became international news, and little by little the board backed down and by September 1923 the children were back in their regular classes. The right of all children to a public school education no matter what their race or nationality or where they had come from had been maintained.

During the 1920s immigration from China, Japan and India was severely limited thereby reducing somewhat the pressure on the schools. Education was not the only arena in which discrimination vs justice was played out; employment and housing were two areas where adults met discrimination, which, of course, affected children.

Under the terms of Confederation, the Provincial Government of British Columbia became responsible for the education of all children within its boundaries, except native children who were the responsibility of the Federal (Dominion) Government. Educators of non-English-speaking immigrant children believed that their task was to 'Canadianize' the children, which could best be done by teaching them English and denying them access to their first language during school hours. Norman F. Black (1913), in a methodology text, believed that 'the keynote to the correct teaching of English to beginners is the practically exclusive use of that language in the classroom'. The depression years of the Dirty Thirties meandered slowly towards the outbreak of the Second World War. While Canadian men and women joined the forces and served with distinction in various theatres of war, those of Japanese origin living within a hundred miles of the British Columbia coast were interned in camps in the interior in case they might prove disloyal, and their goods were sold to provide them with money to pay for their enforced evacuation. Elementary education was provided for the young children; teenagers took correspondence courses under the tutelage of church workers. When the war was over, the men and women in the forces returned home and the Japanese-Canadians in the internment camps spread out across Canada or were repatriated to Japan. There had been no incidents of disloyalty.

After the 1939–45 war, perhaps as a result of the war, society's attitudes began to mellow, resulting in time in a change in the immigration laws and an increase in the numbers of immigrants who were accepted. But changes did not come easily. In 1947 Prime Minister Mackenzie King made his famous statement restricting immigration from Asia on the grounds that the people of Canada did not want to see any fundamental alteration in the character of their population. In 1950 the ban on enemy aliens was lifted – Germans were free to enter Canada – but a quota system was set up to allow only a few Asians to enter each year.

Changes to the immigration regulations in 1962 removed some of the more blatantly racist clauses. The 1966 White Paper on Immigration Policy resulted in new immigration regulations in 1967 which set up a points system. Applicants were required to attain at least 50 of a possible 100 points based on a knowledge of French or English, education, training, occupational demand, occupational skill, age, and having a relative in Canada. The points system was supposed to provide a basis for Canada's economic growth. The result of the new regulations was swift and dramatic; immigration from Asia and third world countries was now possible provided applicants could acquire the requisite number of points.

The new Immigration Act of 1977 set out certain basic principles underlying immigration policy: non-discrimination, family reunion, humanitarian concern for refugees, and the promotion of Canada's social, economic, demographic and cultural goals. The new act established three classes of admissible immigrants: the family class, Convention refugees, and independent immigrants. The federal government decided each year on the total number of immigrants that would be admitted. A recent figure places the number to be admitted at about 250,000, but that figure can fluctuate when internal unrest in various countries causes more people than expected to arrive claiming refugee status, or when the Canadian economy declines.

CHANGING SOCIAL CONTEXT

In 1946, immigration, which had slowed to a mere trickle during the Thirties' Depression and the Second World War, picked up and, due to changes to the Immigration Act, began to alter the demographic composition of British Columbia and the other provinces to a greater or lesser degree. Homes had to be found for the displaced people of Europe. Political refugees from Hungary, Czechoslovakia and Uganda sought entry to Canada, as over the years did people from Lebanon, Haiti, Russia, Vietnam, Somalia and Ethiopia. Economic refugees from many countries sought better living standards and better opportunities for themselves and their families in the booming Canadian economy. All expected the British Columbia school system to teach their children English and prepare them, if possible, for a seat in an institution of higher learning.

The faces of children from around the world could be seen in classrooms throughout BC. The majority could be found in Vancouver, fewer in Victoria, the provincial capital, but small towns in the interior where there were mines or sawmills also attracted 'visible minorities' as some of them came to be known. Many teachers were quite unprepared for the influx of children speaking languages they had not heard before and coming from cultures they knew little about. School districts, sometimes with the help of the BC Ministry of Education, hastily put together information sheets on the backgrounds of children from Vietnam, Laos, Uganda and other countries when the need arose.

The Report of the Royal Commission on Bilingualism and Biculturalism (RCBB, 1969) encouraged French- and English-Canadians to integrate their two societies. According to the commissioners, integration does not imply the loss of an individual's identity or original language and culture. 'The process of integration,' they wrote, 'which contributes to the development of the two societies, should therefore be guided by three conditions: the good of the individual, the good of the society he chooses, and the good of the country as a whole' (RCBB, 1969: 5). However, the commissioners saw immigrants as acculturating rather than integrating into Canadian society – acculturation being the process of adaptation to the environment in which an individual is compelled to live. They wrote, 'Anyone who chooses Canada as his adopted country adopts a new style of life, a particular kind of existence. This phenomenon is easily visible in the immigrant's experience in the work world, in his social contacts with other people, in the schools, where children acquire a major part of their preparation for life, and in all his contact with other citizens and public institutions' (RCBB, 1969: 6). The 1960s was an era when racism seemed to be on the increase. Changes to the Immigration Act had opened the way for more immigrants from third world countries, many of whom were 'visible minorities'.

Book IV of The Royal Commission's report, *The Cultural Contribution of the Other Ethnic Groups* (RCBB, 1969: 9), talked of

> many signs of hostility towards immigrants and even towards Canadians of various ethnic origins whose ancestors arrived in Canada two or three genera- tions ago. Yet some Canadians inflict this totally undeserved suffering upon others. It is particularly deplorable when it occurs in schools, not only because the victims are children, but also because of the risk of implanting long-lasting prejudices in other children.

Workshops on multiculturalism and racism were given not just to teachers and administrators but also to members of other institutions, such as the police and social workers. The report said that the presence in Canada of many people whose language and culture are distinctive by reason of their birth or ancestry represents an inestimable enrichment that Canadians cannot afford to lose, but there were – and are today – some who felt that Canada could get along quite well without them.

The recession in the early 1980s was repeated again in the early 1990s, increasing unemployment and causing a rise in racism and discrimination. 'They take our jobs,' was the cry of the working poor and unemployed. 'They are a drain on welfare handouts,' said the better-off. In fact, neither statement was true, but few could be persuaded. Research on the growth of tolerance in Canada and Toronto (Toronto School Board, 1992) indicated that 'levels of prejudice are diminishing and . . . contact is leading to more positive attitudes'. However, the report went on to state that 'the potential for conflict increases when the proportion of visible minority immigrants increases rapidly' – precisely the situation that occurred in British Columbia with the influx of Chinese from Hong Kong as 1997, the date when Hong Kong was returned to China, grew ever nearer. Racist actions, however, tended on the whole not be directed towards the Chinese who, since the war, had entered the professions and were living in areas which, prior to the war, were occupied by whites only. Discrimination centred on the South-East Asians (formerly known as East Indians) and efforts were made to reduce tensions between whites and South-East Asians through various non-government organisations and through courses and workshops for teachers.

(LACK OF) LANGUAGE POLICIES

Prior to the Second World War, school districts made their own policies covering the education of non-English-speaking immigrant children who, at that time, were known as New Canadians, a name that had to be dropped in favour of English as a Second Language students when children from Quebec entered the BC school system, and could hardly be called 'New Canadians'.

In 1907 the Vancouver School Board, which has consistently received the majority of ESL students in BC, opened its first class designed to teach ESL. Today there are approximately 240 ESL teachers working in the Vancouver school system alone, and many more throughout the rest of the province. Some districts found ESL classes a means of (1) segregating Asian children from Caucasian children; (2) relieving classrooms teachers of the task of teaching non-English speakers English; and (3) satisfying parents that immigrant children were not in a position to slow down the teaching/learning process in the classroom through their lack of facility in the language of instruction. Segregated classes have recently been challenged in some English-speaking countries as discriminatory and therefore against Human Rights legislation.

Following the close of hostilities in 1945, the BC government provided some funds to cover part of the cost of these classes, but there were some restrictions: children under the age of 9 years could not receive assistance in learning English as it was presumed that they would acquire as they mixed with other children, and a limit of one year was placed on a child's enrolment in an ESL class.

The 1960s and 1970s were decades of national, provincial and local reports. In 1969, as mentioned above, the Royal Commission on Bilingualism and Biculturalism brought out Book IV of its report. While this was a federal document, some of its recommendations had implications for the provinces regarding education. Three recommendations bore directly on public schools. Numbers 3 and 5 recommended that the teaching of languages other than English and French be incorporated as options in the elementary and secondary school programs, thus strengthening the voices of those who felt that heritage languages should be the responsibility of schools. Number 4 recommended that special instruction in one of the two official languages should be provided for children who entered the school system with an inadequate knowledge of the language of instruction. The federal government soon made it clear that it would assist heritage language programs by providing funds for the creation of curricula and materials, but it would not fund English as a Second Language/Dialect (ESL/D) programs which, in its view, were the responsibility of the provincial governments. The question of whether the federal or provincial governments are responsible for funding ESL/D programs has still not been resolved. Some provincial governments and district boards of trustees across Canada maintain that as the federal government decides how many immigrants enter the country each year and from which source countries, it should be responsible for English language training of both adults and children. The federal government, however, points out that under the Constitution the provinces are responsible for public school education. The fact that, in recent years, the provinces have been consulted before the federal government makes its decision on numbers and source countries of new immigrants has not changed the positions of the adversaries. The federal government does, however, provide funding for French immersion courses in schools in an endeavour to make Canada a bilingual country, so we have the somewhat ironic position that the federal government will provide funding to help a newly arrived Cantonese-speaking child to learn French, but not English, the language of instruction in most schools in British Columbia!

In 1980 the BC Ministry of Education drew together a committee whose task was to write a resource book for ESL/D administrators and teachers of kindergarten to grade 12. The committee took advantage of their task and wrote a philosophy of the program, the goals of the program, and definitions of ESL/D students. Once these items had been accepted by the Minister of Education, they represented the policy of the Ministry of Education, which had never before been drafted in such detail. The resource book stated: 'The philosophy of the ESL/D program is that all students, regardless of their linguistic and cultural background, will have the opportunity to develop their potential to the fullest extent' (BC Ministry of Education, 1981: 4). ESL/D students were seen as having needs in two areas: language and culture. Integration was preferred over assimilation. ESL/D students were to be placed in situations that would maximise their opportunities to learn standard Canadian English. The final statement of philosophy read: 'The degree of success of the ESL/D program depends, to a large extent, on the amount of interaction and understanding between the student, the school and the student's home' (BC Ministry of Education, 1981: 4).

The goals of the program were to help ESL/D students to develop and maintain a sense of self-worth, to develop and preserve a pride of heritage, to develop communicative competence, to become oriented to those aspects of methodology, curriculum, and extra-curricular activities that differ from those of the student's previous experiences, and to develop an understanding of and appreciation for cultural differences and similarities.

All this was preceded by two all-important definitions: 'English as a second language students are those whose progress in the English-speaking school system is not commensurate with their age and/or abilities, due to the fact that English is not their first language' and 'English as a second dialect students are those whose dialect of English is sufficiently different from that used by the school system so as to restrict their progress' (BC Ministry of Education, 1981: 3). This meant that children born in Canada but brought up in homes where English was not spoken had the right to instruction in English as Second Language.

A closing statement tackled multiculturalism and racism: 'In a multicultural society, it is of paramount importance that the entire student body be involved in a program of mutual exchange of cultural information that will result in an understanding of and an appreciation for the various cultures represented in the school and community' (BC Ministry of Education, 1981: 4).

In 1994 the BC Ministry of Education drew up a 'Language Policy' which covered English Language Education, French Language Education, First

Nations' Languages Education, and Additional Languages Education. It has, however, had a rough road, and has yet to be proclaimed as the province's official policy.

The teaching of heritage or home languages walked a similar rough road for some years, but, as noted above, federal money is now available for writing curricula for heritage languages, which, in most provinces, are usually taught after school or on Saturday mornings, the exception being Ontario where some heritage languages are taught during the regular school day which was lengthened by half an hour in an Act that was not well received.

Skutnabb-Kangas (1988) underlined the importance of heritage languages when she wrote that many minority children were becoming forced to feel ashamed of their mother tongues, their parents, their origins, their group and their cultures and went on to propose a 'Declaration of children's linguistic human rights':

1. Every child should have the right to identify positively with his or her original mother tongue(s) and have his or her identification accepted and respected by others.
2. Every child should have the right to learn the mother tongue(s) fully.
3. Every child should have the right to choose when he or she wants to use the mother tongue(s) in all official situations (Skutnabb-Kangas, 1988: 19).

The BC Teachers' Federation in 1994 carried out some research into ESL through questionnaires and discussion with focus groups. They found that while most districts had policies regarding ESL, several did not, including one large district. Those who responded called for policies in the following areas:

- explicit policies for ESL programming,
- policies regarding the integration of language and content,
- policies to improve intercultural relations among students within schools,
- policies to promote the value of ESL students' mother tongues and cultural heritages,
- policies on the standards of achievement expected of ESL students,
- policies regarding parent and community participation, and
- policies regarding the implementation of home-school delivery of ESL services, that is, that students should attend the school closest to their home.

PROGRAMS

In the 1950s, 1960s and 1970s there were three types of ESL programs in operation across Canada: reception classes; withdrawal or pullout programs for individuals or small groups; and total immersion. In 1988 at least 13 program types were in use across Canada, many of which were, or had been, in operation in British Columbia:

1. *Self-contained programs*
   Full day reception classes
   Half day reception classes
   Bilingual classes
2. *Withdrawal or pullout classes*
   English Language/Learning Centres
   Itinerant ESL teachers
   Tutorials
3. *Transitional programs*
   Subject matter transitional classes
   Vocational/pre-employment programs
   Academic booster programs
   Special Education and ESL/D
   Pre-school programs
4. *Mainstreaming*
   Immersion programs with support
   Immersion programs without support

The late 1980s and early 1990s brought a number of reports. One of the earliest was the Sullivan Report (Sullivan, 1988). The Commission received briefs from the Association of Teachers of English as an Additional Language (TEAL) and from other organisations and individuals concerned with multi-culturalism and/or ESL, but the report made limited reference to ESL, point-ing out the obvious that some children had learning difficulties because English was their second language. One of the commissioned papers on curriculum stated:

> Most school districts in the Lower Mainland have effective ESL programmes for students: but, because of limited resources, they are unable to offer them to parents. Many smaller school districts do not have extensive ESL programmes either because of a lack of resources or a perceived lack of need because of small numbers of ESL children needing such services. We see the need for such programmes and for teachers with appropriate qualifications, continuing to increase in the future. We would encourage the Ministry of Education, local school districts, and the three Faculties of Education to take appropriate measures to meet this challenge.   (Sullivan, 1988: 61)

In January 1989, three external examiners, Jim Cummins from the Ontario Institute for Studies in Education, Jean Handscombe from the North York School Board, and Mary Ashworth, professor emeritus, from the University of British Columbia, published their review of the Vancouver School Board's ESL program. They found that 46.9 per cent of the total school population of 23,732 were ESL, a number that is now over 50 per cent and still climbing; that one-third of the ESL students were born outside Canada; that approx-imately one-half of the elementary and secondary ESL pupils were behind their age/peers in their English language facility; and that approximately 1,500 elementary ESL pupils and approximately 1,400 secondary ESL pupils were receiving less language assistance than they needed. From these and other data collected, the external review team recommended that:

> Given the present composition of the VSB population and the strong likeli-hood that the system will continue to receive increasing numbers of ESL students both through immigration and from homes where languages other than English are spoken, what is required is a recognition that ESL should assume a central position in all aspects of VSB planning and operations.
>
> (Ashworth et al., 1989: 5)

The review team (see Ashworth et al., 1989: 11–20) based its recommendations on five principles:

1. The educational and personal experiences ESL students bring to Canadian schools constitute the foundation for all their future learning; schools should therefore attempt to amplify rather than replace these experiences.
2. Although English conversational skills may be acquired quite rapidly by ESL students, upwards of five years may be required by ESL students to reach a level of academic proficiency in English comparable to their native English-speaking peers; schools must therefore be prepared to make a long-term commitment to support the academic development of ESL students.
3. Interaction with users of English is a major causal variable underlying both the acquisition of English and ESL students' sense of belonging to Canadian society; the entire school is therefore responsible for supporting the learning and interactional needs of ESL students and ESL provision should integrate students into the social and academic mainstream to the greatest extent possible.
4. If ESL students are to catch up academically with their native-English-speaking peers, their cognitive growth and mastery of academic content must continue while English is being learned. Thus, the teaching of English as a Second Language should be integrated with the teaching of other academic content that is appropriate to students' cognitive level. By the same token, all content teachers are also teachers of language.
5. The academic and linguistic growth of ESL students is significantly increased when parents see themselves, and are seen by school staff, as co-educators of their children along with the school. Schools should therefore actively seek to establish a collaborative relationship with minority parents that encourages them to participate with the school in promoting their children's academic progress.

The BC Provincial Ministry Responsible for Multiculturalism and Immigration published in 1991 a document entitled *Settlement services for immigrant children: a needs assessment*, which pointed out that the number of children requiring ESL assistance over the next five to ten years would increase significantly, with the greatest demands being in the urban areas – a forecast which has largely come true.

In 1994, Charlie Naylor of the Research and Technology Department of the BC Teachers' Federation completed his important research project on ESL in BC. One document presented district profiles for 16 school districts having many or few ESL students. Other information was collected from the discussions of four focus groups involving ESL teachers, classroom teachers, parents and students. In 1995 the Richmond BC School District published its review of ESL support services, in which it reiterated its commitment to the inclusion or integration of the specific needs of the ESL students, and what that means in terms of delivery of services and the best practices in instruction. That same year Alister Cumming completed his *Review of ESL Services in the Vancouver School Board*. A number of the recommendations in the 1989 evaluation of the Vancouver School Board's ESL program had been put in place, most notably the Oakridge Reception and Orientation Centre. Cumming's review (1995: 3) was concerned with 'identifying aspects that are noteworthy and exemplary as well as areas potentially in need of change and suggesting means for addressing such changes'. Finally, a review of the Victoria School Board's ESL program was completed in February, 1997, in which I listed 45 recommendations (Ashworth, 1997).

Taken together the reports made the following points:

Policies

There is a need for explicit policies covering ESL programming; integration of language and content; standards of achievement expected of ESL students; intercultural relations among students within schools; the promotion of the value of ESL students' mother tongues and cultural heritages.

Funding

Funding was generally seen as inadequate, which limited staffing and re- stricted flexibility of programs and the ability of schools to cope with changing and diverse situations.

Assessment and orientation

The Vancouver School Board's Oakridge Reception and Orientation Centre was seen as a model that other districts might follow. Schools having no such centre often suffer from a lack of people trained to assess students' English, their first/home language, and their academic ability.

Programs

There is a variety of programs throughout the province, but mainstreaming is becoming more and more popular. The concern is that some classroom teachers have a limited understanding of ESL students' needs and are reluct- ant to take the responsibility for ESL students who are integrated.

Multicultural bilingual home/school workers

These have proved over and over again to be of great value to teachers, students and parents, but unfortunately the moment funding is cut they are often the first to go.

Role and function of ESL teachers

The reports showed that more and more ESL teachers are working with classroom teachers to improve ESL students' English proficiency. In addition to teaching ESL, they are also consultants, coordinators and facilitators within the school to which they have been assigned.

Parents

While an early report pointed to the importance of parental involvement in their children's education, immigrant and refugee parents tended to be less involved than other parents in their children's education. However, parents indicated that they would like to be informed on course content and requirements. They would like their children to have regular homework, and to know how they can help their children at home.

Research

A few districts have a central data bank on all ESL students which provides important information for researchers on different topics such as the time students take to progress through the ESL program, or ESL students' opinions on the effectiveness of the ESL program in helping them achieve their educational goals. Some superintendents, when asked to state the major issues facing their ESL/D program, said lack of data was the major issue, followed by staffing issues, the limits on program organisation imposed by grants, and the varying degrees and levels of effectiveness of ESL/D programs. Some very significant research is currently being carried out in a joint program involving researchers from the University of BC and the staff at the Vancouver School Board's Oakridge Reception and Orientation Centre.

PEDAGOGY

What teachers do in the classroom depends, to some extent, on what they have been taught to do in teacher training courses.

In 1967 and 1968, the Faculty of Education at the University of BC brought in Professor A.V.P. Elliott of the University of London to give the first course in teaching English as a Second Language. Until then, teachers seeking training had had to go to Toronto where the Ontario government offered a three-tiered teaching certificate in ESL. From 1969 onwards, the University of BC's ESL course was staffed by its own faculty members. The course swiftly grew from two sections a year (one in the winter and one in the summer) to six sections a year (two in the winter, two in the spring, and two in the summer). Within a very short time a graduate program was put in place. BC's other two universities, Simon Fraser University and the University of Victoria, started their own courses in ESL. As immigrant children registered in classes in rural areas, professors and graduate students were constantly called upon to provide workshops on both ESL and multiculturalism in many parts of the province, and across the prairie provinces until their universities mounted their own courses.

The 1960s and 1970s saw the demise of the Audio-Lingual Habit Approach. It was replaced by The Silent Way, Total Physical Response, Community Language Learning, and others that came and went. The movement towards combining language teaching and content teaching gathered momentum, and in 1986 the BC Ministry of Education published two ESL resource books which demonstrated how ESL and subject matter could entwine together to benefit the students, based on the work of Bernard Mohan. In his ground-breaking book *Language and Content*, Mohan (1986: iv) wrote:

> These [ESL] students need to learn unfamiliar subject matter in an unfamiliar language. Language teachers must find ways to help these students learn the language needed to study subject matter in English, while content teachers must devise strategies to help such students understand content and become more independent learners.

His work formed the core of a pilot project between the University of BC and the Vancouver School Board based on his Knowledge Framework.

The aim of the Pilot Project (see Chapter 8 for project details) reads as follows (Dunn, 1992: 106):

> The overall aim of the Pilot Project is the effective social and academic integration of ESL students. The research on which this Project is based indicates that for ESL students to integrate academically, learning activities should simultaneously emphasize language and content. Social integration involves the adjustment of ESL students to new social and cultural realities.

EMPOWERMENT

Mastery of English provides individuals with a degree of power denied to those whose oral and written fluency is hesitant and uncertain. For students, power and purpose are related. Margaret Early found in her 1992 study that all the high school students who had been successful in learning English spoke of goals they had set for themselves either in general or in specific terms, such as going to university or becoming a doctor. Only some of the unsuccessful students had set themselves a goal, and a number simply replied, 'I don't know.' The successful students seemed to have a greater sense of control over their future than the unsuccessful ones (Early, 1992: 272).

Cummins (1988: 137–8) wrote that 'minority students are "empowered" or "disabled" as a direct result of their interactions with educators in schools'. He writes of four characteristics of schools which can be analysed along a continuum which will result in more or less empowerment to minority students:

1. Minority students' language and culture are incorporated into the school program.
2. Minority community participation is encouraged as an integral component of children's education.
3. The pedagogy promotes intrinsic motivation on the part of students to use language actively in order to generate their own knowledge.
4. Professionals involved in assessment become advocates for minority students by focusing primarily on the ways in which students' academic difficulty are the function of interactions within the school context rather than legitimising the location of the 'problem' within students.

There is little research data in British Columbia bearing on these four characteristics. But some schools celebrate special days in other cultures; some schools encourage parent volunteers to accompany students on field trips. The pedagogy of the Knowledge Framework encourages students to go beyond learning English to using English. The BC Teachers' Federation's Provincial Specialist Association for ESL sees as part of its objectives that of acting as an advocate for ESL students.

LOOKING AHEAD

British Columbia, more than any other province, has seen its population change from being primarily white and largely British to one embracing nationals and races from around the world. It has not been easy for some of its citizens to come to terms with the major demographic changes that have occurred. It has taken time for the school system to adjust to its multicultural classes, to children who speak one of many languages at home, to new ways of educating children who enter school speaking no English. But it has made many adaptations and will have to make more, for to succeed in school, in college, in professional or vocational employment in British Columbia, a child must have good control of English, social, vocational and academic English, and it is the school's responsibility to produce fluent and literate students in the best way possible.

To keep the momentum going, educators and others must closely cooperate for the good of the students and the nation, for these young people from around the world have much to give once they have mastered one of Canada's official languages, which of necessity in British Columbia is English. Thirteen groups can affect the speed and efficiency with which ESL children master both social and academic English, for they control policy, funding, research, teacher training, methodology, and program planning. They are:

- The Federal Government
- BC Ministry of Education
- BC School Trustees' Association
- BC Teachers' Federation
- BCTF ESL Provincial Specialist Association
- BC school districts and schools
- BC universities
- The Association of BC Teachers of English as an Additional Language
- The Heritage Language Teachers' Association
- Ethnic societies
- Non-governmental organisations
- Parents and Parent Advisory Councils
- Business

Finally, as immigration will remain a factor in the continuing economic growth of British Columbia, regular classroom teachers and administrators must view ESL students not as a phenomenon that will go away, but as a normal component of classroom teaching.

Much has been done but there remains more to be done. Lord Swann (1985: 12), in his report to the British government, wrote:

> Teachers must sometimes despair at being so frequently cast as the people who can set the ills of society to rights, and can resolve dilemmas for which they are not primarily responsible. Nevertheless, second only to the family, they are the people who can most profoundly influence future generations.

Chapter 6

The second language as a medium of learning

Bernard Mohan

INTRODUCTION

The previous chapter reviewed the historical development of the educational situation in British Columbia. This chapter will review our response to that situation, and the thinking behind it. The main points of this chapter can be summarised as follows. Change is needed in assumptions and practices concerned with language as a medium of learning as educational systems become more multilingual and multicultural. This, rather than second language acquisition, is the central issue. Since it takes a considerable time to learn a second language for academic purposes, to learn to use it adequately as a medium of learning content and culture means that ESL students must learn language and subject matter and culture *at the same time.* To meet this goal, *explicit and systematic* integration of language teaching and content teaching is required, a development which could bring educational benefits to students in general. Language as a medium of learning requires a functional theory of language and discourse. Systemic functional linguistics provides one. Within the perspective of systemics, the 'Knowledge Framework' provides a theoretical basis for aspects of language as a medium of learning. It provides links between second language development and first language development, and between language development and educational development generally. The Knowledge Framework takes a functional view of language as discourse in the context of social practice. It supports the functional analysis of discourse and a language socialisation perspective. Two ways it can be applied are: with a focus on knowledge structures, or with a focus on activities and tasks (see the detailed discussion of task in Chapter 11).

LANGUAGE AS A MEDIUM OF LEARNING

As has been mentioned above, the fact that educational systems are becoming more multilingual and multicultural raises the issue of language as a medium of learning, or, to put it in M.A.K. Halliday's words, learning as a linguistic process (Halliday, 1978: 30–1). This, rather than second language acquisition, will be our central focus. Beyond the question of second language learning, language as a medium of learning raises the question of the relation between language learning and the learning of content and culture. Second language learning prioritises the concerns of the second language classroom, where language as a medium of learning draws attention to issues that are shared by all classrooms. Second language learning draws attention to learning by the individual second language student, where language as a medium of learning draws attention not only to the individual learning from the institution, but also to the institution learning from the individual.

Educational systems have a responsibility to deliver educational services to all students. Since language is the major medium of learning, an important further responsibility is to support language as a medium of learning to enable students to be academically successful. It is not difficult to see that this applies to native speakers of English (L1 speakers) as well as Limited English Proficiency (LEP) students. For example, the American researchers Langer and Applebee (1987) responded to nationwide evidence of L1 student weaknesses in writing and in higher level thinking skills, and studied the role of writing in thinking and learning in secondary school content classrooms. They identified a need for a clearer understanding by all students of effective discourse in different subject areas. Any multilingual and multicultural education system needs to address this need with especially systematic attention to language and culture learning.

Because of the length of time it takes to master a second language for schooling, we cannot delay academic instruction until students have mastered L2 skills. We cannot place LEP students' academic development on hold during this period, and language programs alone cannot provide the necessary support to learners. Subject matter teachers and content classrooms must play a large and essential role. We must rely on the cooperation of content teachers from different specialisations at all grade levels.

However, merely exposing students to content classrooms is not an adequate response. It is widely recognised that native speakers of English need support with language as a medium of learning e.g. in reading across the content areas (Vacca and Vacca, 1993) and writing across the curriculum (Crowhurst, 1994). Unprejudiced common sense might suggest that second language learners need similar support, but with a great deal more understanding of language and discourse. Yet it is frequently assumed that second language learners do not, despite the fact that they are learning through their weaker language. Mainstreaming of L2 learners, though mandated in some educational systems such as England (Leung, 1993), cannot be assumed to provide optimal language learning opportunities as a matter of course. Good content teaching is not necessarily good language teaching and may, for instance, fail to help students develop appropriate form–meaning relationships in language. As Swain (1991) points out, such content teaching needs to guide students' progressive use of the full functional range of language, and to support their understanding of how language form is related to meaning in subject area material. The integration of language, subject area knowledge, and thinking skills requires systematic monitoring and planning. This is essential in jurisdictions where full-time ESL classes are allowed, as in Canada and Australia; it is crucial in jurisdictions where they are not, as in England. We will discuss the question of integration through the concrete image of a collaboration between a language teacher and a content teacher, noting that the responsibility to integrate remains, even when there is only one teacher.

There is need for approaches to Language as a Medium of Learning which explicitly incorporate content goals. It is essential to go beyond the perspective of the language specialist, and address interdisciplinary concerns. Approaches which fail to address the goals of content teachers are likely to be rejected by them. Witness Langer and Applebee's (1987) finding that content teachers were reluctant to devote time to writing as a means of learning if such approaches were perceived as a means of fostering the work of the English teacher and did not promote learning of the teacher's own subject. Thus approaches should explicitly integrate language goals and content goals (ILC). Ultimately, this is a question of interdisciplinary curriculum policy which is in the domain of Ministries of Education.

Verbal language is not the only mode of language as a medium of learning. Younger learners often express themselves through multiple media, such as both drawing and text (Dyson, 1986). In the later years, graphic representations and the connections across different modes of meaning should be exploited for the benefit of LEP students rather than ignored (Early, 1989).

Language as a medium of learning raises the question of the functional role of language in learning. It requires a functional theory of language and discourse, such as is provided by systemic functional linguistics. In Australia in the 1980s and 1990s, an important development has been the genre-based approach to teaching writing, which responds to concerns similar to some of those raised by Langer and Applebee. A recent example of this large body of work is the Write it Right Resources for Literacy series (e.g. Write it Right, 1995: *Exploring Literacy in School English*). The genre-based approach helps students to gain control of the literacy demands of major curriculum areas through the analysis of 'genres', the ways texts are systematically organised for communicative purposes in a variety of contexts. In our view the genre-based work is a convincing demonstration of the value of approaching language as a medium of learning from the perspective of systemic functional linguistics, which takes a functional perspective on the study of language, studies the relation between texts and their contexts, and provides analytical tools for the description of discourse and the resources of the lexicogrammar of English.

THE KNOWLEDGE FRAMEWORK

Any concept of Language as a Medium of Learning assumes a functional theory of language. The Knowledge Framework (see Mohan, 1986) works within the general perspective of systemic functional linguistics and provides a perspective on language as a medium of learning which is different from, but complementary to, the genre approach. A brief summary follows.

The Knowledge Framework is a view of language as discourse in the context of social practice. To provide a broad view of learning, we see education as the initiation of the learner into social practices or activities (see Peters, 1966). We start with a general analysis of social practice or activity and then look at the role of language and discourse within social practice or activity. In our view, a social practice or activity is a combination of knowledge (theory) and action (practice). This duality can be powerfully demonstrated through everyday life and events – for instance, getting car insurance. In the detailed example of the social practice of car insurance given in Mohan (1986: ch. 2), the theory was knowledge of car insurance, and the action was driving a car and having a car crash. The example came from a car insurance issue of a newspaper for ESL readers: several of the newspaper articles discussed insurance and a strip story described driving a car and having a crash.

In more detail, the *theory* aspect of an activity typically includes knowledge structures like classification, principles and evaluation, and the *practice* aspect of an activity typically includes knowledge structures like description, time sequence and choice. So, for example, there were newspaper articles on the different kinds of insurance (classification), on causes of accidents (principles and if–then relations) and on good and bad drivers (evaluation). Similarly, in the strip story, each picture was a description, the series of pictures was a sequence, and at several points in the story the characters faced a choice (e.g. after the crash, should they call the police?). A number of these knowledge structures were represented visually in 'Key Visuals' which highlighted main points and the type of knowledge structure. Taken together, these knowledge structures form a 'Knowledge Framework', which is our general analysis of a social practice or activity. The Knowledge Framework is a simple model of a complex issue. It is a basic starting point for analysis, a heuristic. Even so, you can start from two places, depending on whether you emphasise the parts or the whole: you can start from the knowledge structures, or you can start from the activity as a whole. The second way connects directly with work on student tasks. It should be remembered that the Knowledge Framework is an analysis of discourse and social practice, not a teaching methodology. It can relate to classroom practice in a variety of ways. Figure 6.1 gives a visual summary of the Knowledge Framework.

Language as a medium of learning takes a variety of forms. It is much wider than reading or writing across the curriculum. Learning an activity

Activity	Theory	Classification	Principles	Evaluation
	Practice	Description	Sequence	Choice

Figure 6.1   Knowledge Framework

means learning both theory and practice. Verbal, expository learning tends to be associated with theory, and practical experiential learning is associated with practice. You can learn about car insurance both by reading books and articles about car insurance, and by being involved in car driving and crashes (or by observing other people who do this). Language (as extended, less context-dependent discourse) is very obviously a medium of learning in verbal, expository learning. If you learn from a book, you are heavily dependent on language. The role of language as a medium of learning in experiential learning, where discourse interacts with information in other modes like the visual, is different and less obvious, but not to be underestimated. Even action movies can be difficult to understand if you turn off the sound track. Expository learning from 'theory discourse' is obviously very different from experiential learning from 'practical discourse', but a good theory will recognise them both and relate them together.

For the remainder of our discussion, it is helpful to have an additional example which again illustrates a Knowledge Framework analysis of a social practice or activity but reveals some other facets. It is a classroom example of coordination between teachers, reflecting the circumstances in British Columbia that full-time ESL classes are allowed, unlike in England. The example is taken from the work of two collaborating high school teachers: an ESL teacher teaching ESL/social studies to ESL learners about 17 years old who wished to enter the mainstream social studies course, but who lacked the academic and discourse abilities to do so; and a social studies teacher teaching the mainstream Social Studies course that the students would later enter, along with native English speakers. The ESL teacher and the social studies teacher had planned collaboratively to ease this transition, so that the ESL teacher used material from the social studies course to build up the students' ability to work independently on social studies tasks. (We will discuss this collaboration in more detail later.) The material they used was a transcript of the CBC National Radio News for Monday, 30 October 1995:

> Here is the CBC News. I'm Lorna Jackson. Quebeckers are taking part in what is perhaps the most momentous vote in the country's history. The province's destiny and Canada's future lie in the hands of perhaps half a million undecided voters. On the eve of the referendum the race was too close to call as most of the five million eligible voters headed to the polling booths. Shortly after the polls opened some of the leaders went out to vote. Prime Minister Chretien and his wife, Aline, cast their ballots in their home town of Shawinigan. In Montreal, Premier Jacques Parizeau and his wife voted in the posh enclave of Outremont. He expressed optimism that Quebec will be an independent country by the end of the day. The Liberal leader, Daniel Johnson, cast his ballot at a public school in the same neighbourhood. He says he's confident of a 'No' victory.

Second language socialisation vs second language acquisition

The broadcast says something in English about politics. The second language learner who manages to understand the broadcast can thereby learn something about the English language. At the same time, the learner can also learn something about Canadian politics and political culture. The same is true when a child learns its first language through interaction with its mother. The child learns language and, at the same time, learns about the world.

A theoretical approach which captures this simultaneous learning relation is the language socialisation perspective. The language socialisation perspective explains how language and culture (understood to include knowledge of content areas and disciplines) are learned at the same time (Halliday, 1978, 1986; Bruner, 1983; Ochs, 1988). The language socialisation view is based on an account of discourse in the context of sociocultural practices. The learner's participation in discourse in sociocultural activities is not only a means to acquiring language but also to acquiring sociocultural knowledge. Some relevant questions are: Can school tasks be seen as meaning-making sociocultural processes?. How are these processes reflected in the patterning of discourse units beyond the sentence? How is the organisation of content knowledge reflected in discourse?

Approaches to second language acquisition, such as those views of second language acquisition which aim solely at grammatical competence (e.g. Krashen, 1985; Prabhu, 1987), typically ignore content learning and concentrate solely on certain aspects of language learning. These are accounts of second language acquisition only, not of content learning. They see second language acquisition as a matter of learning the second language code (particularly the rules of sentence grammar) through involvement in language use. The role of language use is to provide examples of the language code. A content course, then, is seen only as a source of examples of the language code. However, if code is divorced from message, content is excluded; if form is divorced from function, there is no functional grammar; if language is divorced from discourse, there is no account of larger units of discourse, and so no account of the role of discourse abilities in academic reading and writing, for instance. There is no functional theory of discourse in context. There is no attempt to account for language as a medium of learning, or for content learning.

The language socialisation perspective flows from a functional approach to language, while many approaches to second language acquisition draw upon a formal, Chomskyan view of language.

Functional vs formal approaches to language

To account for language as a medium of learning, we take a *functional* approach to language, starting from discourse in the context of social practice. Functional approaches to language interpret language as a system of meanings and reject the strong separation of 'language by itself' and 'language in use'. They aim to explore how language functions by seeing how meanings in discourse are expressed by the forms of language. In the case of systemic functional linguistics (SFL), Halliday and Martin say that:

> SFL is oriented to the description of language as *a resource for meaning* rather than as a system of rules. . . . SFL is concerned with *texts*, rather than sentences, as the basic unit through which meaning is negotiated . . . SFL focuses on . . . relations between texts and *social contexts* rather than on texts as decontextualised structural entities in their own right.   (Halliday and Martin, 1993: 22)

Formal approaches to the study of language traditionally begin from the formal structure of words and sentences and they analyse 'language by itself' rather than 'language in use'. Hence most formalists exclude the analysis of discourse in social context, concentrating instead on the formal structure of language rules, such as the grammar of sentences. From a strictly *formal* view, the broadcast is a collection of examples of rules of the English language, though it is the rules rather than the examples that are of interest. The broadcast begins, for instance, with three sentences using the verb 'to be' in the present tense ('Here is', 'I'm', 'what is').

Functionally, however, the text is more than a collection of grammatical forms: it has meaning; it gives a message; it has a function in a context; it has content; it is about some topic. A listener cannot be said to understand the text if he or she does not understand this meaning. From a systemic functional view, the broadcast is more than a collection of sentences: it is a text, a construction of meaning, which the sentences combine to build. On the one hand, from the perspective of language, it is an instance of language in use. It builds a simple symbolic opposition or contrast between the separatist leader, Parizeau, voting with the hope of a victory for independence (the 'Yes' side) and the federalist leader, Johnson, voting with the hope of a victory for the 'No' side. On the other hand, from the perspective of social context, it is an event in the social practice of national politics: an announcer for the official national broadcasting company, CBC, is updating the nation's citizens about a current political happening. Listeners are assumed to know a framework of oppositional politics: that the referendum vote concerning independence for Quebec establishes a choice of alternatives (yes or no for independence), two 'sides' for political debate (separatists versus federalists, including some sense of what the sides stand for and why), a 'race' in which commentators can speculate on winners and losers, and a date on which the decision is made. This background of sociocultural knowledge helps to interpret the broadcast report on individual voting.

SFL allows us to clarify the terms 'language' and 'content', which have proved difficult to define. One reason for this difficulty is a failure to distinguish between their meaning at the level of curriculum and classroom goals and their meaning at the level of discourse analysis. With respect to curriculum, our example shows how a rough division can be made between general social studies goals ('develop an understanding of Canadian politics') and general language development goals ('develop the abilities to deal with the discourse demands of social studies and other subject areas'). The relation between these two sets of curriculum goals is a question of curriculum analysis which we will discuss later. With respect to discourse analysis, the everyday terms 'language' and 'content' are replaced by technical analysis within SFL.

The everyday term 'content' is replaced by Halliday's three contextual categories of field, mode and tenor. In the text, the field ('the topic of the text and the social process being achieved by it') is political action, the mode ('the role that language is playing') is a news broadcast ('Here is the CBC News') and the tenor ('the role structure – who is taking part') includes the announcer ('I'm Lorna Jackson').

Field contains knowledge structures. Within the field of political action, the text constructs a structure of meaning or knowledge, a choice or opposition of two alternative votes, and draws on a background of sociocultural knowledge, a related knowledge structure, a choice or opposition of two sides in a political debate. Strategically, as a crude rule of thumb, we find that teachers and students can use knowledge structures intuitively as hinges between content issues and language issues. In our example, both teachers can use the choice in the text as a point of departure.

The text is a broadcast discourse in the sociocultural context of political activity. It illustrates the concept of discourse in the context of sociocultural activity, and can be analysed using the Knowledge Framework. We can develop this analysis further by discussing, firstly, knowledge structures and, secondly, activities.

KNOWLEDGE STRUCTURES

Identify important knowledge structures in curriculum, materials and learning processes

To introduce knowledge structures (KSs) to teachers and to students, our usual approach has been to show how knowledge structures can be found in a teaching unit on any chosen topic. Represented graphically, these KSs can help to make content material comprehensible, develop thinking skills and develop language (Mohan, 1986, ch. 2). Our experience so far has been that the six core KSs (description, sequence, choice, classification, principles, values) are common to most, if not all, subject areas and levels of student. This central idea can be developed in a variety of ways for classroom purposes.

In our example, the news item about the Quebec referendum mentioned three politicians voting. Each of them could be given a further *description*; the vote concerns the conduct of government, the processes or *sequences* of government operation; and each of them is making a *choice* in his vote. A fuller understanding of the news item depends on some depth of background knowledge. The description of each politician should give some reference to the party (the Liberal Party, the Parti Quebecois) to which they belong: the parties give us a basic *classification* of the politicians. Presently the government operations in question – legislation, taxation and foreign affairs – are powers of the federal government. The vote could change this *principle* and make them powers of the Quebec provincial government, thus giving it sovereignty. The mention of the voting choice raises the question of the *values* behind the choice: the Liberal who chooses to stay in Canada and who values a pluralistic society, and the Parti Quebecois who chooses sovereignty and who values a nationalist society.

Another example, illustrating student-designed graphics, comes from the *Key visual dictionary* (Hunt et al., 1991) created by a team of teachers to introduce KSs to elementary school students via common graphic conventions. Student-produced graphics include: a plan *describing* the interior of a pyramid; a pie graph which *classifies* the first languages of students in an elementary class; a personal time-line to show the *sequence* of significant events in the author's life; a line graph which shows the *if–then relation* between two variables – how the student population of Vancouver schools has changed over time; a decision-tree to display the author's *choices* after her parents' divorce; and an *evaluation* grid showing the value of a forest management policy.

The question of finding common elements across the curriculum, such as knowledge structures, is likely to be a matter of special interest to those responsible for curriculum at Ministries of Education, who may be prepared to endorse efforts towards mutual support between different segments of the educational system. As part of its work of curriculum renewal, the British Columbia Ministry of Education had indicated that one of its priorities was a more integrated and holistic approach to the curriculum in general and to communication in particular.

In a recent study, we found that curriculum documents provided evidence for the presence of common knowledge structures (or 'thinking skills') across the curriculum, and thus for one element of a possible common agenda of mutual support, including mutual support between language specialists and *mathematics* specialists, an interesting possibility. A review of curriculum documents produced by the British Columbia Ministry of Education (Mohan et al., unpublished) revealed that both language arts and mathematics were seen as providing a language for science and socials, and that, reciprocally, science and socials provided a context for mathematics and language arts. Some of the specific themes which formed bridges between these two groupings were essentially the same as the KSs we identified above: *classification* and sets; *principles* and functional relations; *choice*/decision-making/problem-solving; and, less explicitly, *sequences* and routines (or procedures, or processes). We strongly suspect that these findings would not be greatly different for other educational systems.

There are several implications to be drawn from these findings. First, there may well be a basis in officially endorsed policy documents for educational systems to support and resource the type of common agenda we have identified as a general policy. Action at the system level is needed to complement action at the classroom level. Second, such a policy should be a multidisciplinary initiative, not a unilateral initiative by language specialists. Decision-making, for example, is an area of interest to a number of disciplines. Third, since mathematics is seen as playing a parallel role to language in these curriculum documents, mathematics and language specialists might examine ways in which they can support each other in their cross-curriculum responsibilities.

Develop graphic means of representing knowledge structures

We understand and construct meaning both verbally and visually, and knowledge structures appear in both modes. Teaching and learning processes could be greatly helped if we were more aware of this. The referendum news item quoted above was from CBC national radio. When the item played on CBC national TV, we saw film clips of each of the politicians voting: the discourse of the item was given a visual context. There were also certain general parallels between the discourse and the film: there was a *description* of each politician by words in the discourse and by a picture in the film; the *sequence* of voting – going to the booth, casting the ballot, and so on – was referred to by words and by the sequence of pictures in the film. Even the *choice* of vote – 'Yes' for independence or 'No' – was picked up in contrasting remarks for and against independence by the politicians and by contrasting shots of them voting.

The more general and abstract information required to understand the background to the referendum vote is expressed again both visually and verbally in 'in-depth' magazine articles and in textbooks. We may be told in a comparison of Canada's two largest provinces that in Ontario about 53 per cent of the population is of British ethnic origin and 8 per cent of French descent, while in Quebec about 80 per cent is of French ethnic origin and 8 per cent of British descent. Or we may be shown tables and figures of the Canadian population *classified* by ethnic origin, or of demographic and immigration trends which could *cause* the decline of French, or a comparison of the relative importance of such *values* as francophone cultural survival to citizens in Quebec and Ontario.

Thus we have a number of conventional and unconventional ways of representing KSs visually as well as verbally. This has implications for reading comprehension, for example, and graphics have been shown to be an important factor in reading comprehension, but reading research also shows that these implications have been neglected: many teachers and many students ignore graphics (Reinking, 1986; Evans et al., 1987). It should not be taken for granted that teachers and students have the skills and attitudes to make appropriate use of graphics. Instruction to develop these skills and attitudes is often needed.

How do ESL students use graphics to communicate about learning? Gloria Tang has investigated this question in several studies (Tang 1989, 1991a, 1991b, 1992). In an ethnographic study of grade 7 ESL students in Vancouver, she found that the students essentially ignored graphics (see Chapter 7). They saw graphics as decorative artwork rather than a way of communicating knowledge and exploring ideas – a view that probably corresponds to priorities in schooling which are biased against the arts as reflective modalities and towards a narrow concentration on the words on the page, priorities that ultimately hold back progress in literacy.

Tang also investigated the use and awareness of graphics in Hong Kong in an ethnographic study of secondary students and classrooms with both Chinese and English medium instruction. Like Vancouver, there was a rich learning environment of graphics, and learning materials illustrated a full range of KSs. Moreover, Tang found that all of the KSs that appeared in her sample of Chinese social studies textbook materials also appeared in comparable Canadian materials. An important additional finding was that many of the graphic forms of KSs in the textbooks (such as line graphs, pie charts, classification trees and time lines) were common across textbooks in the two languages. However, by contrast with Vancouver, it appeared that teachers and students made more frequent use of graphics, recognised their importance more, and were more systematic in their use. When Tang interviewed the students, they displayed a high level of graphic literacy, showing an awareness of different graphic representations and an ability to construct meaning from different graphic forms. Why was there a difference between students in the two cities? It is possible that Hong Kong students, influenced by their bilingual teachers, have developed strategies for their biliterate reading which make intelligent use of graphics. Consider this remark by a Hong Kong student, commenting in Chinese on some graphics in English: 'I have never come across these diagrams before. But I have seen similar ones in my own language. I recognise some words and symbols. I know some English. I put two and two together from my previous experience.' It is possible that some of these students have understood the possibilities of using graphics as a bridge between their education in Chinese and their education in English: that graphics of KSs in Chinese-medium situations can build transferable knowledge for English-medium learning, and vice versa.

Can a knowledge structures approach be applied to the teaching and learning of languages other than English? Huang (1991) demonstrated the feasibility of this approach in a beginner's course in Mandarin for English-speaking elementary students, where the classroom activities, as for ESL students, were centred on themes organised by KSs and graphics. This opens up possibilities for teachers of different languages to share materials and strategies to a greater extent, and for bilingual learners to access knowledge more easily in their different languages.

Explore the links between knowledge structures, discourse and graphics

Graphics have a considerable potential for supporting students' work in writing and reading, and increasing their awareness of language. But this potential has largely been unexplored because of deep-seated biases that graphics means drawing and drawing is only for young children, or again that meaning is only expressed verbally, not visually. There has been a failure to relate students' powers of visual interpretation and expression to their powers of verbal interpretation and expression, to relate graphics and words as means of thought rather than to separate them. There needs to be a major shift in perspective, such as is provided by significant work by functional linguists that analyse both graphics and discourse as semiotic systems (see Kress and van Leeuwen, 1996).

Students can build on this relation as a natural part of class process (Early, 1989, 1990, 1991; Early and Hooper, in press). In Early's case study of a class of grade 4/5 ESL students, the teacher had designed a combined science and socials unit on the theme of 'Fish', and organised the content around KSs and corresponding graphics. Graphics used included a diagram of the parts of a fish, a classification tree which located fish within the animal kingdom, and a chart that organised information about fish as pets. The teacher skilfully combined discussion, teacher questioning and the construction of graphics to sustain a process of academic talk and writing over a number of weeks. With the animal classification tree, for example, the teacher helped the students to draw their own classifications of familiar objects, she elicited their knowledge of animal classification to draw a scientific classification, then guided a discussion of the various ways to explain the tree in words, and this bank of expressions, along with the tree, became a resource in later writing process discussions. Thus the teacher skilfully made the link between visual and verbal language a conscious focus of attention, using means which included direct instruction and discovery methods. The students enthusiastically engaged in their discussions about language, perhaps because it was functionally related to their own language production.

Connect knowledge structures and genres

The process of working on the link between graphics and words offers important insights into the complexities of meaning and wording that are part of constructing written discourse. In the following example, two different groups of writers, grade 10 ESL students and native speaker university students, were given a chart graphic about early European exploration and asked to write a short essay on the topic, using a classification pattern of organisation, grouping by country sponsoring the exploration. Only the first few lines of the examples are given.

(a) Chart

SPONSOR	EXPLORER	DATE	AREA EXPLORED	PURPOSE
England	Drake	1578	South America	Gold and silver
England	Cabot	1497	North America	Trade route
[continued . . .]				(spices, jewels)

(b) Classification essay (Grade 10 ESL student – a basic writer)
In 1578 South America was explored by Drake who was looking for gold and silver sponsored by England. Also in 1497 Cabot explored North America for a trade route of spices, jewels and he was also supported by England . . .

(c) Classification essay (native speaker university student – a skilled writer)
Three seafaring countries sponsored major voyages during the early exploration period of the late 15th and early 16th century.
England sent ships and men to points in both South and North America. Drake sailed in 1578 in search of gold and silver and Cabot reached North American shores in 1497 seeking spices and jewels. . . .

This contrast between an unskilled and a skilled writer reveals something of the complex, and only partly conscious, discourse decisions a skilled writer makes, and an unskilled writer needs to develop. Both writers are using essentially the same information, but they have shaped it into discourse in very different ways. The ESL simply follows the chart line by line, and writes a sentence for each line. The native skilled writer starts with a general introductory paragraph, then gives a more limited generalisation, and then finally brings in the specific chart information, creating a discourse pattern which suits the requirements of the classification essay genre. The basic writer uses a few devices repetitively. The native writer uses much richer language resources to create the 'texture' of the discourse. For instance, the basic writer creates cohesion by using 'also' repetitively, whereas the skilled writer creates cohesion through lexical harmony, as in the verb phrases 'sponsored major voyages', 'sent ships and men', 'sailed', 'reached North American shores'. Similarly, the basic writer awkwardly shifts between the area 'In 1578 South America' and the explorer 'in 1497 Cabot' whereas the skilled writer signals the 'themes' of the discourse very clearly: 'Three seafaring countries', 'England', 'Drake', 'Cabot'. This type of contrast can be taken much further by drawing on work in systemic linguistics which offers detailed discussions of genres, discourse 'texture' (theme, information focus and cohesion), and functional grammar (see Halliday, 1985, 1994; Martin, 1985, 1992; Christie and Rothery, 1989).

A number of teachers in British Columbia now help their students to work out their meaning in graphics and then construct written discourse. They find that they can build on the opportunities provided for learners to share ideas about how they put their meanings into words. Further, they find that students' graphics form a natural bridge between organisational work on the knowledge structures of information and detailed work on discourse genres like that available in Australian materials inspired by systemic linguistics, such as Christie et al. (1990). This appears to be a fruitful way of working functionally on the grammar and lexis of writing, and an important step in overcoming the gap between the teaching of grammar and the teaching of writing.

We have looked at graphics and writing in detail, but similar comments can be made about graphics and reading. Many teachers are familiar with the idea of exploring reading comprehension by encouraging learners to express their understanding of a reading passage in a graphic (Novak and Gowin, 1984). This idea can be developed much further by using graphics which express knowledge structures and by adding the sophisticated understanding of discourse offered by systemic analysis.

Explore knowledge structures in oral discourse

There has been very little work which explores knowledge structures in oral discourse and factors, such as graphics, which might sustain knowledge construction in group discussion, despite the fact that these issues are vitally important to academic discourse development. Here is a classification conversation (Liang, 1999) between two students in Home Economics who are finding examples for food categories and writing them on a chart. They are identifying examples for the 'MEAT' category: beef, pork, chicken, hamburger (an understandable suggestion) and tofu (an interesting idea!):

A: Meat, beef.
B: OK.
A: Pork, meat. Chicken.
B: Right, chicken.
A: Will hamburger do?
B: What are you thinking of for hamburger?
A: I mean the meat. . . . Tofu.
B: [*pointing to their chart*] She said to put these two categories together. Tofu might belong to that category. This category is meat.

This example makes two points: that knowledge structures like classification (e.g. classification of kinds of meat) show up not only in written discourse but also in oral discourse; and that the students are using the chart to orient and guide their discussion, a type of visual/verbal support strategy which has been studied very little so far. These are future directions for both research and for classroom action.

ACTIVITIES

Relate 'activity' and student task

It is equally possible to start to apply Knowledge Framework analysis to the classroom by foregrounding the activity as a whole instead of the knowledge structures which are contained in the activity. The choice depends on the educational situation. The aim in both cases is to find a basic pattern of meaning which can be foregrounded to awareness, which teachers and learners can use for intentional work, and which teachers and learners can intuitively unfold into greater complexity. The tasks that students do in school can be seen as parts of a larger activity or social practice. When students listen to the broadcast as a task in a social studies course, this is part of the activity of doing the course. Earlier we said that a social practice or activity is a combination of knowledge (*theory*) and action (*practice*). Our analysis of activities applies to tasks as well. A student task, obviously enough, requires a student to do something. It also usually requires a student to know something. In other words, a task combines action and knowledge, or theory and practice. In our example, the broadcast task required students to listen, regardless of whether they were in the ESL class or the social studies 11 class. The same action was required. But interestingly, there was a difference in the knowledge requirement. Socials 11 students were explicitly assumed by their teacher to have background knowledge gained in social studies 9 and 10. For the ESL students, no background knowledge was assumed by their teacher, and the teacher was prepared to explain it to them as necessary. They had not attended social studies 9 and 10, and in any case, they had little exposure to Canadian political culture. In other words, they lacked content knowledge and cultural knowledge for the task.

Several comments on this are in order. First, background knowledge is not the sole consideration. Just as students may lack background knowledge for a task, so they may also lack familiarity with doing a task. Just as they may be short of theory, they may also be short of practice. Second, we should not overlook the knowledge and experience that ESL learners bring with them to the classroom. They may not know about politics in Canada, but they may well know about politics in their home country.

Use task as a shared planning unit

The news broadcast was used in both the social studies class and the ESL class, but in different ways. In social studies, students were to listen to it for homework; in ESL, students did in-class comprehension and discussion work on it, building up their ability to listen to it independently. The ESL teacher and the social studies teacher had planned collaboratively, and used the broadcast task as a common bridge: the task abilities and information that were assumed in the social studies class were a target of development in the ESL class. The task was used as a shared planning unit for collaborative language and content goals. A single teacher with responsibility for both language and content goals could plan in a similar way.

Research recognises the importance of student tasks in the operation of content classrooms and language classrooms. *In content classes,* task is a basic unit of analysis of student work. From the student standpoint, the curriculum is 'a collection of academic tasks' (Doyle, 1983). *In language classes,* task as a unit of analysis can provide a coherent approach to 'all six phases of program design: needs identification, syllabus design, methodology design, materials writing, testing and program evaluation' (Long and Crookes, 1992). But we cannot assume that language teachers and content teachers plan for the same tasks or look at tasks in the same way. Educational tradition treats language and content separately rather than relatedly. The possibility of using a task as a shared planning unit is just that – a possibility not a certainty. There is no reason to believe that teachers will automatically interpret their courses in terms of tasks, nor that content teachers and language teachers will automatically identify shared tasks that are common to their work. Adequate time, training, and commitment for reflection and collaboration are required.

Develop a teaching/learning task model

The 'Teaching and Learning' task model developed by Margaret Early and Hugh Hooper (see Chapter 8) is intended to help to achieve a number of goals (for related earlier work, see Morris and Stewart-Dore, 1984). We can show this by relating its four stages to our example:

1. Building background knowledge, where the aim is to help students to connect their prior knowledge to the task in hand. In our example, students could discuss their ideas about a part of a country seceding, drawing on their knowledge of their home countries.
2. Thinking through the topic, where the aim is to help students to interact with task information. In our example, students might summarise main ideas from referendum speeches they have heard, and sort them into 'for' and 'against' separation. Then they might collect the supporting reasons given by the class for each of the ideas and sort the ideas into strongly/ weakly supported.
3. Reconstructing knowledge, where the aim is to help students to organise their knowledge into a coherent pattern. In our example, the students might map out the ideas they have worked through (the arguments for and against, the reasoning which backs them up, their own opinions). The teacher might support their work in doing this.
4. Expression and application, where the aim is to help students to organise their knowledge into cohesive discourse. In our example, the students might compose a letter to a Quebec voter and the teacher might help them to turn their map of ideas into discourse appropriate to the letter.

The teaching/learning task model is, in part, a way of building bridges to, and developing, the 'theory' or background knowledge that students have. It is also a way of helping students to become familiar with a social practice. As James Gee (1992: 33) suggests: 'Discourses are not mastered solely by overt instruction, but by enculturation ("apprenticeship") into social practices through scaffolded and supported interaction with people who have already mastered the Discourse.' The task model can be extended beyond discourse to familiarise students with differences in the classroom culture of education. Parents are not unaware of such differences. As one Chinese parent in British Columbia said, comparing Hong Kong with BC: 'Hong Kong is the basics. There are a lot of tests and you have to memorise a lot of things. But the creativity part is not that emphasised. Here, we are emphasising teamwork and creativity.' The teaching/learning task model provides opportunities for teachers to help students to become more familiar with and aware of such differences.

Work towards the integrated assessment of tasks

The ESL teacher and the Social Studies teacher planned collaboratively. They did not, however, evaluate student work collaboratively, a process which can be very challenging. Yet they did have some basis for collaborative evaluation within their work. Both were concerned with critical analysis by the students. The ESL teacher asked her class to react to an opinion statement from the broadcast material, agreeing or disagreeing and giving a reason. The Social Studies teacher asked her class to use the broadcast and other material as sources for a discussion, with reasoned examples, of their point of view about 'distinct societies' within Canada. Both teachers felt that the link between opinions and reasons was important.

Evaluation is an area which shows very clearly the need of bringing together a language perspective and a content perspective. Testing in school systems usually requires students to perform some sort of task, in many cases a writing task, and there is now an increasing awareness of this in learner assessments conducted at the state or provincial level. An important emerging issue is the role of language in the assessment of subject knowledge. Can students express what they know or is language a barrier? This is a vital question for second language learners, but it is also a major problem for native speakers. The assessment of communication skills and the assessment of subject areas such as science have typically proceeded as separate enterprises. Tests of social studies are one thing; tests of writing are quite another, even though students need to display writing skills in order to respond to subject area assessments. Yet educational systems often lack assessments of communication skills in the functional context of academic tasks in subject areas.

A relevant case from science evaluation is an assessment of 'point of view' in social issues in science (Gaskell et al., 1993). In this task, the student watched a video prompt which presented two points of view on an issue (e.g. for or against logging the forests intensively; for or against animal experiments). Then the student was expected to write an opinion response dealing with *both* sides of the argument – a requirement which many students found difficult. This task clearly relates to the theme of decision-making or reasoned choice. These student responses have been assessed from the standpoint of science. Our interest is to assess student responses like these from the standpoint of discourse and language, and to do so in a functional way which strengthens the relation between science education and education in communication.

This leads on to the issue of collaborative assessment, by ESL and content area specialists, of ESL writers who demonstrate content learning through written assignments. As more teachers become responsible for teaching and evaluating both the language and content learning of second language students in mainstream classes, collaborative assessment may become an essential tool for fair and consistent evaluation practices. In a study of collaborative assessment of writing, Mohan and Low (1995) found that, while different teachers marking independently typically assume that they share a common understanding of the evaluation criteria, the dialogue between teachers in a collaborative process often brought to light differing assumptions about the perspectives on language that teachers have. Where one teacher felt that meaning was most important, another might feel that grammatical correctness was paramount. As one teacher said: 'I know we don't teach in a vacuum, but we often mark in a vacuum.' Although they did not find collaboration easy, the teachers were able to learn from each other and develop greater shared understanding. However, collaborative assessment needs to move forward to a new stage where collaborating teachers join in a focused dialogue with functional discourse analysts.

Turning from evaluation in the classroom and school system to evaluation for research purposes, the integrated assessment of oral tasks is also a central, though little acknowledged, problem. The area of student group work on tasks, and cooperative learning in particular, shows the need of bringing together a language perspective and a content perspective. *In content classes,* cooperative learning methods can improve the effectiveness of student learning of subject matter (Kagan, 1990). This is typically evaluated by scores on achievement tests. *In second language classes,* group work can increase both the quantity and quality of student talk (Long and Porter, 1985). This is evaluated by discourse measures. If cooperative learning is to be used for collaborative language/content goals (McGroarty, 1989), then how is it to be evaluated? Here we particularly mean an examination of the task discourse of cooperative learning applied to tasks with authentic content learning goals. This calls for functional discourse analysis of the oral interaction to evaluate both language learning and content learning. To our knowledge no such analysis has been performed.

This seems to be an issue with which researchers have difficulty. Those whose hopes were raised when the field of Language for Specific Purposes gave attention to discussing task (Hutchinson and Waters, 1987; Swales, 1990) will find that, unfortunately, Hutchinson and Waters concentrate on tasks in the language classroom rather than tasks in the content classroom, arguing that it is necessary to design *learning tasks in the language classroom* which act as vehicles to help the learner to develop the ability to do the target task, and they do not offer any discourse analysis which applies an ESP perspective to content tasks.

The questions raised for cooperative learning research also apply to learning strategies research. Student performance on *content tasks* can be improved with learning strategies (Weinstein and Meyer, 1985; Derry, 1989). Student performance on *language tasks* can be improved with language learning strategies (Oxford, 1990). If we ask how strategies can be used for tasks with both language and content goals (cf. O'Malley, 1988: 51), we face the same issue of research evaluation.

See tasks in the context of wider activities

We said above that an individual task may often be part of a larger pattern – part of a wider activity which can extend as far as a whole educational program and beyond. In our example, politics is a broader social practice or activity that provides the context for the broadcast, and the Social Studies course is a narrower one. When citizens listen to the broadcast or vote in an election, these are individual parts of the activity of politics. When students listen to the broadcast as a task in a Social Studies course, this is part of the activity of the course. The course aims to initiate students into the activity of politics; they are to learn to participate in politics more fully. The course assumes that students can see how the broadcast task fits into politics; if they cannot, the work becomes pointless. Seeing how tasks fit into a larger whole is a concern for all students, but there is reason to believe that it is particularly of concern for second language students because of language difficulties.

Mohan and Marshall Smith (1992) qualitatively investigated the case of a group of students from China studying in Canada who successfully completed a graduate course in adult education program planning, even though they lacked a knowledge of the field and a suitably high TOEFL score. Students particularly praised the organisation of the course. Among other things, the instructor organised the course so that the assignments simulated the parts of the adult education program planning process, and thus formed a coherent series of tasks, central to the topic of the course, with earlier assignments building a context for later ones.

It is interesting that the question of how students see that tasks fit into a larger whole is not very important in formal views of second language learning. From this perspective, it is enough if the task exposes the learner to language input at the sentence level. From a functional point of view, however, it is important to understand how students grasp the context in which they work.

How, then, do ESL learners perceive and act upon their educational experience? One of the few explorations of this question is Early (1992), who analysed themes arising in semistructured interviews with 15 more successful and 11 less successful students. One theme was time: many of the more successful were not only doing assigned homework but were spending extra hours in disciplined study. Another was help: where the less successful students drew more on family and friends, the more successful made greater use of teachers. Overall, the successful gave an impression of greater purpose and power and of larger vision and self-organisation. As one student said: 'It's not enough to know what to do; you must understand it.' Another said: '[A teacher should] care about the students and be especially well organised.' A third said: 'If I were the teacher, I would also give my students confidence, and try to help them know their goal and believe that they can do it.' A central implication for teachers is how to help students take more control over their own learning, and have access to resources and a sense of direction, not simply at the microlevel of the brief task, but at the macrolevel of the longer cycles of academic work.

CONCLUSION

As we have argued above, the difficulties of second language learners have drawn our attention more clearly to the role of language as a medium of learning in education generally, and to the need to address the related responsibilities of the education system much more effectively. The insights that a deeper understanding of meaning and discourse will provide can allow greater mutual support between language development and educational development, not only for second language learners but for all students. In this chapter we have outlined the Knowledge Framework, and some of its implications. As an analysis of discourse and social practice, the Knowledge Framework can relate to approaches to language as a medium of learning in the schools in a variety of ways. The next chapter will describe cases of teachers using one approach in their classrooms based particularly on knowledge structures.

Chapter 7

Knowledge Framework and classroom action

Gloria Tang

INTRODUCTION

It has been noted earlier that unless ESL students develop language and content simultaneously, they will be denied the full benefits of education due to their low proficiency in English. Many ESL students, particularly those at the upper intermediate and secondary levels (i.e. grades 7 or 8 and above), have difficulty understanding and expressing content knowledge in English. How can we help students to learn new content knowledge, written or spoken, in English? This chapter will describe an approach using the knowledge structures of the Knowledge Framework, and, in particular, visual representations of knowledge structures, to help ESL students to work constructively and independently with the literacy demands and conceptual demands of content areas of the middle and high school curriculum.

This approach is consistent with the strategies of visual tools for constructing knowledge, recommended for students in general, which address criticisms of mainstream education by promoting critical and creative thinking (e.g. Hyerle, 1996; Schwartz and Parks, 1994). These criticisms take a constructivist view of knowledge, placing emphasis on a student-centred, developmental, and interactive approach to learning; their visual tools for constructing knowledge range from representations of specific content to thinking process maps and move towards the development of a common visual language for learning; and they aim to restructure schools by integrating teaching, learning and assessing, and by 'displaying alternative views of knowing and thus restructuring, from the ground up, how participants in a learning community develop ideas, communicate and negotiate meanings' (Hyerle, 1996: 5). They thus aim to change schools where learners passively memorise material for examinations without understanding, critical thinking, or active relation to their lives. They aim to move from the transmission of inert content or subject matter to the construction and communication of knowledge.

These strategies for constructing knowledge are based on the assumption that students and teachers can relate visual tools to the meanings expressed in content textbooks and to other forms of educational discourse. But Hyerle (1996) and Schwartz and Parks (1994) do not discuss how meaning in visual tools relates to meaning in discourse. The approach in this chapter addresses this assumption directly: it is specially concerned to explore the connections between visual meanings and discourse meanings. This is a particularly urgent problem for ESL learners while they are developing the language of learning, but it is also an important issue for all students, who must continuously develop language as a medium of learning throughout their educational lives and who must connect visual and discourse meanings in increasingly complex ways. Throughout this discussion my emphasis is on the relation between content or knowledge and discourse and language, and specifically on the relation between knowledge structures in visual form and knowledge structures in discourse form.

These strategies for constructing knowledge must also take account of students' prior learning. It would be comforting if research indicated that students could fully develop the potential of visual tools in their classroom environments spontaneously and without support. Unfortunately this is not the case, and in fact research has revealed some major impediments to this development. In a number of cases, students appear to have learned to ignore and even to reject visual tools, perhaps as a result of a bias towards the written word. This will be discussed later in the chapter. Teachers need to adopt a positive and active role to overcome these impediments, and this chapter will document the work of two teachers who have taken that role and created a more favourable learning environment. Their work provides examples of careful, sustained and systematic support for students. Teachers working in different contexts will need to adapt these examples to their own philosophies and to the circumstances of their own classrooms. I would also like to document the corresponding work of their students, as they think critically, discuss deeper understandings of subject material, and express their ideas graphically and in writing. Regretfully, space limitations prevent me describing student work in any detail.

The classroom approach described in this chapter is based on the knowledge structures of the Knowledge Framework. It uses knowledge structures as the central link to graphic representations, to thinking and the construction of knowledge, and to discourse and language. It includes five components which can be sequenced in a variety of ways:

1. Explicit discussion of knowledge structures and text organisation.
2. Explicit discussion of graphic representation of knowledge structure.
3. Explicit discussion of the language of knowledge structures and cohesion in discourse.
4. Engaging students in tasks which involve constructing graphics from expository prose.
5. Engaging students in tasks which provide opportunities for them to practise constructing expository prose from a graphic.

The remainder of this chapter cites two case studies to show how teachers create this approach in (1) grade 7 social studies classes and (2) secondary science/computer science classes.

USE OF THE APPROACH AT THE INTERMEDIATE LEVEL

A teacher from the Burnaby School District introduced some of the components of this approach into her grade 7 social studies class and found the strategies successful. The textbook I refer to is *Other Places, Other Times* (Neering and Grant, 1986), a social studies textbook widely used in public schools in Vancouver.

The teacher planned her lesson according to the Knowledge Framework (Mohan, 1986). She read each chapter to determine the top-level structure of the text, to organise the content according to the knowledge structures in the Knowledge Framework, and to prepare a structured overview or graphic organiser which best summarises the content of the chapter.

Chapter One is about early civilisation and the development of the four major classifications of early humankind: Homo habilis, Homo erectus, Neanderthal Man and Cro-Magnon Man. The macro structure of the chapter is a temporal sequence of descriptions and the structured overview that best represents the chapter is a time line (Figure 7.1). The graphic helped her to plan the content as well as language associated with the time line, e.g., 'lived from . . . to . . .', 'began in . . . and ended in . . .', 'inhabited the earth for . . . years', 'during that period'. In presenting the chapter overview, she explicitly introduced the knowledge structure 'sequence' and the language used in sequence texts.

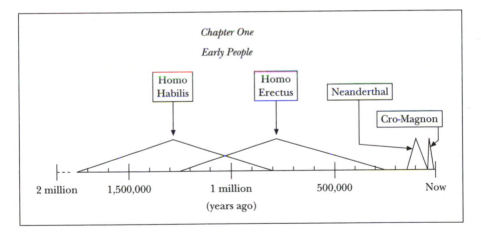

Figure 7.1 Time line to accompany 'Early People', Chapter One of *Other Places, Other Times*

She divided the chapter into four sections according to the four major groups of early people. Each section describes one group of early people, their way of life, the change and development they experienced, and the impact the environment had on them. She put the information in each section in a graphic and since similar information can be extracted from each of the sections, she organised the information in the same web-like graphic form

Figure 7.2   Graphic representation of Homo Habilis to accompany *Other Places, Other Times*

for all the sections (Figure 7.2). Use of the same graphic form allowed the teacher to use the same language repeatedly, thus reinforcing learning.

The teacher presented the first of these completed graphic organisers (Figure 7.2) on the overhead projector (OHP). She used the language of description consistently to answer the questions When? Where? What? After the graphic presentation, she referred students to the text, explicitly drawing their attention to the knowledge structure, description, and the language specific to that knowledge structure. In presenting the next two major groups of early people, she varied her strategies. She built up one of the graphics on the OHP while presenting the section, and she built up the other cooperatively with the students by assigning the paragraphs to be read and by asking the questions When? Where? What? She focused on verbs in the past form, e.g. 'were', 'was', 'lived', 'ate', 'hunted'; adjectives and adverb phrases of comparison, e.g. 'longer than', 'short', 'erect', 'sharp', 'pointed', 'different from', 'the same as', 'similar to', 'as large as'. She then allowed the students to work in groups to construct the fourth graphic. Building the graphic together with the students, she was helping them to make the link between the graphic and the text, and to see that the two are giving similar information but in different forms. She was also exposing students to the real language of description found in textbooks, a step towards managing school knowledge independently.

To bring the whole chapter together, she prepared a table (Figure 7.3) and asked students to complete it using the information in the webs. Using

	When	Where	Tools	Food	Shelter	Clothing	Art
Homo Habilis	From 1.75 million to 800,000 years ago	Eastern Africa and Southern Asia	Used sharp stones for tools and weapons – no fire	Berries, birds' eggs, wild pigs	Built shelters of branches	No clothes	No art
Homo Erectus	From 1.25 million to 250,000 years ago	Africa, Asia and Europe	Fire, flint blades, pointed wooden spears	Wild animals – elephant – cooked meat	Probably built shelters of branches	No clothes	No art
Neanderthal Man	From 130,000 to 30,000 years ago	Europe, Middle East	Knives, borers, spear sharpeners – made from stone	Wild animals – bear – cooked meat	Lived in caves	Animal hides for clothes	No art
Cro-Magnon Man	From 30,000 to 10,000 years ago	Europe, Asia, Africa, North and South America, Australia	Chisels, knives, spearpoints, needles, fish hooks, harpoon heads, lamps	Hunted animals and gathered wild plants	Lived in caves	Probably made coats from animal skins	Painting on cave walls, necklaces from shells and animal teeth, flutes and whistles from animal bones

Figure 7.3 Review of Chapter One of *Other Places, Other Times*

such a graphic, the teacher was moving the students from managing information in isolation to managing the relations of information. The table provides further opportunities for students to use language to compare and classify.

The teacher taught the students to build similar graphics on their own after working cooperatively with her a number of times. For example, the teacher introduced the time line in Chapter One and her ESL students could build up a time line on their own when they came to Chapter Five. To construct the time line, the students had to try to understand the chapter. They had to interact with authentic textbook language which is an important resource for writing expository prose. To give students practice in writing a coherent passage from a graphic, the teacher provided familiar graphic representations of familiar knowledge structures and asked students to write an essay based on the graphic. She provided language support and ensured that students knew 'how to link sentences together . . . and how to present and focus information' (Mohan, 1986: 94).

The graphic and the text are 'semantically comparable' (Mohan, 1989b); they convey similar information; they have the same knowledge structure. But in order to convert the graphic into expository prose, students have to translate the lines, arrows, and spatial arrangement, which are graphic representations of linguistic and cohesion devices, into linguistic and cohesion devices in text form. Figure 7.4, for example, is a cause–effect graphic of 'Events leading to the end of the Roman Republic'. The title and the headings give the signal that it is a table showing a series of causes and effects and the left – right sequence of each row represents 'caused' or 'brought about' or 'resulted in' or 'leading to' or 'so' or 'because' or 'The effect of . . . was . . .' or 'As a result of . . . , . . .'.

The teacher had taught the knowledge structure of cause–effect and exposed the students to cause–effect tables. She had also pointed out relevant

Events leading to the end of the Roman Republic	
Cause	Effect
Rapid expansion of the Roman Empire	Romans had to spend a lot of time and energy defending their empire from invaders
Angry Italians wanted the advantages of Roman citizenship. They threatened to rebel and attack Rome	The Romans granted citizenship to the Italians
Many internal problems: – poor people were starving – government officials became corrupt – consuls were assassinated – slaves rebelled against rough treatment from masters	Republican system was weakened

Figure 7.4   A cause–effect table

language features many times and given the students practice in constructing text passages from graphics. The students could write a coherent passage on the events leading to the end of the Roman Republic and they could produce expository prose using language features of cause–effect, e.g. 'cause', 'the reason was', 'so', and 'because' (see Figure 7.5).

There were three major events leading to the end of the Roman Republic. First, the rapid expansion of the Roman Empire caused the Romans to spend a lot of time and energy defending their Empire from invaders. The second reason was that angry Italians wanted the advantage of Roman citizenship. They threatened to rebel and attack Rome. The government survive without them so the Romans granted citizenship to the Italians. Last, the Republican system was weakened because poor people were starving, government officials become corrupt, consuls were assassinated and slaves rebelled against rough treatment from masters.

Written by

Jerry

Figure 7.5   Student-generated text

Teachers have used the approach described above not only in social studies classes at the intermediate level but also across a range of subject disciplines and levels. The following is an account of a secondary school teacher's work to integrate the teaching of computer skills, academic language, and science through graphics (computer graphics) in an ESL class at the secondary level. This teacher was both an ESL teacher and a mainstream science teacher. He was also a computer expert.

USE OF THE APPROACH AT THE SECONDARY LEVEL

The course was a beginner ESL science course specifically designed for ESL students who found the academic language of science demanding. The subject matter was based on the science textbook used by regular classes and the topic was life functions.

The teacher organised and rewrote the material for the Macintosh Classic microcomputer. Using this as a basis, the teacher integrated the teaching of three subject disciplines: he was teaching computer literacy through science, science through the computer, and English through science and computer literacy. He employed the Knowledge Framework (KF) to organise his lessons and to effect the integration of language and content. In the presentation of knowledge, the teacher made use of knowledge structure graphics both on the chalkboard and on the computer screen. He used graphic representations to lower the language barrier for the students, to enhance the visual impact, to elicit background knowledge, and to make the links in the integration. He was aware of the principal knowledge structures of each phase of instruction and used the language items characteristic of those knowledge structures.

While presenting science knowledge, the teacher systematically drew the students' attention to the language of particular knowledge structures, e.g. sequence and classification.

Not only did the teacher base his lessons on the KF, but he also explicitly taught students about knowledge structures and the language of the knowledge structures using graphics. He taught science concepts using the language of sequence and, at the same time, taught the language of sequence by discussing the human digestive system. In presenting the different steps of working on the computer, such as copying a card or writing a script, he used the language of sequence, such as action verbs and adverb phrases of time. The KF was, thus, the device which effected the link across computer skills, science knowledge and academic language.

Students were expected to learn the parts and functions of various systems, including the respiratory system and the processes of life functions such as digestion and blood circulation, and principles such as response to stimuli. The tasks which the students had to perform and the knowledge which they were expected to acquire included labelling diagrams, completing charts, constructing sentences to show cause–effect, and writing paragraphs to show sequence of events. The tasks set on the same topic were related. Each task was based on a graphic and built on a previous one. For example, they had to label a diagram of the respiratory system. Then the students had to make a chart, to sort, to sequence, and to write down the name and functions of each part of the system beginning from the nasal cavity. The next task was to write a paragraph based on the information in the graphic they had just completed titled *Respiration,* following the path of air from the nasal cavity to the lungs and out again. Before the students started writing, the teacher told them explicitly that the paragraph involved writing about a process and that there were special language features for that type of writing. While going over the passage of air through the respiratory system, he drew the students' attention to the present tense form of the verb, the third person singular, conjunctions, and adverb clauses. He put the following on the chalkboard: When air enters, first it goes ... Then it passes ... Next ... etc.

This process was integrated around the computer by creating a cycle of tasks which included creating 'cards' in a Hypercard stack (computer skill), copying a diagram onto the card (computer and content), labelling the diagram (content and language) and writing a paragraph based on the diagram (language and content). The end product was a stack of cards which the students made or responded to on the computer showing (1) the knowledge they had acquired regarding life functions and (2) the language they had learned to demonstrate their knowledge.

To check how students responded, I interviewed them and examined their written work. It was evident from the questioning in the interviews that the students could recall the information from their short-term memory. All the students could understand the concepts presented when the teacher employed graphic representation of knowledge structures to present content knowledge. They showed understanding of the processes of the various life functions; of the cause–effect relation of stimulus and response; and of the functions of the systems learned. The examination of their written work revealed that they had also learned to express in short paragraphs their understanding of the information, such as the digestion of a hot dog and the functions of various organs. Some samples of the first drafts of student writing are shown in Figure 7.6. It is true that there were mistakes in their writing, but they produced cohesive texts: the teacher had explicitly taught them language aspects of the knowledge structures and text cohesion and had given them practice. The final drafts were almost perfect in accuracy because the students were alerted to errors and inaccuracies during individual conferencing when the teacher provided immediate feedback.

Nancy's Respiration Paragraph

When I inhale the air, it enter my Nasal Cavity to breath in oxygen and it passes through to the pharynx. The it goes to Epiglottis, from the Epiglottis it moves down to the larynx and that the air goes to my Trachea. Then from the Trachea it goes to the Bronchi and the airs spreads out all through the lungs into the Alveoli. The oxygen from the air it goes to the alveoli. From the lungs.

*   *   *

Kristina's Respiration Paragraph

When air inhaling, it enter to my nasal cavity. Air passes through the pharynx. Next the epiglottis open to let air go to larynx and passes through the trachea. After this it go down to bronchi. Then it spreads out all through the lungs. It goes to alveoli.

Figure 7.6 Students' paragraph writing

The foregoing examples have concentrated on teacher initiatives in the sense that the teachers in both situations started by explicitly teaching the students about knowledge structures, as well as graphics and discourse representing the knowledge structures. However, it should be emphasised again that the aim of the approach is to help students to work with increasing independence. In conducting research with both intermediate and secondary school students over the past ten years, I have noticed that, as a result of teachers employing the approach, students have become more aware of the language representing knowledge structures and they have created graphics without instruction and prompting. An example from the second case study follows.

Steven and Alan, two Chinese boys, aged 16, were working on the same computer. They were looking at a computer graphic of an eye in which the pupil expanded or dilated in response to the amount of brightness. Alan had noted down what was on the computer by constructing two sentences: (1) If the pupil smaller, then you increase the brightness. (2) Pupil bigger, then decrease the brightness. Steven noticed an error and offered this unsolicited advice to Alan.

S: I think your sentence is wrong.

A: Wrong? Why wrong? 'If the pupil smaller, then you increase the brightness.'

S: Should be 'If you increase the brightness, the pupil become smaller.' The brightness is CAUSE and the smaller is the EFFECT.

Steven continued his explanation in Cantonese by constructing a chart as follows:

CAUSE	EFFECT
If...	then...
If...	then...

Alan was concerned about the correctness of the concept but Steven pointed out that Alan was expressing the concept incorrectly. Having learned knowledge structures, graphics and the language which represents the different knowledge structures, Steven had gained in language awareness. He was able to explain the language of a knowledge structure, i.e. cause–effect, and was able to represent a knowledge structure in graphic form. His explanation drew on a common visual language of learning.

DISCUSSION AND CONCLUSION

In the above cases, the teachers and students effectively integrated the learning of English and the learning of content employing the Knowledge Framework. However, I should reiterate that students need explicit teaching and practice to acquire the skill of using graphic tools for understanding and expressing content knowledge and academic language. The teacher case studies described above can only be fully appreciated against a backdrop of the way in which students typically fail to take advantage of graphics in classrooms.

Research shows that we cannot assume that exposing students to a large quantity of graphics will automatically facilitate learning (Herber, 1970; Vacca, 1981; Hunter et al., 1987; Levin et al., 1987; Winn, 1987; Holliday, 1975; Peeck, 1987). In a study of the role of graphics in intermediate classrooms (Tang, 1991), I too discovered that exposure is not enough. The students in the study were exposed to a large quantity of graphics and textbook illustrations which represented all knowledge structures. However, when the students encountered graphics in textbooks and other instructional materials, some passed over them after a quick look, others did not even look. Although some textbook illustrations are visual summaries of the text on the same page, the students did not seem to associate the illustrations with the information in the text: they did not realise that the text and graphics were giving the same information in a different form, or that the illustrations were a device 'by which the authors clarify their exposition' (Herber, 1970: 104). It appears that students indeed 'tend to skip over visual aids entirely or pay only cursory attention to them' (Vacca, 1981: 208) unless there is real curricular need. Few interacted with the graphics they encountered unless the teacher or the assignment required them to study, write about, or reproduce them.

When the teacher gave them information in both text and graphic form, the students chose to look for information in text passages. They found it simpler and more direct to copy answers to questions from the text. In studying for tests, too, nearly all the students depended on the printed word. Given a choice, not many of them chose to study the graphics or answer the questions in graphic form. It may be true that schools and teachers are biased towards verbal forms of representation, and that students have been forced into the verbal format of learning by tradition (Winn, 1987), and that 'because teachers, parents and students tend to assign an inflated value to the printed word' (Fleming, 1962, cited in Holliday, 1975: 22) students are unwilling to invest their time and attention in graphics.

The teacher encouraged the students to use multiple resources in an assignment which involved understanding, interpreting and explaining graphics. He engaged the students in research by setting the topic, giving instructions on the requirements, arranging for them to use the library, and leaving them on their own. Both the process of the research and the final product indicated that the students did not know how to use graphics to explain, represent, reinforce (Hunter et al., 1987), organise or interpret (Levin et al., 1987) knowledge. Even when they had gathered relevant or related data, they had difficulty organising and presenting them. They had no idea what format to use and what categories and information to select. It is often assumed that students are capable of processing and producing illustrative material when they are simply told to do so. However, this assumption is questionable for 'competency in adequately dealing with illustrations develops only gradually' (Peeck, 1987: 133), and only with explicit help and guidance from the teacher. It was only after the students had been systematically shown many times how to represent information graphically, that the whole class finished the assignment without difficulty. Explicit guidance in graphics also changed the students' attitude towards graphics.

How, then, can we help students to learn new content knowledge written or spoken in English? This chapter has suggested that teachers can recognise the power of graphic representation of knowledge structures. They can explicitly teach knowledge structures and their graphic representations; draw students' attention to linguistic signals of knowledge structures; and provide practice in constructing graphics from text and text from graphics in content classes as a means to help to increase students' ability to read and write academic discourse. By taking the initiative and providing guidance in this way, teachers can create an environment in which ESL students can make independent and constructive use of knowledge structures and graphics to work with the literacy demands and conceptual demands of content areas.

Chapter 8

Implementation of the Vancouver School Board's ESL initiatives

Margaret Early and Hugh Hooper

INTRODUCTION

Earlier in this volume, Mary Ashworth (Chapter 1) provided a description of the history and development of ESL programs and services within the Vancouver School District. This chapter situates itself within the broader context of that work and reports on a set of initiatives undertaken in that district from 1987 to 1997. During this period a group of educators/researchers at the University of British Columbia (UBC) worked collaboratively with educators in the Vancouver School District to develop an integrated approach to the teaching of language and content (Early et al., 1986; Mohan, 1986) and to deliver a carefully considered program and services for the instruction of children for whom English is a second language (Hooper, 1990).

This chapter reports mainly on the implementation of two large-scale projects and on the work cycle of in-service for educators during the period mentioned above. It also provides an update on the current context for ESL services in Vancouver and presents some lessons/insights learned over the years. Thus the chapter has four parts. First, it reports on Phase I of our work, a three-year district project concerned with the language barrier to academic achievement for ESL students. Second, it describes Phase II, a large-scale pilot project designed to inform the development of programs and services to support ESL learners which took place over a four-year period in selected schools. In the third section, we report briefly on Phase III, current initiatives underway in Vancouver. Finally, some understandings and insights gained from our work over the past decade will be drawn.

The objectives of Phase I were to increase the academic achievement of ESL students by developing their cognitive/academic language skills and to train a body of teacher curriculum developers who could disseminate the approach and materials throughout the system. Our central aim was to develop a core of teachers who took ownership of the ideas and strategies we explored mutually, who used them in their own classrooms, and who were enabled to work with stakeholders in the educational community.

The goals of Phase II of the work were more far reaching than Phase I and included: developing strategies for providing social and academic integration

138

of ESL students; intensifying staff development programs; developing recommendations for level of service; and developing strategies that would encourage parents to work in partnership with the school in their children's education. The first phase of our work, 1987–90, is described below.

CONTEXT

In the early to mid 1980s British Columbia received a steady flow of ESL learners. Many ESL teachers were finding that the strategies and methods that had once served them well were not providing their students with the necessary skills to be successful in the academic classroom. ESL teachers in Vancouver schools had begun to experiment with the use of subject area 'content' in their classes. Still, mainstream teachers complained that ESL students did not have the 'English' to face the academic demands of their classes. At the same time Mohan published *Language and Content* (Mohan, 1986) and the Provincial ESL Coordinator, Margaret Early along with Wakefield and Thew published an integrated language and content resource book for the BC school system (Early et al., 1986). Shortly after these books were published Mohan and Early (now at UBC), in partnership with the Vancouver School Board (VSB), secured a large grant from the Ministry of Education to fund a project to increase the academic achievement of ESL learners (K-12). This was, of course, designed as a means to take the work of both the UBC team and teachers further. The Knowledge Framework was central to the project and provided the theoretical perspective for our ongoing dialogue with teachers. This framework has been described in theory in Chapter 2 and illustrated in practice in Chapter 3 of this volume. The reader is referred to these chapters for a detailed account of the substantive nature of the ideas inherent in this framework. It is, as stated above, the implementation of the working ideas inherent in this particular approach to the integration of language and content, rather than its essence, that is the focus of this chapter.

PHASE I (1987–90): THE LANGUAGE AND CONTENT PROJECT

Vancouver is a large district; it is composed of approximately 100 elementary and 18 secondary schools. There are some 58,000 students in the district, 28,000 of whom are designated ESL students, and has some 3,200 teachers. From the outset, it was our intention to be directly involved with a small number of schools and key personnel within those schools. Our operating principles were to be involved with approximately one-tenth of the elementary schools, and one-fifth of the secondary schools in the district. It was intended that these schools be included on a volunteer basis, and that the members of each of the volunteer schools work in teams. As for the administration of the project, Mohan was the Research Director, Early acted as Project Director and Hugh Hooper assumed the role of ESL Project Manager and liaison with the School Board.

The project began in March 1987. For most of that school year and the whole of the next year, 1987–88, we worked with eight elementary and four secondary schools. Teams were established in each of these schools and each team consisted of both ESL and mainstream teachers, including those who had expertise in social studies, science and computers as well as an administrator and a person known for facilitating a collaborative spirit within the school. In all there were approximately six team members from each school – 75 educators in all. We broke these into three groups of 25 each – two elementary groups, one secondary group – to make it easier for all participants to get to know each other. Substitute teachers were provided each time teachers attended workshops. (The same substitute teacher was provided for a participating teacher whenever possible to minimise disruption for the students.) The general shape of this action research project is shown in Figure 8.1, and the process was structured in the form shown in Figure 8.2. The basic plan of our in-service program consisted of a series of workshops for groups of elementary and high school teachers, and for other educators who worked for schools. During the first year, between March and June 1987, workshops were provided for three groups of teachers – 25 secondary school teachers in one group, and 50 elementary school teachers who were divided into two groups of 25. Six workshops were given for each group, making a total of 18 workshops. Later, overview workshops were given for administrators, teacher-librarians, and speech language pathologists.

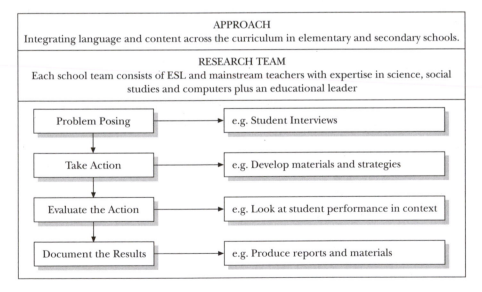

Figure 8.1   Language and Content Project: partial overview

During the summer, many of those teachers, administrators, librarians, and speech pathologists voluntarily took a two-week material writing workshop and developed units based on Mohan's Knowledge Framework. Between September 1987 and July 1988, ten workshops were again held for three

March–July 1987: 6 team workshops × 3 = 18 workshops *Summer*: 2 weeks material writing *Overview workshops for*: Administrators, teacher-librarians, speech language pathologists
September–July 1988: 10 workshops × 3 = 30 workshops (3 groups × 25) *Summer*: Language and Content Summer Institute (5 days: for new teams) *Overview workshops for*: Administrators, teacher-librarians, department heads of Social Studies and Science, and ESL teachers
September–June 1989: 10 workshops × 3 = 30 workshops (2 groups × 60) *Summer*: Language and Content Summer Institute (5 days: open to all) *Overview workshop*: Administrators

Figure 8.2   Structure of the in-service process

groups of elementary and secondary school teachers. Overview workshops were again held for administrators, teacher-librarians, and department heads of social studies, science, and ESL teachers at secondary schools. During the summer of 1988, new teams of elementary and secondary teachers were organised into a Language and Content Summer Institute. The following September to June 1989, two new groups of 60 teachers received ten workshops each. Overview workshops were again held for administrators. In the summer of 1989, a five-day Language and Content Summer Institute was again open to all teachers and administrators.

We developed an in-service model which we called the Framework for Teaching and Learning (see Figure 8.3) and conducted a series of workshops, the topics of which ranged across such diverse areas as: the relationship between knowledge structures, discourse and graphics; thinking process; the multiple uses of key visuals; and issues in task-based language learning

KNOWLEDGE FRAMEWORK	KEY VISUALS	TASK DESIGN FOR TEACHING AND LEARNING
	1. Building background knowledge 2. Thinking through the topic 3. Reconstructing knowledge 4. Expression and application	

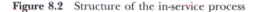

Figure 8.3   Framework for teaching and learning

including cooperative learning. Reading and writing exposition, discussion, developing talk, vocabulary building and assessment were also addressed. We tried to model good teaching/learning and designed tasks which were interactive and went through a cycle of building background knowledge on a particular topic; thinking through the topic; reconstructing/accommodating the new knowledge and articulating and applying the new learning. Readings were sent out in advance for consideration and response. Initially, we chose topics; but later, to be more democratic, the sessions were led by different school teams who chose the topics and the readings. Learning logs and reflection sheets were encouraged. Many teachers kept logs, portfolios and diaries as part of the reflection/action research process.

We also conducted a series of research studies to assess and better understand the work we had undertaken. Here are but a few examples.

Early (1992) conducted a series of interviews to see how more and less successful ESL learners perceive and act upon their educational experiences. Hooper (1988) conducted a qualitative and quantitative study of a science teacher and an ESL teacher working collaboratively to simultaneously develop grade 7 students' knowledge of biology, the language of classification and the use of a computer database program. Early (1990) conducted a case study of grade 4/5 ESL students working on a science and socials unit on the theme 'Fish', organised around knowledge structures and key visuals. Tang conducted a series of quantitative and qualitative studies on ESL students' use of graphics. (She examined such issues as their attitude towards graphics as a learning strategy; the effect of graphics on students' ability to comprehend social studies text; and the cross-cultural bilingual (Cantonese/English) potentials for the use of graphics in developing bilingual academic talk.) A large-scale study was also conducted by a team including Mohan, Early and Hooper in social studies and in science in several secondary schools to

- assess the effects of instruction and practice on structural patterns of knowledge and their realisations in graphics and texts on high school ESL students' comprehension of social studies and science textbook materials;
- to assess the effects of this instruction on the quality of ESL students' expository writing.

Because we presented our workshops on a frequent, regular basis it allowed us the opportunity to integrate the findings from our research.

At the closure of this project, we had some products and some insights and understandings. We had, we felt, come close to meeting the goals *and* purposes of our agenda. In summary, we had developed teaching strategies and curriculum resources, and provided models and packages for staff development. Also, from our research, we had gained a better understanding of what hinders and facilitates the integration of language and content teaching. Perhaps even more importantly, we had institutionalised our ideas on a small scale. As a result of the work people, in particular, well-respected educators in a number of schools had taken the ideas on board and were very interested to put them into practice. Moreover, they did this in a way that gave them a sense of ownership in the development, refinement and expansion of these ideas. Thus, the products of our work seemed sound and promising and encouraged the School Board to:

- build our work into the ongoing staff-development program – entire schools committed three of their possible five professional development days to in-service in this area;
- build the work into a new ESL Pilot Project (Phase II) which was currently being designed.

It would be wrong of us to let the reader think that everything ran smoothly and that we did not have to make changes along the way. We came, in time, to understand that while the implementation of ideas on paper may be fine, in reality they play out in somewhat similar but yet quite unique ways as they are applied to different cultures of teaching – that is, 'according to the guiding beliefs and expectations evident in the way a school or particular subject area within a school operates' (Fullan, 1993). So we made adaptations for elementary/secondary teachers, for science teachers, mathematics teachers, etc. Moreover, we came to a deepened appreciation of Hargreaves' (1992) concept that when we think about the notion of cultures of teaching, we need to consider both the 'content' of teachers' cultures and the 'form' of teachers' cultures. By 'content' he means what teachers say and do (their beliefs and practices). This is the area where he sees most cultural diversity among teachers. The 'form' of teachers' cultures is 'the particular articulation of relations between teachers and their colleagues', i.e. the way in which teachers relate, communicate and establish a shared vision. He argues that his distinction is important because creating change in beliefs and actions (content) is not merely related to the way teachers interact, but is in fact highly dependent upon changing the pattern of relationships, interactions and opportunities for discussion, i.e. the form of teaching cultures. Neither of these changes in teaching cultures (content or form) is a small feat, as Cuban (1986: 109) clearly warns us:

> Teachers' repertoires, both resilient and efficient, have been shaped by the crucible of experience and the culture of teaching. Policy makers [staff-developers] need to understand that altering pedagogy requires a change in what teachers believe, getting professionals to unlearn in order to learn, while certainly not impossible, is closer in magnitude of difficulty to performing a double bypass heart operation than to hammering a nail.

The difficulty of changing the nature of working relationships is equally on par. For example, in our work it not only entailed having an ESL teacher move from teaching a grammar-based syllabus to an integrated language and content approach, but also moving from teaching in isolation to a more cooperative and collaborative working relationship with mainstream teachers. Neither move is easy to effect but both are necessary if the innovation is to succeed. In our work the strength of the Knowledge Framework was that it helped to bridge the gap between the two cultures of teaching; it was the 'common currency' by which they could share their knowledge and jointly plan their work.

We therefore learned at the end of Phase I that while successful, the success of our innovation was and would be limited if it addressed only the 'content' as we had been doing, and did not consider and provide adequate support to change both the content and the form of the relationships in the culture of teaching. By this we meant that one of the most positive things we could do was to deliberately build into our in-service work the notion of the school as a 'learning organisation, i.e. a place where people continually expand their capacity to create the results they truly desire . . . and where people are learning how to learn together' (Senge, 1990). In other words, to build into the next phase of the plan the central and critical notion of the school and its community as a network of people who are resources.

As a building block for this idea, however, we had laid some very important groundwork in the first phase of our project. We had indeed, as stated earlier, begun to establish a strong network of people as resources. This was a positive and vitally important outcome of Phase I – indeed a legacy within the district to this day, as will be discussed later.

PHASE II: THE ESL PILOT PROJECT

As reported earlier in this volume (Chapter 5), in 1989, in response to unprecedented ESL population growth and unrelenting pressure from stakeholder groups, the VSB commissioned an external review of their programs and, as a result of the review, among other things, new district staff positions were established (one ESL Program Administrator and five teacher consultants). The ESL Program Administrator (Hugh Hooper) was charged by the newly established ESL Coordinating Committee (ESLCC) with the responsibility for devising a plan for implementing the review recommendations. The ESL team, in the spring of 1990, proposed a four-year plan for making substantive changes to ESL program delivery. This plan and the accompanying costs were later endorsed by the ESLCC and the school trustees. A central component of the plan was the development of a large-scale ESL Pilot Project.

Schools were required to apply to be a pilot school. They had to be prepared to make a sizable commitment to the pilot project goals. This time, six elementary schools and four secondary schools were chosen as pilot schools. Each of the schools established an ESL Pilot Project steering committee which considered a number of goals and prioritised them for their unique school context. The purpose and goals of this project were as follows:

- Develop strategies for providing social and academic integration of ESL students.
- Develop recommendations for levels of service that will adequately serve the language needs and long-term development of the academic potential of ESL students.
- Identify and develop teaching strategies that will allow all students to reach their academic potential.
- Identify and develop curriculum resources for teachers and students.

- Identify and develop effective staff development programs.
- Identify and develop strategies for encouraging parents to work in partnership with the school in their children's education.

In order to address these goals the Board provided ESL pilot schools with support, staff development training in instructional strategies (integrating language and content and collaborative consultation – introductory levels for school staffs and advanced levels for pilot staff) and curricular materials.

Phases I and II differed in a variety of ways. In the first place, in Phase I only teams of teachers were involved in the project, whereas in the ESL Pilot Project (Phase II) all teachers at the elementary schools were involved and 30–40 per cent of the teachers at each of the secondary schools. Unlike the Phase I schools, the ESL pilot schools received from two to four additional teachers for the duration of the project. These positions (English Language Support Teacher and ESL Resource Teacher) were new to the District and were designed by the ESL district team. All of the teachers who assumed these roles had experience of using the Knowledge Framework and were willing to learn additional collaboration skills. After the district ESL team presented workshops on the Knowledge Framework at each of the pilot schools, the ESL pilot teachers were involved in supporting follow-up efforts. In order to support, steer and own the changes in the school, each school set up an ESL Pilot Project Steering Committee composed of teachers and administrators.

Figure 8.4 summarises the conceptual framework for these goals and purposes.

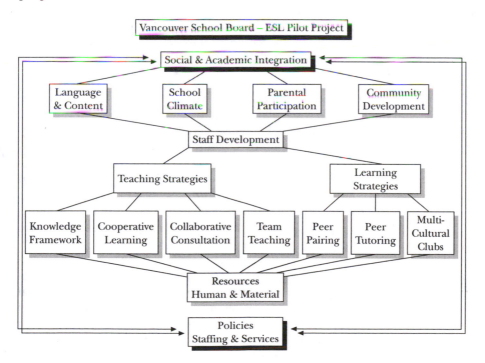

Figure 8.4

In relation to the UBC teams' involvement in this phase of work, apart from ongoing discussions with Hugh Hooper (now District Principal – ESL for the VSB), Mohan and Early had obtained Social Science and Humanities Research Council (SSHRC) funding to continue their efforts to understand issues around the integration of language and content. They therefore undertook one part of the overall evaluation of the pilot project and examined the implementation in detail in one high school and one elementary school.

As was mentioned earlier, collaboration or the changing of the form of the relationships within cultures of teaching emerged as centrally important to the success of our work in the schools. Indeed, there is generally a growing recognition that the job of teaching may require more collaboration between teachers and their colleagues *and* indeed between teachers and parents than has been recognised. Several studies (Dempsey, 1994; Hurren, 1994; Helmer, 1995; Mohan and Early, 1996) were conducted on the mainstream and ESL teachers collaborative efforts. These studies reflected the complex nature of collaboration and the necessary conditions for its success, and helped us to understand that collaboration is no easy feat.

In addition, the Vancouver School Board conducted a large-scale evaluation of the ESL Pilot Project just one year after its commencement (Dunn, 1992). In that study, questionnaires were given to teachers, administrators, and students in the pilot schools – some 900 participants in all. Many different aspects of the pilot project were considered; but, for the sake of brevity, here are some of Dunn's general comments regarding the pilot's success rate:

> All groups rated the success of the pilot in working towards its long-term goals of academic and social integration of ESL students into regular classes. 79% of elementary teachers and 72% of secondary teachers rated the pilot very or moderately successful. 92% of administrators and 95% of district staff rated it very to moderately successful. (Dunn, 1992: 1)

A major emphasis in the project was to have as many teachers using the Knowledge Framework in their planning and teaching as possible. A second critical theme was encouraging ESL teachers and mainstream teachers to share their expertise in a collaborative planning process. The ultimate goal was again for ESL students to enjoy more social and academic success. As with the first phase of our work, we learned many lessons. Here, we learned more about the implementation/collaboration process of trying to effect change in a whole school context. In keeping with Fullan, these are insights which we believe are important to remember when engaging in innovative work: change is a long-term process – do not expect dramatic results overnight; change requires constant dialogue and communication among all participants, including students and parents in the process; change requires an atmosphere of trust and respect; it is resource hungry – time is an important resource for reflection and collaboration; and without something to anchor the process, i.e. a framework of some kind – in our case we used Mohan's (1986) framework and our framework (cycle of in-service) for teaching and learning – change can be very chaotic.

As an example of how this worked out relative to the need for communication and the need to provide resources, in one particular instance the school principal changed the teachers' preparation time in order to support collaborative planning time – a deliberate change of the timetable. This principal also used his extra staffing allocation to create support positions for this work.

Moreover, we also learned that consideration of these factors in themselves is not adequate. Collaboration between teachers is complex. For successful collaboration to take place, certain conditions need to be in place. These include: collaboration must be voluntary in nature; there needs to be shared broad goals; there needs to be parity in roles and responsibilities (i.e. each person's contribution needs to be equally valued and there needs to be an equal distribution of power among collaborators); the rewards must outweigh the work and the risks; there needs to be organised institutional support; and there needs to be trust and mutual respect (Dempsey, 1994).

Over time, the Knowledge Framework (Mohan, 1986) which we originally used as a conceptual tool, has 'metamorphosed' and has been applied variously as we have engaged critically with this framework in practice for over a decade. It has continued to serve us well as an 'anthropological lens' by which we can consider or 'see', however fleetingly, multiple perspectives across cultures of teaching and epistemological positioning of teachers.

PHASE III: CURRENT CONTEXT FOR ESL SUPPORT AND SERVICE INITIATIVES

And so to the present. At the end of the ESL Pilot Project, ideas, resources and service models were 'owned' by the district and implemented across the district in the sense that the district implemented the ideas through workshops provided for district teachers and for teachers and trainers from school districts all over British Columbia, other provinces and other countries. In some large measure the UBC team, while actively conducting research in the district and in constant communication with key personnel, had become dispensable, their role no longer central.

While these in-service models and instructional strategies were receiving positive attention, a variety of events were occurring that would change the face of ESL services in Vancouver. In 1995 the VSB undertook another review of its ESL programs and services. While the quality of the programs received commendations, the most significant recommendation was to ensure that ESL learners had the opportunity to attend their neighbourhood school. To bring this change into effect meant the devolution of responsibility for ESL learners from the district ESL office to each of the neighbourhood schools. Although the majority of ESL learners attended their home school, many did not and were given financial support for transportation. Teachers and school administrators were adamant that if ESL students were to attend their home schools, then high-quality services would be made available to them, e.g.

that ESL staffing would be in place. From 1995 to 1997 the district ESL staff created a plan to implement a new program delivery model in the Fall of 1997, one in which, it was hoped, schools would assume more responsibility for their ESL learners who would now be 'theirs'. This plan incorporated all of the positive elements learned from the two projects described above.

At the same time as the ESL review was conducted, a review of centralised district services concluded that these services should be provided closer to the schools. Recommendations were made to concentrate previously central-ised district staff resources in four area offices.

While these large-scale changes were being debated and discussed, it was announced that the Vancouver School Board faced a multi-million dollar shortfall going into the year of implementation. To meet its obligations the district cut over 350 full-time positions from the budget. There were now 100 fewer positions to reallocate to the four area offices. Moreover, the dis-trict office staff was seriously reduced and the entire ESL team was disbanded; as such there was no ESL team to support the implementation of the new plan.

There is no doubt that the materials, resources, models of service delivery and resource teacher/leaders who were closely involved in the ESL initiatives described in Phases I and II are being used throughout the district but in ways deemed appropriate by individual sites. Area and district consultants (only one of whom is designated as an ESL specialist) are acting as facilitators, while the teachers in classrooms who have developed particular knowledge and skills over the years will be used as 'teacher leaders' in the exchange of expertise with colleagues. This model, which squarely places responsibility to meet ESL students' needs in the hands of each school community, has great potential to: give ownership of the initiatives to the schools; tailor the services for students and professional development needs of teachers to the individual school; bring about greater integration of ESL students and their families into the school and community; firmly establish home–school responsibility for all ESL students since this is their neighbourhood school where they will be in attendance for the long term.

However, like everything else in education, this service model may be implemented well or poorly, and there will likely be variation across schools depending upon expertise and priorities of teachers and administrators. The total devolution of centralised district ESL program personnel and resources was not without its heated controversies and strong opponents, especially since it was felt that not all schools were equally well prepared for such an instant change. However, time will tell, and this new phase may well be the ultimate test of the degree of success of our earlier initiatives in terms of what has been learned about the implementation of language and content; the complexities of teacher collaboration; the change process and the imple-mentation of innovations. In summary, therefore:

- The focus in Phase I was on the innovation itself. Here the emphasis was on the teacher and the classroom, on a perspective which showed the possibility of integrating language and content, and the strategies for doing so.

- The focus in Phase II was on the school and community as a network of resources. Here greater emphasis was placed on collaboration between the teachers in the project and other teachers and other participants, and on the conditions for collaboration.
- The focus in Phase III was on the cooperation between different stakeholder groups while supporting and maintaining the elements of phases I and II.

However, radical changes occurred in the administration of the school district, particularly the disbanding of the central ESL team. In effect, this changed the service model to a devolved model. At present, the results for school-based teacher development are unknown.

REFLECTIONS: INSIGHTS AND UNDERSTANDINGS

This book discusses issues of theory, practice, policy and implementation in the education of linguistically and ethnically diverse children. This chapter has discussed the well-resourced and well-planned implementation of a set of innovations, within a wider context (detailed in other chapters of this volume) of one school district's ongoing attempts to effectively deliver a quality program which integrates the instruction of language and content to ESL students. From our experiences, we would argue that there is no substitute for implementation. Policy alone is simply not enough, although policy is clearly critical.

Referring to the history of school-change initiatives in Canada and the USA, Fullan has warned that government (and, we would argue, all forms of 'government') policies, on their own, are no guarantee of success:

> Almost all education policies that governments pass fail to make any difference in improving schools and combating school failure.
>
> (*Globe and Mail*, 11 September 1997)

For policies to work, he warned, there needs to be a combination of pressure and [implementational] support from the governing agency so that teachers, students, parents and the wider community have the capacity and context to improve the culture of a school.

In this light, then, it becomes particularly vital to be reflective about implementation procedures and to learn from our experiences. The obvious first point is that the innovations described here are not simple, but are of considerable complexity. The second point is that these innovations required a great deal of commitment and creativity from the experienced teachers with whom we worked in partnership.

We hope that it has been clear from our description that the approach we took was not static; and our implementation process was a journey, not a blueprint (to paraphrase Fullan, 1993). Even as our ideas became institutionalised, it was critical to be fluid to adapt and to listen 'with our hearts' and minds to the perspectives and wisdom of the other participants in the process – teachers, students, parents, administrators and the community.

In the end, although there are units, models, resources and packages of various forms, there was no legacy of a 'package' of implementation. What we are left with is the knowledge that we acted as catalysts and facilitators for a community to become reflectors-in-action.

CONCLUSION

In this chapter we have attempted to set out how and in what ways we responded to issues and needs in particular situations, but this is not a prescription. We believe, however, that at the heart of any successful implementation is the development of a core of teachers who own the ideas and use them in their classrooms. These teachers need to be provided with a context whereby they become workers/change agents within their communities and they must be given institutional support in their new role. Part of this role is to engage in dialogue with all invested stakeholders, establishing a shared broad vision and trusting in the organisation's efficacy (ability to 'pull it off') is vital. If we have learned anything, it is the need to appreciate the unique nature of contexts and yet to recognise the interdependency of communities and the need to connect. We have also learned, as others elsewhere, that ultimately the direction, intensity and continuation of an innovation will be dependent upon the teachers. If we support them to shape their vision and transform their reality collaboratively, the innovation will be owned and take root. The long-term effects of our work in Vancouver are about to face that test.

Part III

ENGLAND

Chapter 9

England: ESL in the early days

Constant Leung and Charlotte Franson

THE 1950s AND 1960s

Until the 1950s the bulk of English Language Teaching (ELT) work was done in overseas countries: EFL in countries where English was a foreign language, e.g. Sweden or Japan and ESL in countries where English was a second or an official language, e.g. Kenya and India. But this offshore character of ELT started to change in the 1950s with the arrival of the Asian and West Indian immigrant workers and their families. For instance, Spring Grove School in Huddersfield was reported to have made special reception arrangements for non-English speaking students as early as 1958 and by 1961 it had set up full-time English classes for those whose English was regarded as inadequate for normal studies (Hawkes, 1966, cited in Derrick, 1977). There was little planned and systematic response to the educational needs of the new arrivals. Some observers argued that many of the difficulties experienced by schools were in fact due to the fact that there was no central policy to meet the needs of non-English-speaking children in schools (Tomlinson and Tomes, 1983).

While there was no formal declaration on long-term educational policy as far as the immigrant children were concerned, it was evident that the tacit expectation was eventual cultural and social assimilation. The central goal of the education provision was to turn all in-coming children into 'ordinary' British or English students as quickly as possible. The aim was to help the immigrant child to

> become 'invisible', a truly integrated member of the school community, sharing the traditional curriculum and participating in regular classes as soon as possible.
> (Derrick, 1977: 16)

The Plowden Report (DES, 1967: 71), for instance, advised that:

> The curriculum of the primary school with a substantial intake of immigrant children should take account of their previous environment, and prepare them for a life in a different one ... It is ... important to introduce the younger children to their new environment. Visits to shops and factories, to the local fire station ... and the country can provide a useful background to their school work.

Since the major educational concern was to bring about the assimilation of immigrant children, the lack of English language skills was seen as a major obstacle. The Plowden Report stated categorically that 'It is absolutely essential to overcome the language barrier.' A survey of the arrangements for immigrant pupils in a number of LEAs, *Immigrant Children in British Schools* (Hawkes, 1966, cited in Derrick, 1977: 5) argued strongly for the improvement of English language teaching to immigrant pupils.

> The language barrier is concrete and superable. Tackling it in a rational and socially conscious way is essential to a social unity in future, in which the children and descendants of the most recent wave of immigrants will enjoy the same opportunities in life as those who were here before them.

Policy concerns in the early 1960s started to focus on the teaching of English to non-English-speaking students, and English language teaching began to receive more official support and encouragement. During the first part of the decade Local Education Authorities (LEAs) and individual schools developed approaches to teaching English as a second language. Practices included both peripatetic teaching and withdrawal classes; however, in many cases the provision was fairly *ad hoc*. Circular 7/65 (DES, 1965: 2) recommended that 'Where a school contains a number of children with little or no knowledge of English, it is desirable to arrange one or more special reception classes in which they may learn English as quickly and as effectively as possible.'

By the 1970s almost all local education authorities with appreciable numbers of non-English-speaking background students were providing some form of ESL facilities albeit on a very limited scale. Townsend (1971) reported that there were four main types of ESL provision:

1. Full-time language centres where intensive language courses were offered. The general aim was to improve the non-English-speaking background students' English as quickly as possible so that they might join their neighbourhood school and take up normal studies. The most common length of stay at such centres was reported to be one year.
2. Part-time language centres where non-English-speaking background students from ordinary schools attended for about half of the school week. In terms of organisation, staffing and student in-take these centres were similar to the full-time centres.
3. Full-time language classes within ordinary schools. These classes were often referred to as language units. Students normally stayed in such classes between two and six terms and as soon as they were judged to have mastered the requisite English language skills they were integrated into the ordinary subject classes.
4. Part-time language classes within ordinary schools. These classes were normally conducted on a withdrawal basis. Students who were deemed to be in need of additional or special language study were taken out of their normal curriculum studies for part of their school time to study the English language.

NATURE OF THE EDUCATIONAL RESPONSE:
NUMBERS AND RESOURCES

Perhaps it should be emphasised that the provision of ESL in the state education sector at this time was very much a response to a rapidly emerging need
at the local government level and not a planned national development based
on anticipation. As a result, the overall ESL provision for immigrant children
was patchy and varied.

A major official preoccupation during this period was to do with the organisation of staff and physical facilities. The pamphlet *English for Immigrants*
(Ministry of Education, 1963), the first official statement regarding immigrant
pupils, offered teachers advice on practical and organisational matters such
as deployment of staff, teaching arrangements and use of materials within
schools (Derrick, 1977; Wallace, 1987).

We are not suggesting here that no educational principles were considered.
On the contrary, decisions were made on the basis of many well-practised principles, but by and large they tended to be on the level of resource deployment. For instance, the choice between setting up reception centres and
language classes on a full-time or part-time basis within schools was often
influenced by the number of non-English-speaking background pupils, staff
availability, and so on. This approach was underpinned by an unquestioned
assumption that the arrival of non-English-speaking background students
represented a threat to the maintenance of academic standards and scholarly
attainments of the indigenous students. The second report of the Commonwealth Immigrants Advisory Committee in 1964 (cited in Tomlinson and
Tomes, 1983: 16–17) stated that:

> If a school has more than a certain percentage of immigrant children among its
> pupils, the whole character and ethos of the school is altered. Immigrant pupils
> in such a school would not get as good an introduction to British school life as
> they would in a normal school.

The authors of this document also stated that: 'the presence of a high proportion of immigrant children in one class slows down the general routine
and hampers the progress of the whole class' (*loc. cit.*).

Whatever the merits of these views, they were translated into a sort of
'numbers' game. DES Circular 7/65 (DES, 1965: 4) suggests that:

> It is inevitable that, as the proportion of immigrant children in a school or class
> increases, the problems will become more difficult to solve, and the chances
> of assimilation more remote ... Experience suggests ... that ... up to a fifth of
> immigrant children in any group fit in with reasonable ease, but that, if the
> proportion goes over about one third either in the school as a whole or in any
> one class, serious strains arise.

This perceived need to spread the load, as it were, led to some LEAs adopting administrative measures such as dispersal (spreading out non-English-
speaking students to a number of schools to prevent high concentration,

often involving bussing) and redrawing catchment area boundaries to ensure an even distribution of non-English-speaking students.

At the same time there was an official recognition of racial disadvantage in Britain. The 1966 Local Government Act (LGA) was introduced to enable the central government, through the Home Office, to make support grants (under Section 11 of this Act) to local authorities (both counties and city boroughs) to promote race equality by making additional provision for ethnic minority communities and to employ additional staff 'in consequence of the presence within their areas of substantial numbers of immigrants from the Commonwealth, whose language or customs differ from those of the rest of the community' (LGA, 1996, cited in Bourne, 1989: 40). This 'additional' provision included meeting the linguistic and cultural needs of pupils of New Commonwealth heritage. The interpretations of the funding requirements, and application for funding, were left to the LEA's discretion. In the 1980s the Home Office conducted an extensive review of Section 11 provision which resulted in the implementation of criteria demanding much greater accountability. The exclusive focus on New Commonwealth pupils was removed in 1993. The bulk of ESL work is still partly funded by the central government working in partnership with local authorities under an administrative mechanism known as Ethnic Minority and Travellers Achievement Grant (EMTAG).

EARLY ESL: A READY-MADE PEDAGOGY?

At this point it may be interesting to ask what ESL meant in terms of content and method. Systematic and comprehensive information is hard to find on this point, but given the rich and long experience of ELT (particularly in overseas contexts) in this country, and the potential availability of seemingly suitably qualified staff, it would seem that the newly emerging ESL profession did not need to go far to look for a subject identity. The Ministry of Education (1963: 18) advised that:

> The teacher, through his own clear and natural speech should set a constant example of the normal intonation, rhythm and pitch of ordinary conversation, using pictures, objects, actions and improvised dialogues to ensure comprehension and to enlarge vocabulary. The pupils should be expected to imitate what the teacher says, preferably in whole sentences, with as reasonable a standard of pronunciation and information as it seems appropriate to expect . . . Most teachers experienced in the teaching of English as a second language would stress the importance of basing oral work on a carefully graded vocabulary and carefully introduced sentence patterns.

The Plowden Report (DES, 1967: 71), by contrast, offered a methodologically slightly less confident view:

> [The English language barrier] is less serious for a child entering the infant school. He rapidly acquires, both in the classroom and outside, a good command of the relatively limited number of words, phrases and sentences in common

use among other children. He can then learn to read with the rest, by normal methods.

Immigrant children who arrive later in their school life have much greater problems. They need to learn a new language after the patterns and often the written forms of their own language have been thoroughly mastered. This calls for special techniques and materials and poses problems to which little research has been directed.

The Schools Council Project in English for Immigrant Children (1969) focused on sentence patterns and preselected vocabulary. Oral practice was emphasised. Townsend (1971: 40), in a discussion on the work of language centres, observes that:

> The main emphasis in teaching was placed on language work in listening, speaking, reading and writing. Some centres were excellently equipped with language laboratories and a wide range of audio-visual equipment such as language-masters, tape recorders ... Teaching was generally by direct-method.

There did not seem to be a single dominant method. ESL in the state sector simply followed the time-honoured British ELT tradition of being flexible and undogmatic. It was happy to accommodate different methods as long as they suited its purpose. As Strevens (1977: 56) puts it:

> Within British ELT it is a basic assumption that the nature of learning and teaching in any given teaching situation is affected by a great number of variables, and that in consequence a different choice among a wide range of possible procedures and methods will turn out to be appropriate in different teaching/learning situations.

He calls it 'pedagogical professionalism'. If there was no one dominant teaching method, there was nevertheless a distinct subject area – the English language system itself. As a teaching syllabus, it largely consisted of grammatical structures and preselected vocabulary. Recommendations for teaching ESL in the mid 1960s focused on a systematic, graded, structural approach with an emphasis on drill methods and the development of oracy skills before reading and writing (Derrick, 1977). Thus, language learning was typically viewed as 'the achievement of a proper degree of cognitive control over the structures of a language, assuming that a facility to use the language will develop automatically' (Wallace, 1987: 121). In the climate of assimilation many teachers expected the newly arrived non-English-speaking pupils to acquire a knowledge of English fairly quickly and, having accomplished that, nothing further needed to be done about their English language development in the wider context of schooling.

1970s: A WIDENING PERSPECTIVE

The ESL provision put in place in the 1950s and 1960s was being challenged increasingly in the 1970s. The results of the surveys conducted by the Department for Education and Science (DES, 1971, 1972) indicated that the initial English language teaching was not effective in preparing the students to integrate into the mainstream classroom. The issues concerning the teaching of English to beginners had been conceptualised as practical and organisational matters, but with the passage of time this organisationally oriented response was shown to be inadequate.

There were two main background reasons, one sociocultural and ideological and the other intellectual, to account for this development. First, the British education system has always been wary of segregation along racial and language lines. In the 1960s, the Ministry of Education (1963: 9) suggested that:

> As far as the school is concerned, whenever it is desired to treat immigrant children in a rather different way from our own children, for example by putting them in a special class for intensive English teaching, the parents should be briefed as fully as possible about the school's purposes; otherwise it may be cited as an example of racial discrimination.

In connection with the policy of dispersal, Circular 7/65 (DES, 1965: 5) gave the following advice to the LEAs:

> It is important for the success of such measures that the reasons should be carefully explained beforehand to the parents of both the immigrant and the other children, and their cooperation obtained.

The same circular (DES, 1965: 2) makes the point that

> . . . the Secretary of State wishes to emphasise that on suitable occasions the children should join from the beginning in the normal social life of the school and gradually take their place in the ordinary classes as their command of English allows.

The Bullock Report (DES, 1975) represents an interesting transitional point in the pedagogical response. It maintained the Plowden Report's (DES, 1967) concern with the learning of the English language by the immigrant children; but unlike Plowden it was slightly more sanguine about the nature of the teaching task:

> There is by now a considerable body of methodology available and some very useful materials, at least for the initial stage of learning English as a second language . . . considerable practical knowledge has been contributed to the field by teachers and college lecturers returning from teaching posts overseas. . . .
>
> (DES, 1975: 289)

The above passage would suggest that Bullock's conceptualisation of second language pedagogy was not very different from the one adopted by Plowden a decade or so earlier. (In passing, the Bullock Report argued that in order to overcome staff shortage 'more should . . . be done to make it easier for teachers returning from overseas postings to be recruited into language teaching for immigrant children' (DES, 1975: 289). This rather suggests that the mainly overseas ELT practice was seen as directly applicable to ESL within England.) However, the integrationist debate of the 1970s clearly had an impact on Bullock's thinking on issues concerning the types of educational provision for the immigrant children:

> Common sense would suggest that the best arrangement is usually one where the immigrant children are not cut off from the social and educational life of a normal school . . . [English language teaching in special centres] is often carried out in complete isolation from the child's school . . . Specialist language teachers need to work in close liaison with other teachers. In whatever circumstances they operate, they should be given time to consult with these teachers in the schools and to be in touch with the child's education as a whole.
>
> (DES, 1975: 289–90)

Thus the learning of English was no longer the exclusive consideration; the access to the 'normal' school environment and curriculum was now an issue. On practical grounds the Report also began to question the efficacy of the specialist language centres:

> Another worrying aspect of this *initial* provision is that it absorbs almost all the trained teachers . . . Very few are to be found giving sustained language help to immigrant language learners beyond the *initial* stage . . . In most cases . . . it is unrealistic to think that the immigrant can reach that level of proficiency in English [to participate fully in the 'normal' school] in 18 months or so. His whole experience of English, the language and the culture, has more or less to be mediated through school. The Indian child virtually goes home to India every night . . . Although after a year he may seem able to follow the normal school curriculum, especially where oral work is concerned, the limitations to his English may be disguised; they become immediately apparent when he reads and writes. . . .   (DES, 1967: 290)

A more mainstream-integrated and language across the curriculum approach was endorsed:

> We were impressed by the efforts of schools . . . where the specially appointed language specialists had devised a flexible co-operative system within the school. They functioned both as teachers and consultants, sitting in on subject classes, analysing the linguistic demands made on immigrant learners in different areas of the curriculum, and offering running help to the children as the class proceeded.   (DES, 1967: 291)

The Swann Report (DES, 1985b) emphasised its 'fundamental opposition' to separate provision for ethnic minority children and envisaged ESL specialists working alongside their colleagues in the mainstream classroom. The Calderdale Report (CRE, 1986) held that separate ESL provision was against the promotion of equality of access to the mainstream system and as such it was racially discriminatory in outcome (if not in intent). The issues surrounding ESL teaching had become overtly political and ideological, directly tied up with issues concerning equal opportunities and anti-racism within educational institutions.

The second reason for the move away from the earlier system of separate language teaching draws its arguments from the more recent debates in linguistics in general and in communicative language teaching in particular. In the two or three decades leading to the 1970s a great deal of work in linguistics in English-speaking countries concerned itself with the language system, i.e. grammar. This holds true for the traditional prescriptive grammars as well as the relatively modern Chomskyan universal grammar. Developments in the adjacent disciplines of anthropology, philosophy of language and sociology, however, had eroded this insularity and by the mid-1970s there was a sea-change in the way language was perceived in some areas of sociolinguistic and language pedagogy. 'Correctness' now meant more than just grammatical accuracy, it also meant whether an utterance was appropriate in a given context. (See Hymes, 1974, for an example of this discussion.) Once the monolithic definition of correctness was challenged, it was possible to let in considerations such as graded communicative competence as goals of language teaching. The learners were encouraged to use language for a genuine communicative purpose in the learning process.

The Schools Council Project in English for Immigrant Children (1969) stated that the teacher 'does a disservice if he tries to impose language without regard for the child's communicative needs . . . .' (cited in Derrick, 1977: 18) The Bullock Report (DES, 1975) voiced the concern about learners who were superficially fluent but whose literacy skills indicated limited competence. Such learners needed extra help across the curriculum subject areas. This view was further strengthened by the White Paper *Better Schools* (DES, 1985a) which stated that ethnic minority students would achieve more if they were given the opportunity to acquire English while participating in the mainstream curriculum.

The Swann Report (DES, 1985b: 426) echoed the principle of 'language across the curriculum' as defined in the Bullock Report a decade earlier, stating that

> the needs of English as a second language learners should be met by provision within the mainstream school as part of a comprehensive programme of language education for all children.

1980s: MAINSTREAMING – REFOCUSING AND RELOCATING PEDAGOGY

In the change of emphasis to 'language education for all' there was a subtle but significant shift of focus of pedagogy:

> We believe that the language needs of an ethnic minority child should no longer be compartmentalised . . . and seen as outside the mainstream of education since language learning and the development of effective communication skills is a feature of every pupil's education. In many respects, ethnic minority children's language needs serve to highlight the need for positive action to be taken to enhance the quality of the language education provided for *all* pupils . . . Since . . . we have the additional resource within our society of bilingual . . . communities, it is surely right and proper that the education system should seek to build on the opportunities which this situation offers. Linguistic diversity provides the opportunity for all schools, whether monolingual or multilingual, to broaden the linguistic horizons of all pupils by ensuring that they acquire a real understanding of the role, range and richness of language in all its forms.
>
> (Swann, 1985: 385–6)

There seemed to be a two-part reasoning involved: language learning could be seen as part of the wider development of communication skills and, probably in an attempt to redress the 'ESL as deficit' view, the children from linguistic minority backgrounds were now seen as linguistic capital of the education system which could be used to enrich the language learning of all pupils. The 'linguistic diversity as capital' argument was often seen as a statement about the benefits of being bilingual or multilingual; but the formulation in Swann (see above) would suggest that it was the English-speaking majority pupils who would benefit from the presence of this diversity. In any case, these two lines of argument were not intrinsically connected, but once articulated together and presented as a pair of linked propositions they had the effect of moving the focus of pedagogical concern away from the individual second language learner's needs; thus suggesting the process of second language acquisition could be subsumed within first language (English) development within a curriculum context. The identification of learner needs were now to be found in the mainstream classroom processes and not within the individual pupil.

It was this refocusing and relocating of language teaching and learning that had enabled, on the conceptual level, ESL to change its direction. Bourne (1989: 64) comments:

> ... English as a second language learning has come to be perceived as part of a continuum of language development, not in itself a very different process from extending the repertoires of a first language across an increasingly differentiated range of domains ... Unlike the Bullock Report ... which had to accept a very different teaching strategy for 'ESL' based on the different language learning theories for mother tongue and second language acquisition current at that time, Swann ... was able to return English language learners to the mainstream classroom.

By the mid-1980s full-time language centres were all but a thing of the past. The few remaining part-time centres were being phased out. In-school withdrawal language classes no longer received official encouragement except in the case of absolute beginners. Indeed, ESL teaching carried out on a withdrawal (from the mainstream classroom) basis was regarded as somewhat morally offensive and socially divisive. There was a great deal of emphasis on equal opportunities and anti-racism. In the English context these ideological ideals were interpreted, in educational terms, to mean equal access to the mainstream curriculum and classroom by the second language students. Throughout the 1970s and 1980s there was a strong body of opinion arguing in favour of promoting multicultural education. One of the tenets of multiculturalism was to promote greater awareness and tolerance of different cultures within British or English society in schools. Among other things, this led to an increased awareness of the multilingualism of the pupil population. Interestingly, however, there were no national census figures for the number of speakers of other languages than English in England. In a survey of LEAs, Bourne (1989) identified over 209,000 pupils speaking a language other than

English at home. Furthermore, the concentration of bilingual pupils in LEAs across the country ranged from 4 to 26 per cent. As Bourne (1989: 32) concludes, 'in talking about bilingual pupils one is not talking about exceptional cases in a few urban authorities, but about a substantial proportion of the school population'. To this day detailed figures are conspicuous by their absence. DfEE (1997b) states that a tenth of the pupil population is from ethnic minority backgrounds and over half a million pupils do not speak English as a first language. In some urban areas it is not uncommon to find schools with 80 per cent or more linguistic minority pupils.

For many years the pupil's first language had been seen as a source of interference, but with the shift of emphasis to language as communication (e.g. Dulay et al., 1982) and more positive findings in studies in bilingual education (e.g. Cummins, 1984), bilingualism was seen as a potential educational advantage. ESL staff were encouraged to explore ways and means of tapping and developing this potential and, in this connection, even the label 'ESL' was being questioned. Increasingly the term 'bilingual' was being adopted as the positive aspects of children's experiences of speaking other languages were being stressed (Linguistic Minorities Project, 1985).

ESL AS AN AGENCY OF SOCIAL AND EDUCATIONAL CHANGE

Given the decentralised nature of the English schooling system at the time, there was no specific central government policy statement on educational multiculturalism and withdrawal ESL teaching. The cumulative effect of professional exhortation in the form of official reports or reviews and local government action was that there was a *de facto* policy and practice in the 1980s of mainstreaming ethnic minority students who were learning English as a second language.

> Despite an absence of central funding or co-ordinated national policy, LEAs during the later 1970s began to initiate policies specifically for ethnic minority children, following the lead taken by the Inner London Education Authority, which produced the first LEA document on multi-ethnic education ... The authority had taken seriously the relevant sections of the Race Relations Act 1976, which for the first time in race legislation required LEAs to take positive action to eliminate discrimination, and promote equal opportunity, understanding and good relations.   (Tomlinson and Tomes, 1983: 23)

Finally, ESL, arguably more than any other subject, had taken direct responsibility to tackle racism in schooling education. The climate of opinion was inexorably moving towards the integration into mainstream classes of pupils who were learning English:

> Policy for bilingual children was, within Swann, clearly framed in a broader approach to multicultural education, and to the dual aims of broadening and reorganizing the mainstream to accommodate more of ethnic minority cultures, meeting minority demands, while at the same time working towards educating the whole society in order to alleviate racism and hostility.   (Bourne, 1989: 9)

Collaborative teaching was seen as a useful pedagogical response for the reconceptualised multilingual and multicultural classroom. (For a time there was no clear definition of collaborative teaching, but broadly speaking it meant the ESL teacher working alongside the subject teacher in bi- or multilingual classrooms providing language support teaching to those who needed it.)

> With social cohesion as the main theme, stress was laid on provision for bilingual pupils within a mainstream system responsive to linguistic diversity, but within a curriculum framework common to all pupils.   (Bourne, 1989: 9)

The 1988 Education Reform Act, which is the legal instrument for the introduction of the National Curriculum, explicitly endorses this practice by stating that second language students are expected to follow the National Curriculum as a matter of entitlement and that speaking English as a second language is not in itself grounds for exemption from it. Furthermore, staff training materials (e.g. Bourne and McPake, 1991) finally provided collaborative teaching with a clear articulation within an approach now known as partnership teaching. The general idea is that the ESL teacher (now commonly known as language support teacher) and the mainstream class teacher should work together on planning, classroom teaching, assessing students' work and progress and producing teaching/learning materials. This approach is intended to create opportunities of change both at the whole school level as well as at the classroom level.

1990S: IN THE MAINSTREAM – DIFFERENT PRIORITIES AND DIFFERENT QUESTIONS?

One of the consequences of mainstreaming ESL in this particular context is that ESL is no longer regarded as a distinct subject area. ESL and the needs of ESL learners are subsumed in the mainstream curriculum. It can be readily observed that the mainstreaming as an educational response is a genus open to different uses and interpretations. It allows policy-makers and teachers to make the claim that equality of access to educational provision has been achieved; and at the same time it effectively removes the need to commit curriculum space and resources explicitly to address the specific language and learning needs of the pupils. The English (subject) National Curriculum has been written without explicit reference to second language learners, except to suggest that, 'where appropriate, pupils should be encouraged to make use of their understanding and skills in other languages when learning English' (DFE, 1995a: 2). In the revised version of the National Curriculum (DfEE, 1999a) there is a general requirement for all teachers to take account of the English language needs of pupils whose first language is not English; but this requirement is not reflected in the programmes of study or the level descriptions. As a curriculum area ESL has not been allowed a distinct discipline status; there are no ESL curriculum specifications and no national ESL scale for assessment. In the past few years the funding for ESL has been reduced repeatedly and the cuts have always been justified on financial grounds. These can be seen as indicators which point to ESL's loss of academic status and curriculum value in the official view, and with it the privilege to argue for its protection and development.

This is ironic. As mentioned earlier, one of the motivations to mainstream ESL was to offer second language learners equality of access to the mainstream provision and to avoid marginalisation. To the extent that the second language learner is now in the mainstream curriculum, it has been a success; and many more mainstream teachers now have some awareness that the second language learners in their classes have additional language needs, but ESL itself may disappear as a distinct professional practice in the process. In the next chapter the pedagogical issues of mainstreaming in the English context will be discussed in greater detail.

Chapter 10

Mainstreaming: ESL as a diffused curriculum concern

Constant Leung and Charlotte Franson

INTRODUCTION

The 1980s saw the development of a pedagogical approach to second language learning in the mainstream which advocated enquiry-based activities, small peer group work and the use of pupils' other languages to support their second language learning (see Edwards and Redfern, 1992, for a discussion). It was thought that ESL learners, working in the mainstream curriculum environment, with real opportunities for expressing needs and communicating with their peers in the context of appropriate activities, would learn English in the best possible way. The Swann Report (DES, 1985b) supported the move towards mainstreaming and recommended that the needs of ESL learners should be met within the mainstream context as part of a language policy for all pupils, reiterating the view of the Bullock Report (DES, 1975) that all teachers have a responsibility for meeting the language learning needs of ESL pupils.

This view was endorsed by Her Majesty's Inspectors (HMI) who stated that ESL pupils should be considered as 'members of ordinary classes and taking part in as full a range of activities as possible within and outside class' (DES, 1988: 2) and the National Curriculum document, *English for Ages 5 to 16* (DES, 1989), which stated that 'all pupils must have access to the same attainment targets and programmes of study for English' (op. cit.: 10.6) and that 'where bilingual pupils need extra help, this should be given in the classroom as part of normal lessons' (op. cit.: 10.10). The Office for Standards in Education report (OFSTED, 1994) on educational support for minority ethnic communities also highlighted the value of collaboration between mainstream and language support teachers in providing effective lessons for ESL learners in the mainstream. This view continues to have a powerful impact on ESL provision.

The claim that bilingual pupils would learn English in the best possible way under this policy is a very strong one. Few, if any, qualifications are made upon this claim. It is not suggested that individuals might learn in different ways, or that different aspects of English might be learned in different circumstances, or that some learning conditions might be less helpful than others. One might expect that such a broad claim and the policies that flow from it, affecting such a large number of pupils, would be the subject of large-scale, careful, responsible, thorough and long-term evaluations of its effectiveness in the school system. Unfortunately this is not the case (cf. see OFSTED, 1994, 1997; Blair and Bourne, 1998). In these circumstances, a sober and sceptical examination of some of the issues arising from this claim and these policies is an important step in moving towards a responsible analysis and evaluation.

MAINSTREAMING: A SPECIFIC INTERPRETATION

In the English context 'mainstreaming' has come to mean placing the ESL pupil in an age appropriate classroom in which the medium of learning is English and the content is the National Curriculum. Although mainstreaming may have initially been a response to the ideological and pedagogical criticism of the provision of specialist English language centres and separate English language teaching which was not related to the wider school curriculum, the participation of all pupils in the classroom is now regarded as a necessary prerequisite in ensuring that all pupils have equality of access to the educational provision. In the mainstream classroom, the ESL pupil and the class teacher may be supported by an ESL support teacher. However, this additional support is not a statutory obligation of the school or local education authority.

In other countries 'mainstreaming' can be defined in several ways. For example, in the USA 'mainstreaming' can refer to the exiting of ESL pupils into the mainstream classroom after an intensive programme which may last up to three years. If there is no intensive ESL programme and no other instructional option, pupils are placed in the mainstream but are withdrawn for specialist ESL teaching programmes for language development work (Carrasquillo and Rodriguez, 1995). It is understood that although the mainstream classroom can offer purposeful, authentic input and many social opportunities for interaction with native speakers, specialist ESL teaching can offer language instruction and opportunities for language learning more appropriate to ESL learners' levels and needs. In the USA context, the debate is about clarifying pedagogical and social values and objectives in *different* learning contexts (Harklau, 1994; Destino, 1996). (For an Australian and Canadian perspective, see the earlier chapters of this volume.) In England the discussion is focused on how to make the mainstream classroom a helpful environment for second language development.

This move towards mainstreaming ESL learners has necessarily meant the mainstreaming of ESL teachers. As a result of the increased emphasis on integrating ESL learners into mainstream classrooms, the definition of the role of ESL teachers, who are often referred to as language support teachers, has changed to include (Bourne, 1989: 107–8):

- a 'remedial' teaching role where the English language support teacher provides individualised ESL support so that the pupil may complete the mainstream task;
- a 'specialist' model where the English language support teacher uses her expertise to intervene in the pupil's language development;
- a 'catalyst' role where the English language specialist tries to effect change in policy and curriculum planning to enhance overall language development; and
- a 'good teacher' role where the English language support teacher works towards promoting the language development of all pupils in the classroom.

PARTNERSHIP TEACHING

The current approach to mainstreaming ESL learners and ESL support teachers is commonly known as 'Partnership Teaching', in which ESL and classroom teachers work together to 'develop a curriculum response to the language needs and abilities of all pupils, whether monolingual, bilingual or multilingual' (Bourne and McPake, 1991: 8). It promotes both collaborative teaching in the classroom and a whole school approach to meeting the language learning needs of all learners. A number of statements in the Partnership Teaching (Bourne and McPake, 1991: 357; for a slightly revised view see Bourne, 1997) in-service training materials suggest the view that second language teaching is indirect and complementary to individual learning which arises in process-oriented group work:

> The main principles of a cross-curricular reponse to multilingual classes can be briefly analysed as follows:
>
> - learning is often best achieved through enquiry-based activities involving discussion . . .
> - some curriculum subjects are structured in such a way that they themselves give support to children learning English (e.g. through the patterning of certain activities and thus of certain linguistic structures)
> - one of the main strategies, then, for both curriculum learning and language learning is the flexible use of small group work . . .

This view is frequently echoed in the professional literature. For instance:

> Children have more to gain from from working collaboratively in the classroom, than from being withdrawn in small groups, for English is related to and drawn from the learning contexts and curriculum activities in the classroom.
> (Barrs et al., 1990: 42)

> Provide plenty of small group collaborative activities where talk and interaction are central to the learning going on. The new arrival may initially take a passive role but she or he will be learning a lot whilst listening.
> (Hampshire County Council, 1996: 4)

A stated aim of the model of partnership teaching is the development of a curriculum response in which

> teaching methodologies which have developed – or are developing – in response to mixed-ability classes, are, by definition, appropriate to the needs-and-abilities of bilingual learners.   (Bourne and McPake, 1991, Introduction: 9)

In this approach, language support work is viewed as a form of action-research

> where observation, discussion with pupils and parents, experimentation with new approaches and careful evaluation can lead to an improved, shared understanding of classroom processes and of the responses of individual pupils within these.   (Bourne and McPake, 1991, Introduction: 6)

A great deal of professional in-service training has been devoted to the promotion and development of the 'good teacher' role in which the English language support teacher helps the class/subject teacher 'fine tune' the curriculum to meet individual learner needs in a particular curriculum context. (Davison and Williams, Chapters 2 and 3 this volume, have problematised the notion of the mainstream curriculum as the basis of ESL development.) At the same time the support teacher is encouraged to take the 'catalyst' role seriously to promote whole school curriculum change and staff development. All this demands far greater participation of the English language support teacher at all levels of school organisation and activities than previously experienced.

At first sight, the collaborative/partnership approach seems to offer an elegant answer to the demands of maximising learning opportunities and providing equal opportunities of access to the mainstream. There are indeed some excellent examples of successful partnerships where both teachers involved share a high level of common understanding of the needs of the learners and work together on all important aspects of teaching (see Bourne and McPake, 1991, for examples). Individual cases of successful partnership notwithstanding, there are some key pedagogical issues which have to be addressed. Some of these issues are directly related to professional practice and others are concerned with the conceptualisation of language teaching. Before we turn to these issues perhaps it would be useful to point out that until very recently a vast majority of the ESL support teachers were organised as service teams within a county or city and they were assigned to individual school(s) in the local area on the basis of need. Under the current funding arrangement (DfEE, 1998b and 1999b) ESL teachers are expected to be employed by schools directly. This new arrangement may, if anything, throw the issues raised in this chapter into sharper relief. Given that there is no mandatory requirement to provide ESL support, the level of provision varies in different schools and different areas. In terms of the everyday working reality of an individual ESL teacher, he or she may work in one or more than one school – one day each week in one school and two days in another, and so on. It is within this working context that the following issues are discussed. The arguments in the following sections have been informed by a focused discussion with a number of experienced ESL colleagues as part of a year-long in-service staff development programme. The statements made by teachers will be used where appropriate to highlight points of arguments; the teacher quotations came from three teachers, Tania, Ros and Jill (pseudonyms). The main purpose of this discussion is to problematise some aspects of the current conceptualisation of ESL work.

PROFESSIONAL RECOGNITION

One of the long-term difficulties with English language support work has been the ESL teacher's lack of professional training, status and authority. There is no national mandatory pre-service subject specialist training for ESL teachers and, thus, practitioners have entered the ESL teaching field by various routes. (There was a highly organised non-mandatory in-service training scheme validated by the Royal Society of Arts for serving teachers to develop ESL teaching skills in multicultural schools; but this scheme, in its original form, is no longer in operation due to the lack of financial support.) The ESL teacher could be an EFL teacher with overseas working experience, a former Special Educational Needs teacher resuming work after a career break, or a class/subject teacher who has been offered an opportunity to make a sideways move. This does not mean that ESL support teachers are not good at the job of teaching ESL but there is no commonality of training and expertise that the classroom teacher (working in partnership with the ESL support teacher) can recognise and draw on. In this way, ESL support teaching can appear idiosyncratic, inconsistent and even 'disappointing', as one research report puts it (Blair and Bourne, 1998). Sometimes this lack of recognised and recognisable training has led to difficulties in establishing the credibility of the ESL teacher among school staff.

The significance of the lack of professional recognition cannot be underestimated. A successful working relationship between the language support teacher and the class/subject teacher has to be built on a mutually recognised sense of professional identity and expertise. Without this it is difficult to develop collaborative roles and responsibilities in the classroom. (See Chapter 12 for a further discussion.)

LIAISON TIME

From the perspectives of both the language support teacher and the class/subject teacher the working reality of collaboration is more complex than some of the training literature may suggest. On the practical level, to collaborate effectively it is necessary for the teachers to share the preparation of classroom materials and to work out teaching strategies jointly and, just as importantly, to share specifically designed in-service training. These are precisely the two 'luxuries' that most teachers, ESL or mainstream, do not have as a matter of entitlement. Adequate opportunity (and time) for liaison is widely acknowledged as a crucial element of successful collaborative teaching; but it is often missing from the work schedule. Often ESL teachers are required to work with several colleagues, in a range of teaching contexts, with very little opportunity to discuss their classroom practice and pedagogical views and establish a working relationship. Even when a language support teacher is appointed full time to one school, regular discussion and planning time may be difficult to establish. Since there is no official time-tabling allowance for staff liaison, it is often carried out on an *ad hoc* basis. ESL staff who work in a number of schools and a large number of classes sometimes experience severe difficulties in maintaining a sense of continuity and working knowledge of classroom events. As one ESL teacher, Tania, remarked,

> and if you have had time to talk to them [teachers in school] you go in next week and find that the planning isn't happening, or they say, 'I forgot you were coming' or 'we've done that last Friday' or 'we're just finishing this up' . . .

Yet, as an OFSTED report (1994: 3) states, in-class support teaching was

> more productive when [ESL support] teachers and mainstream teachers devised the programme together and each complemented the other in the teaching of it.

When there is a lack of collaboration, or time for planning the collaboration, there is also less effective in-class support. One result is that language support teachers find themselves mediating between the class teacher and the pupils often in hushed voices at the back of the classroom. Even in well managed classes the ESL support teacher role, under such circumstances, is reduced to a teaching assistant. In lessons where the teaching and learning activities and the work materials are disorganised, the contribution of the ESL support teacher may be reduced further. The OFSTED report (1994: 4) states this point explicitly:

> The efficacy of the work of the [ESL] staff depended largely upon the effectiveness of the mainstream teachers with whom they were working. Poor classroom management and organisation by the class teacher . . . inhibited progress.

TEACHING PURPOSE

For an ESL teacher working in the mainstream classroom the attempt to maintain a clear language teaching focus may be problematic. There are two levels of potential difficulties and pressures. The first is concerned with the class/subject teacher's view of learning and knowledge. From the class teacher's point of view it is 'normal' that one should focus on the curriculum content knowledge and skills. The fact that some pupils might not be able to understand the content because their current level of English language development is, in this view, a problem to be fixed. Very often the ESL support teacher is expected to deal with the language difficulties. Ros, an ESL support teacher, made this point:

> You can be presented with a chapter from a science book, for example, and told this is what we're doing in the next four weeks, can you take them [ESL pupils] away and go through it with them?

It might be argued that this is an extreme case, but the point here is that it raises a number of fundamental issues of the nature of pedagogy and professional collaboration. In terms of collaboration this means that there is a different interpretation, namely that the ESL teacher is to collaborate with the class teacher by teaching the language of the subject content as some sort of priming for the real moment of learning. At the heart of this perception is that language is learned separately from the content and that two unrelated and different processes are involved.

The second level is concerned with the often unquestioned use of curriculum space and time. It is therefore all pervasive and yet invisible. It has been suggested that one of the most powerful arguments for mainstreaming, as we have seen earlier, is that it provides naturally occuring opportunities to use and develop language through purposeful use. Yet in the mainstream classroom the main teaching purpose is to get on with the curriculum content. The classroom exchanges are primarily concerned with curriculum meaning; language development work is not necessarily the focus of attention (Harklau, 1994; Destino, 1996). Through the skilful use of adjusted talk, realia, graphics and role play, teachers can make even very complex information accessible to ESL pupils. There is, however, little reason to assume that comprehension of content ideas at a broad level would automatically lead to an ability to use English to carry out academic tasks effectively. In other words, receptive ability is related to but not the same as productive ability. Swain (1995) points out that the pupil may make use of subject- or topic-related contextual clues and paralinguistic signals when trying to understand what is being said. In contrast, when trying to use language to express meaning, the pupil has to attend to all aspects of the language system in order to communicate effectively; and the development of this ability requires at least some teacher input, meaningful use and practice and helpful feedback. In a classroom perceived to be crowded with curriculum content the opportunity to develop this aspect of productive language use may not be 'naturally occurring'. Therefore the focus on the delivery of the curriculum content may preclude the focus on language development. Whenever this happens, the ESL support teacher is constantly seeking to find curriculum space and time to make a contribution but the uptake from the mainstream teacher cannot be taken for granted. Professional experience suggests that in most cases the two teachers involved tend to settle for a 'negotiated' understanding which provides some opportunity for language development, but it should not be assumed that such 'negotiation' always leads to arrangements and practices which maximally promote second language development.

CLASSROOM LEARNING PROCESSES

Although there is no official articulation, it would seem that the implicit support for the mainstreaming of ESL draws on aspects of work in a number of fields: general learning theory (e.g. cooperative or group learning), first language development (e.g. the importance of talk), second language acquisition (e.g. comprehensible input) and bilingualism (e.g. the positive effect of bilingualism on cognitive development and L1–L2 transfer of language knowledge and skills). Professional literature and in-service training materials tend to take certain principles – such as, learning is best achieved through enquiry-based and/or hands-on activities and learning a language requires participation in its meaningful use – as axiomatic. (For a more detailed discussion of these principles, see Edwards and Redfern, 1992.) These principles are no doubt sound in general but the real issue is that they are stated at such a high level of universality that they are not very helpful when considering individual pupil needs. Furthermore, there is little attempt to differentiate the applicability of these principles in terms of age, the learning context, the learning task and the pupil's learning style. An example of this application of generalised theories of learning to ESL learners is found in one of the training video programmes (programme 3) disseminated with the Partnership Teaching materials (Bourne and McPake, 1991). Two classroom situations are presented in which the topics of the teachers' discussion include the planning and liaison between the two teachers, the implementation of group activities in a mixed ability class, the organisation and composition of groups, the effect of gender on group activities, pupil participation and roles within the groups, and the value of group work in promoting talk and cooperation. There is very little discussion of explicit language learning objectives for the ESL learners involved.

Another example is the principle of learning through enquiry-based curriculum activity, which, when stated at a high level of generality, does not offer any guidance on the language focus in respect of any curriculum content; nor does it say anything about the second language learning needs from the point of view of the learner. Tania's description of an instance when teaching has gone well is quite revealing:

> I think the best time for me is when the children start to question me. I think that's terrific because then you know they've really taken on board what's been going on and they want to know why . . . and that's the sign for me when they're confident . . . to look at the content of what they're doing and their situation and generally the world around them . . .

There is clearly a real sense of progress when children begin to show interest in what they are doing and want to know more. The point here is that the same evaluation could have been made by a class or subject teacher who may not be directly concerned with English language development. There is little concurrent and explicit focus on language use and language development in context beyond the general notion of communication.

The proposal that the doing of the activity and the discussion generated as a result of activities, i.e. meaningful use in context, will provide language learning opportunities for the ESL pupil should also be scrutinised. In a self-evaluation of her lesson, Jill, an ESL teacher, commented:

> I had the 'hands-on' element, in other words we actually had real bricks for the children to lay together. So I thought, well, this is a very important element for second language children.

Of course the opportunity to handle materials physically can be very effective in helping ESL learners to participate in the learning activities, but, as Jill observed, the ESL learners did not know enough about bricks and patterns and the attendant language to discuss their work or exchange ideas. She said: 'I should have provided more linguistic props, both orally and written.' In the absence of specific language objectives the results of activities were often expressed in terms of social or personal outcomes. Language learning outcomes were taken for granted or subsumed under general communication. One often hears comments such as the pupils 'enjoyed' the activity and they were 'really keen'. At the end of her self-evaluation, Jill concluded,

> The most successful bit, and I think perhaps the thing that was really successful, was that the children's interest was maintained . . . the children enjoyed it and were very keen.

One of the popular classroom strategies to develop writing skills is 'draft and redraft'. The use of the generally sound technique of 'draft and redraft' for literacy development is often regarded as good practice based on the principle of meaningful use. No doubt this is a very useful technique in itself but its value for ESL learners must be judged with reference to the learners' current level of knowledge of the target language. To engage in meaningful redrafting, learners need to have at least some knowledge of different conventions of language use and forms of presentation – in other words, a knowledge of registers and genres. For learners with a limited repertoire, redrafting without the necessary support teaching (and language learning) of the new language and cultural information must leave them somewhat puzzled as to the purpose of the exercise. Yet, the assumption is that all pupils will go through a similar process of writing development.

McLaughlin (1992) states that it is a myth to assume that all pupils learn a second language in the same way. Pupils from diverse linguistic, cultural and, in some cases, educational backgrounds require a variety of different teaching approaches to meet their emerging and changing learning needs. Recent research has shown that variation in factors such as learning strategies, social skills and personality, as well as variation in the curriculum setting and variation in the target language speakers, also influence the second language learning process (Ellis, 1994; Lapkin, 1998; Oxford, 1990, 1996; Spolsky, 1989). The work of Gregory (1993, 1996) has pointed to the need to take account of both pupil and teacher expectations and background assumptions when considering teaching approaches. Classroom practices are inevitably influenced and shaped by specific cultural values. Therefore it would be important not to assume that pupils, particularly ESL pupils, automatically understand classroom practices and subscribe to the values underpinning them.

ESL PEDAGOGY

The absence of a more explicit and rigorously defined pedagogy often leaves the ESL teacher without a language explicit working agenda on the everyday level and, indeed, the professional language to talk about their work. Because of this, mainstream teachers often find it difficult to see the specialist contribution of the ESL teacher. A job description for an ESL teacher will often include reference to working collaboratively with mainstream teachers, making teaching materials, liaising with parents and the community of the ESL pupils, and maintaining appropriate records and monitoring pupil progress. When asked to describe what makes their roles distinct from that of the classroom or subject teacher, the ESL teachers often speak of promoting confidence, encouraging participation in classroom activities, providing grammatical input, modifying curriculum content and developing materials. Successful teaching is often described in personal development and affective terms. Tania, one of our ESL teacher discussants, puts it in the following way, which is fairly typical:

> Giving the children the tools to express themselves, you're liberating them, and when they progress you see the smiles on their faces . . . it's great . . .

The need to rediscover a more pedagogically explicit and pupil-sensitive ESL practice within the mainstream context is urgent. There are two key aspects which require attention:

* different pedagogical responses to different levels or stages of ESL development in different phases of education and
* a systematic and principled approach to curriculum content-language integration.

The first of these will be discussed in the remainder of this chapter. The second will be taken up in the next chapter.

PUPIL-SENSITIVE ESL RESPONSE

The stages of ESL development have been variously defined by different assessment systems, both within the UK and elsewhere. For the purpose of this discussion we will simply refer to three broad categories: beginning stage, second stage and advanced stage. At the beginning stage a pupil is new to English; at the second stage a pupil has acquired spoken English for day-to-day communication and an emergent ability to read and write English; and at the advanced stage a pupil is able to use English effectively in most social and school situations, but there is a need for further development in academic uses of English. The ESL needs of the first-stage pupils may be regarded as immediate; they need to develop an initial communicative ability quickly. The needs of the pupils in the second and the third stages, to various degrees, are more diffused. Our current practice recognises that individual ESL pupils are at different stages of language development. However, the mainstreaming approach does not attempt to respond to the different stages of language development needs in a systematic way; the actual pedagogical response is left to the individual teacher and school through a set of process-oriented principles as discussed above. This does not mean that there is no effective and appropriate pedagogical response, but it does mean that the response could vary from case to case and much depends on the level of staff expertise and staff availability on a local basis. It would be professionally more responsible and, from the point of view of pupil entitlement, more socially and educationally equitable if there were a more whole-system approach based on an analysis of language needs. Davison (Chapter 2, this volume) suggests a pedagogical response which varies according to pupil needs:

ESL needs	*immediate* ←——————————————————→ *diffused*	
Curriculum focus	*ESL integrated with content* ←————→ *content integrated with ESL*	
(content = curriculum content)		

In the English context this view can be interpreted to mean that when working with beginners who have a high level of need in terms of the English language for both everyday communication as well as for academic learning purposes, the focus should be on providing language input and learning opportunities to promote such development in the pupil. Given that all pupils are entitled to the National Curriculum, it is incumbent upon the teachers to develop second language learning materials and strategies which would take full account of the curriculum content (including the English literacy programme) and the appropriate use of the non-National Curriculum time (approximately 20 per cent of the total school curriculum time). At the same time, when working with pupils who are able to use English for everyday and general learning purposes but who are still in need of some support for specific uses of academic language (second and third stages), the focus should be on developing the ability to understand and use English appropriately and effectively in spoken and written forms in different curriculum areas. There is, therefore, a continuum which suggests a need to prioritise the pedagogical focus which has an implication in terms of classroom pedagogy.

Campbell and McMeniman (1985: 32, see Chapter 1, Figure 1.1) categorise ESL teaching in terms of direct and indirect assistance. Direct assistance includes, inter alia, tuition by ESL specialists which involves programmes of systematic language development and/or subject-specific language and tasks. Indirect assistance includes providing in-class opportunities for receptive and productive use of English through pupil participation in learning activities and teachers using language with a view to (a) helping pupils to understand and (b) providing models of language use. This conceptual distinction is very useful as an analytical device. However, the term 'direct' could be interpreted to mean direct language teaching methods in the sense of using language drills. Such an interpretation would be too narrow. Therefore, it would be more helpful to adopt the curriculum-oriented terms of 'contextualised language teaching' and 'language-conscious content teaching' (see Davison and Williams, Chapter 3, this volume).

It would seem reasonable to suggest that the distinction between 'contextualised language teaching' and 'language-conscious content teaching' can be mapped onto the immediate and diffused needs continuum:

ESL needs   *immediate* ⟵————————————⟶ *diffused*

Classroom assistance $\left(\begin{array}{c}\text{contextualised}\\\text{language teaching}\end{array}\right)$ ⟷ $\left(\begin{array}{c}\text{language-conscious}\\\text{content teaching}\end{array}\right)$

Seen in this light it suggests that, with students who are at the beginning stage of learning English, the teacher may have to provide more language-focused input to facilitate the development of communicative language use in the school context. This means that the mainstream curriculum, both in terms of content and time, has to be explored and exploited for opportunities for language teaching and learning. In the traditional conception of 'survival' English, often devised to meet the needs of first-stage ESL students, the teaching content tends to consist of so-called basic vocabulary and expressions for general everyday social functions; the language selection tends to be based on a mixture of teachers' perceptions of these students' needs, common sense and existing teaching materials. While these should not be discarded, there is also a need to take into account the more specific language and communication demands of the classroom and the curriculum. With students who are able to use English more or less effectively for everyday and general learning purposes, the focus of ESL teaching may be embedded within subject- or discipline-specific language use. In this case the mainstream curriculum content and the classroom language use will be used as the basis of the ESL teaching and learning agenda. In other words, we are concerned with content and language integration. We will address this issue with reference to the English context in the next chapter.

Chapter 11

Evaluation of content-language learning in the mainstream classroom

Constant Leung

INTRODUCTION

In the previous chapter we have seen that the mainstreaming of ESL pupils represented a significant educational development. The mainstreaming process itself has, however, generated new issues and challenges. We have raised the question earlier of the lack of systematic evaluation of the present policy in England. In this chapter the main focus is on identifying the key issues which should be considered in an evaluation of content-language learning in the mainstream context. This is a first step towards forming a critical agenda for responsible evaluation and development of policy and practice. The discussion in this chapter will assume the stance of a critcal evaluator with a declared theoretical perspective. It will be argued that a language socialisation perspective and a task-based approach would allow for an analysis which integrates curriculum content and language learning in the mainstream classroom context. A number of key pedagogical and research questions will be highlighted from this point of view.

KEY ASPECTS OF PEDAGOGY IN THE MAINSTREAM CLASSROOM: SOME EVALUATIVE QUESTIONS

Classroom learning environment and school ethos

Second language pupils enter school from a variety of backgrounds. Some may have a highly developed knowledge of literacy skills in their first languages; others may only have oral communication skills in their first or home languages. Some may have schooling experience in another society; others may enter school as bilingual minority community language speakers. The concern here is that irrespective of the pupils' backgrounds, the school should offer as supportive a learning environment as possible.

It is generally held that the pupils' perceptions of how others in the school regard them in terms of ability, achievement and personal worth are important factors in shaping learning behaviour and achievement (Blair and Bourne,

1998: chapters 4 and 5). Teacher expectation is particularly important in this respect. There is some evidence that teachers' behaviour reflect different expectations towards different groups of pupils. Teunissen (1992: 98) puts it as follows:

> Teachers create a warmer emotional climate with children they have high expectations of (the 'highs' as contrasted to the 'lows'). 'Highs' get more and more difficult learning tasks, more feedback and also feedback with a richer content. 'Lows' get fewer questions in class, less difficult questions, less opportunity for response and less opportunity to pose questions than the 'highs'.

In this connection the following evaluative questions are germane: *What is the variety of backgrounds of pupils in the school and are teaching approaches, teacher expectation and task organisation responsive to this variety?*

While an individual teacher's expectation and behaviour are crucially important in creating a positive learning climate, the ethos of the whole school is equally significant. For the second language pupil in the mainstream school, it is important that the distinction between second language development and cognitive/academic ability is clearly recognised by teachers. Where this distinction is not clearly understood, it can lead to a school decision, with the best of intentions, which puts second language pupils in low ability sets or streams. Such decisions are often justified on the grounds that the 'easier' or slower pace of learning in these classes provides more and better opportunities for the second language pupil to work on his or her language and subject content knowledge. However, many teachers are familiar with the scenario of seeing apparently highly motivated and able second language pupils adopting anti-social and anti-learning behaviour when they have been put in the 'bottom' set or stream. The key evaluative question is: *Is the distinction between second language development and cognitive/academic ability clearly understood at school policy level and translated into practice accordingly?*

A related issue is the belief that language pupils cannot cope with the full range of the curriculum until they have acquired sufficient English language. This in itself can lead to a lowering of teacher expectation. Since there is no principled way of establishing what constitutes sufficient English language in terms of participating in, at least some, content learning, this could produce a convenient explanation or excuse for the absence of pedagogical action to improve learning and achievement. There is no doubt that second language pupils will need time to develop their target language, but, as we have argued (see chapters 6 and 7), language and curriculum content learning can take place at the same time. In any case, in a mainstream situation second language pupils do not have the luxury of delaying content learning while improving their English. The content of the school curriculum moves on from term to term and from year to year. The question therefore is whether the teaching method(s), presentation of material and classroom task organisation are responsively developed to meet the needs of the pupils.

Second language pupils' achievement within the curriculum is often under-recognised. Indeed, the current National Curriculum assessment procedure for English has no built-in mechanism for recognising the difference between first and second language development (although there is some advice for teachers to help second language pupils to engage with some of the assessment tasks). The achievement in content areas is assessed and reported according to a set of universal criteria or measures. Given that the second language pupils' still emerging ability to use English may have a deleterious effect on test or assessment performance, this can put their achievement in a less than favourable light. Schools, however, can consciously devise additional assessment and reporting procedures which highlight the achievement of the second language pupils. For instance, all teachers and pupils within a school community can recognise the achievement of someone who has progressed from knowing no English to being able to take part in class activities within six months. Publicly displaying a pupil's first language knowledge and skill by making bilingual story books is another example of recognising achievement in the primary phase. In the secondary phase it may be possible to ask pupils who are literate in their mother tongue to translate a newspaper or magazine article on a familiar topic but which has a different cultural perspective. School assemblies and school reports, for example, can be used to disseminate information about such efforts. These are just some examples of possibilities. In other words, a positive commitment to recognising development and achievement of the pupil rather than a practice of judging achievement from the point of view of monolingual English norms can make visible the work and the scholarly standing of the second language pupils within the school community. An evaluative question here is: *Does a school acknowledge and publicly display second language pupils' achievement in culturally and linguistically sensitive ways?*

Classroom interaction and language communication between teachers and pupils

Interaction between teachers and pupils has long been recognised as an important aspect of second language acquisition. (Peer interaction and communication among the pupils will be discussed in the next section.) Long (1983) suggests that interaction involving an exchange of information provides the opportunity for the second language pupil to provide feedback on his or her lack of comprehension which may generate further interaction. In the classroom this process helps the pupil and the teacher to engage each other in an attempt to adjust the language so that the information is understood by all concerned. The teacher modifies his or her output (e.g. slowing down and repeating and reformulating information) so that it becomes more comprehensible to the pupil; and the pupil tries to make his or her own output progressively like the target language in order to be understood. This process of negotiated adjustment, if successful, provides comprehensible input and, at the same time, an opportunity to use the target language for the pupil. Swain (1985) argues that comprehensible output, meaningful use of language in context by the pupil, is as important as an understanding of meaning. Second language development requires both. Allwright and Bailey (1991: 123) put it this way: '... it is the work required to negotiate interaction that spurs language acquisition rather than the intended outcome of the work....' (For a wider discussion, see Ellis, 1994: chapter 13.) Thus the research literature suggests that both comprehensible input and comprehensible output are important in second language development and content learning.

There has often been an assumption that the mainstream classroom is in many ways an ideal situation for second language pupils because it offers them the opportunities to use language for purposeful communication. While this may be a valid assumption on a general level, research evidence tends to show that a great deal of class time is taken up by teacher-fronted or teacher-led activities. For instance, Flanders (1970, in Coelho, 1992) reports that 68 per cent of class talking time is taken up by teacher-led presentation, 20 per cent to pupil discussion and 12 per cent to 'silence and confusion'. Tizard et al. (1988) find that 65 per cent of all teacher–pupil contacts are accounted for by pupils listening to the teacher either as a class or on a one-to-one basis, and 69 per cent of all teacher–pupil contacts are concerned with the task at hand with the teacher engaged in explaining, informing, demonstrating, questioning or suggesting ideas. Galton et al. (1980) report that while the pupils' work is often individualised, the teacher's interaction with the individual pupils tends to be focused on task supervision, instruction and other routine matters. It has also been found that teachers do not use open-ended and high-level cognitive questioning on a frequent basis. In much of the teacher-led exchanges, pupil participation is limited to single word or phrase utterances (Harklau, 1994; Leung, 1993).

Furthermore, as Harklau (1994) observes, the input received by second language pupils in a mainstream classroom suffers from a major drawback: it is primarily aimed at native speakers of English. In a case study of classroom language use, Harklau (1994: 249) reports that

> ... mainstream high school classroom teachers seldom adjusted input in order to make it comprehensible to L2 pupils ... Pupils had particular difficulty understanding teacher talk which contained puns or was sarcastic or ironic. Pupils were also frustrated with teachers who habitually spoke very fast, who used frequent asides, or who were prone to sudden departures from the instructional topic at hand.

It would seem that a great deal of class time is taken up by the teacher providing whole-class or group input on content-related or other matters. Much of this kind of input has been found to be quite difficult to follow by many second language pupils. In so far as the more individually focused teacher–pupil interaction is concerned, there is a tendency for the teacher to initiate and for the pupil to respond in very short utterances.

On the available evidence it would seem that although the use of language in the mainstream classroom is purposeful and meaning-oriented, it does not always produce the desired negotiation of meaning and form conducive to second language development.

It has also been argued that, in one-to-one exchanges between the teacher and the pupil, speech adjustments – such as reducing the complexity of speech, increasing repetition of points of information and pausing to check comprehension – are all helpful to the pupil. Teachers may be able to provide greater language using opportunities and feedback by making speech adjustments. Chaudron (1988: 45) provides a list of such adjustments:

- repetition: an exact repeating of a previous string of speech (either partial or full, and either a self- or other-repetition)
- expansion: a partial or full repetition which modifies some portion of a previous string of speech by adding syntactic or semantic information
- clarification request: a request for further information from an interlocutor about a previous utterance
- comprehension check: the speaker's query of the interlocutor(s) as to whether or not they have understood the previous speaker utterance(s)
- confirmation check: the speaker's query as to whether or not the speaker's (expressed) understanding of the interlocutor's meaning is correct
- repair: an attempt by a speaker to alter or rectify a previous utterance which was in some way lacking in clarity or correctness (either self- or other-directed)
- model: a type of prompt by a speaker (usually a teacher) intended to elicit an exact imitation or to serve as an exemplary response to an elicitation.

Rueda et al. (1992) advance the argument that in group or whole class settings the learning process in the classroom can be scaffolded by instructional conversations in which students' efforts to communicate nascent knowledge and to express partial understanding are built on and developed by helpful teacher management of participatory talk. Instructional conversations have a number of key features which include: responsiveness to student contributions, maintaining thematic focus and eliciting more complex language and expression.

For evaluative purposes we should therefore ask whether teachers in the mainstream classroom provide:

(a) *content-based comprehensible input,*
(b) *opportunity to use language appropriately for the full range of naturally occurring purposes such as recounting an experience, justifying a decision, describing a process and giving instructions, and*
(c) *opportunities for the pupils to receive feedback on appropriate language use and to act on such feedback.*

Group work, task organisation and peer communication

The opportunity in the mainstream classroom for pupils to engage in sustained meaningful language use with the teacher, as suggested in the discussion earlier, seems to be limited. On the assumption that, say, 20 per cent of class time is used for individual questions and answers, in a 40-minute period 8 minutes would be available for teacher–pupil interaction. In a class of

25 pupils, this could work out to be an average of 19.2 seconds per pupil. While this putative average is unlikely to represent reality, it does indicate the paucity of opportunities for the pupil.

One way of increasing the opportunity for active and purposeful language use in the classroom is to promote collaborative group work. McDonell (1992) argues that group work promotes second language development because it offers, inter alia, the pupils:

- more comprehensible input through peer interactions;
- opportunity to develop better listening skills as a result of responding to and acting on what has been said;
- instant response from others to their output;
- longer conversational turns than in a whole-class teaching situation;
- opportunity to initiate their own questions, articulate their needs and interests;
- opportunity to develop an awareness of audience, purpose and social context;
- access to more varied and complex use of language;
- continual comprehension checks and clarification requests;
- opportunity to use communication strategies and paralinguistic support such as facial expression, drawings and diagrams to enhance understanding and expression of meaning.

(Also see Donato, 1994; Pica, 1994.)

Perhaps the strongest argument for group work is that it provides the pupil with the direct experience of using language for content-based school tasks, which is critical for academic success.

Professional experience has shown that simply putting pupils into groups does not automatically produce collaborative group work. Pupils must interact not simply to talk to one another but to negotiate meaning (Pica et al., 1993). Two related factors may militate against the natural development of collaborative group work: the individualistic and competitive culture of the school (and wider society) and the pupil's background experience and assumptions. In schools where pupils are streamed or set according to test results (or other forms of assessment) and where recognition of merits is based on teacher assessment of individual effort and achievement, the ethos of the school may not be conducive to collaborative work which involves sharing and pooling of ideas and work. In such a situation the pupils may not actually know how to work together. In addition, some second language pupils may have had experience in a different educational environment where learning is regarded as an individual 'passive' mental activity of assimilating and memorising given facts. These pupils may, initially, find working collaboratively with others an unfamiliar practice. Additionally, the process of developing an idea, making a decision and producing an output in a group situation necessarily means that all the participants need to have language and communication skills in discussion and negotiation. Some second language pupils may not have fully developed such knowledge and skills.

This, then, suggests that group work has to be carefully planned, organised and supported with reference to the context of learning and the pupil's readiness. In organising tasks for group work four features or characteristics should be considered: role responsibility among the participants, role requirement, goal orientation and outcome option (Pica et al., 1993). *Role responsibility* refers to whether the participants are required to hold, request and/or supply information in order to achieve the task. *Role requirement* refers to whether requesting or supplying task-related information is obligatory or optional. *Goal orientation* refers to whether participants are expected to share the same goal or whether multiple goals are accepted. *Outcome options* refer to whether a single outcome or a range of different outcomes are acceptable.

Clearly any group task which requires all the participants to hold, request and/or supply information to one another, which obliges all participants to exchange task-related information, and which has only one goal orientation and one acceptable outcome is the most conducive for the generation of comprehensible output, comprehensible input and feedback. A group task of putting a jigsaw together is representative of this type of task. An opinion-forming task (say on the topic of the best lifestyle) which neither obliges all participants to share information nor to share a single goal or outcome, represents the opposite: there is a possibility that little negotiation will take place, some participants may take little or no part and one or two individuals may predominate. At the same time there is a need to consider whether the conditions under which a task is carried out would allow the pupil to attend to both meaning and language form. (Attention to language form may not be desirable in all tasks; this is a matter for teacher judgement.)

Second language pupils can benefit from collaborative group work to the extent that they are able to participate in the process of negotiation of meaning and exchange of information and that the process itself provides the appropriate opportunity for language use. Theoretically, a beginning ESL pupil in a secondary school who has relatively little experience in collaborative group work might, all other things being equal, benefit from taking part in a group task which requires all participants to exchange information (which is pre-supplied as working materials) and which has only one allowable goal and outcome. In reality the teacher will have to make a case-by-case decision with reference to the pupil's learning style and the language and content knowledge required by the task. It may well be the case that a pupil, at a particular point in time, prefers to observe others and to rehearse language before use. In such a case the teacher may decide that it would be more helpful for this pupil to participate in a task which makes the exchange of information optional and which has only one allowable goal and outcome. For instance, a problem-solving task concerned with the different ways of reducing air pollution to a particular level in cities may be designed with these task and communication features in mind. This kind of task may offer the pupil the opportunity to observe others at work, to gain some experience of the process of working together with others and to take part selectively in some of the group activities, particularly in the production of an outcome. Thus, two important evaluative questions here are: *What proportion of class time is devoted to group work?* and *Is group work organised with explicit reference to participant role, responsibility and task outcome in a way that is sensitive to pupil needs?*

Student tasks

The notion of task as a unit of analysis for curriculum design and classroom methodology has attracted a great deal of attention recently (Candlin, 1987; Long and Crookes, 1992; Nunan, 1989, 1991; Mohan, 1990; Crookes, 1986; Crookes and Gass, 1993; Skehan, 1996, 1998; Winne and Marx, 1989; among others). This notion, however, springs from a long tradition going back at least as far as John Dewey's seminal concept of education as an introduction to the activities of the community (see Mohan, 1986: 44–9, for a discussion). Tasks have been defined variously, for example:

> one of a set of differentiated, sequencable, problem-posing activities involving pupils' cognitive and communicative procedures applied to existing and new knowledge in the collective exploration and pursuance of foreseen or emergent goals within a social milieu.   (Candlin, 1987: 10)

> a piece of work or an activity, usually with a specified objective, undertaken as part of an educational course or at work.
>   (Crookes, 1986: 1, cited in Kumaravadivelu, 1993)

> a piece of classroom work which involves pupils in comprehending, manipulating, producing or interacting in the target language while their attention is principally focused on meaning rather than on form.   (Nunan, 1989: 10)

> a piece of work undertaken for oneself or for others, freely or for some reward. Thus, examples of tasks include painting a fence, dressing a child, filling out a form, buying a pair of shoes ... borrowing a library book ... typing a letter, weighing a patient, sorting letters, taking a hotel reservation, writing a check, finding a street destination and helping someone across a road. In other words, by 'task' is meant the hundred and one things people do in everyday life, at work, at play, and in between. Tasks are the things people will tell you they do if you ask them and they are not applied linguists.[1]
>   (Long, 1985, cited in Long and Crookes, 1992: 43–4)

> ... a task is an activity in which:
> * meaning is primary;
> * there is some communication problem to solve;
> * there is some sort of relationship to comparable real-world activities;
> * task completion has some priority;
> * the assessment of the task is in terms of outcome.   (Skehan, 1998: 95)

Thus it can be seen that the notion of task (for language learning) has been interpreted in different ways by second language researchers in terms of formal features, and the degree of real-life authenticity and purpose. They all share, however, a common concern for learning processes and purposeful activities. In the mainstream context, teachers (including ESL teachers) tend not to have the autonomy to be able to select tasks for language learning purposes only. What we need is a template which is capable of superimposing a language focus on the continuous flow of classroom activities. Therefore, the concerns for process and purpose are helpful here. In this discussion tasks are seen in the context of the mainstream curriculum. For Doyle and Carter (1984: 130) 'a task has three elements: (a) a goal or product; (b) a set of resources or "givens" available in the situation; and (c) a set of operations that can be applied to the resources to reach the goal or generate the product'. This characterisation of a task, at a rather high level of abstraction, is particularly helpful because it allows us to define and operationalise the concept relatively easily from the point of view of the pupil. It allows us to frame classroom level questions analytically. So questions such as 'what tasks are pupils engaged in in the classroom and what tasks are assigned for homework?' can now yield helpful information.

Within this conceptualisation we define a task as a piece of work carried out by a pupil, either individually or with others, within the curriculum context for learning purposes. A task can consist of a single activity, e.g. reading a story, or a number of activities, e.g. reading, discussing and developing a story.[2] Tasks are, therefore, located in the mainstream curriculum; they are not separately and specially designed for language learning purposes. In the school context most curriculum-generated or curriculum-related tasks have a goal, e.g. to learn about the water cycle, and/or a product, e.g. a written account and a diagram of the water cycle. A product need not be restricted to things with a physical manifestation; it could be an intellectual product such as an appreciation of a poem or a solution for a maths problem. School tasks are, to various extents, supported by human and material learning resources such as teacher and peer time, paper, books, worksheets, maps, computers and laboratory apparatus. These resources are made available for use by the pupil in the process of accomplishing a task.

This pupil-oriented perspective is important for two reasons. First, it requires all curriculum content and classroom process issues to be considered from the point of view of the pupil and his or her learning needs. It is, after all, at this level of the classroom reality that the pupil experiences the curriculum of content and language learning. Second, it elegantly sidesteps the epistemologically complicated arguments related to the issues of how a task is to be conceived in terms of curriculum hierarchy: is it a topic or is it a unit of content consisting of a number of topics (e.g. development of overseas trade, industrialisation and population changes within the theme of growth of cities)? These questions are redundant here because we are not concerned with the formal structure of the curriculum.

So far we have discussed the task-based approach in general terms. From the specific point of view of ESL pedagogy, the task-based approach provides the basis of exploiting the advantages of being in the mainstream curriculum. There are at least five positive arguments for this approach.

(a) Language and content relevance

In a mainstream classroom, learning tasks in the content areas are not generated on the basis of any special language learning agenda. Teachers and pupils are meant to be getting on with 'doing' the curriculum. Second language pupils are in effect novices being introduced to a set of socially and culturally established knowledge and practices. This process is mediated, to a great extent, through language. (This issue will be given greater elaboration in a later section on language socialisation.) The pupils are expected to learn to perform tasks in the curriculum subjects. Each of the subject areas, as interpreted and presented by textbooks and teachers, has it own way(s) of organising activities and presenting information; the way or ways in which language is used also vary accordingly.[3] A task-based approach which is located in the curriculum would ensure that the focus of (language and general) learning (and teaching) is based upon, or at least related to, the requirements of the curriculum. After all, it has long been argued that language development should take place across the whole curriculum range (DES, 1975). The task-based approach offers a specific realisation of that idea (cf. Davison and Williams' caution against an unproblematised view of the usefulness of the mainstream curriculum, Chapter 3, this volume).

(b) Identifiable units of analysis for learning and teaching content

One of the difficulties for ESL teachers in the mainstream situation is that there does not seem to be any principled way of organising the language teaching input. In a sense every aspect of the English language is urgently required by the pupils. The task-based approach will help to narrow down the focus to what is required in terms of the task at hand. For instance, instead of teaching writing skills in general, one would now be concerned with the writing activity within a task in, say, geography. The functions and notions of language involved, e.g. explaining the concept of gravity, are a constituent part of the content. The target language expressions in terms of vocabulary, register[4] and text types[5] are, in this very special sense, pre-selected. This does not mean that teachers and pupils should ignore other areas of language knowledge and skill within the classroom context; but this approach promotes a principled way of prioritising the teaching and learning content.

The key evaluative question for (a) and (b) above is: *Is the language requirement of the mainstream task clearly understood by both the content and language teachers?*

(c) A common working agenda between content and language teachers

Professional experience, as indicated in the previous chapter, has shown that collaboration or cooperation between the content and the language teacher is often difficult to achieve. One of the reasons is that the two teachers may not share the same goals. The content teacher is primarily interested in delivering the curriculum content and the language teacher aspects of the target language. The task-based view raises the question of a shared focus for both teachers. Since much of what is taught and learnt in content terms is mediated through language, it is possible for the two teachers to discuss ways of organising and presenting the content tasks which would promote active participation by the second language pupils and create a language-using and learning opportunity at the same time. On this view, learning the content means learning the language and vice versa. The key evaluative question here is: *Do the language teacher and the content teacher discuss ways of organising tasks for both language and content goals, according to some common agenda?*

(d) A common agenda for teacher training and professional development for subject and ESL specialists

Since the second language pupils are in the mainstream curriculum it follows that both the content teacher and the ESL teacher are responsible for all aspects of the learning experience of such pupils. It does not make sense to say that the ESL teacher is only responsible for English language development and the content teacher is only responsible for the learning of the curriculum content when, in reality, both content and language occur at the same time. We have argued that language cannot easily be separated from content. However, one of the difficulties in sharing this overall responsibility has been that the two teachers concerned often have had very different professional training. (The situation is further complicated by the fact that some ESL teachers were originally specialists in other subjects such as science and their professional training in the ESL field is of an in-service and short-term nature.) This difference in expertise has often led to a degree of mutual exclusion. The task-based approach creates a common platform for the two teachers to share their expertise: from the content teacher his or her knowledge and skill of the subject matter (which inevitably involve language expressions) and from the ESL teacher his or her knowledge and skill in developing pupils' target language appropriately within the task context. The content teacher can inform the ESL teacher what a task entails in terms of thinking processes, practical activities and specialist language use; the ESL teacher can use the task to promote understanding of the content knowledge and content-related language, and to generate language development opportunities. In this way we can create a clear area of professional overlap. This area of overlap can be explored in teacher training and development programmes for mainstream as well as ESL teachers in order to develop a modus operandi, both at pre-service and in-service levels (Leung, 1995). The key evaluative question here is: *Is there any evidence of a common (language-content) agenda in teachers' experiences of teacher training and professional development?*

(e) Language assessment in context

Second language pupils are often assessed according to language descriptors and criteria which are related to the curriculum in a general way, e.g. 'can take part in a class discussion' or 'can produce writing independently'. While such assessment may produce a helpful general indication of a pupil's overall second language development, it does not offer any specific information as to his or her ability to perform curriculum tasks. The task-based approach provides a principled basis of making explicit what is required in terms of task outcome and the language knowledge and skills involved. The task used in an assessment does not need to be contrived or specially developed; it is perfectly feasible to choose a task, perhaps with superficial changes or adjustments, which is already in the curriculum and is regarded as an important part or aspect of the curriculum content. In such an approach it would be possible to specify in advance the expected language use in respect of skills (e.g. speaking or writing), functions (e.g. explaining or describing), registers and text types. A pupil's ability to use language appropriately and effectively to accomplish a task can be assessed against such specifications. This kind of assessment would yield useful information on the pupil's language development with reference to curriculum demands. Given that such task-based assessments should only be carried out within the normal teaching and learning environment, we can be reasonably sure that we are sampling language performance in an authentic way in respect of the communicative context.[6] Therefore the assessment outcome is likely to reflect the pupil's ability to use language within the curriculum fairly realistically. The need to generalise or extrapolate from a contrived test or assessment is thus avoided. In the longer run this approach can provide an opportunity to gather authentic information on the full range of pupil performances. Such information would be useful for the long-term mapping of second language pupil development.[7] (For a discussion on the development of curriculum task-based assessment, see Cameron and Bygate, 1997.) The key evaluative question here is: *Is there any evidence of systematic task-based assessment being conducted in the mainstream context?*

Task-based evaluation: some specifics

In the previous section we have discussed the concept of the task-based approach and the potential benefits it offers. In this section we shall explore the planning and implementation issues. The discussion is primarily concerned with preparation, organisation and management of teaching.

(a) Size of task

Since we define a task as a piece of work to be done by the pupils, there should be no language-based restrictions as to the size of a task. A task should be derived from the curriculum goal and curriculum content, for instance, carrying out and writing up a science experiment, doing a maths exercise or telling a story. Seen in this light, a task could be a short activity lasting a few minutes or a large project spanning over several lessons. The issue then is: *Is there a conscious recognition of what tasks are being used?*

(b) Analysis of a task demand

The key questions here are: *What is to be accomplished?* and *What is the expected outcome?* In other words, we are concerned with both the process of doing a task and the product of the activity. We should consider these questions with reference to the two related aspects in any task: content and language. For instance, in a geography task of identifying suitable sites for a shopping centre, the process may involve listening to a teacher-fronted introduction of the principles involved, reading through the accompanying written and graphic materials, discussing choices in a small group and making a written recommendation with supporting reasons in an assumed role of a town planner. In this case the evaluator will need to consider the following factors:

1. The thinking skills involved in the content, e.g. describing (a shopping centre), evaluating (the suitability of different sites), choosing (a site) and explaining (a decision). (Refer to Chapters 6 and 7, this volume, for an account of the Knowledge Framework.)
2. The content-obligatory language expressions (Snow et al., 1992). These expressions are instances of language use essential for understanding the content information and doing the task. In this case we will be concerned with topic-specific terms such as 'planning permission', 'commercial land' and 'volume of traffic flow'; at the same time we will also be interested in the discourse (at and beyond the level of the sentence) used for describing, evaluating and explaining.
3. The appropriate registers for the discussion and the written work (Gibbons, 1998). Furthermore, there will be a need to clearly identify the language skills involved, e.g. listening and speaking to the teacher and peers, reading the supplied information and writing a formal recommendation, from the pupil's point of view. The notion of mode as discussed by McCarthy and Carter (1994) should be considered here. The division between spoken and written language is not clear cut in terms of discourse features. 'Mode refers to choices that the sender (of a message) makes as to whether features normally associated with speech or writing shall be included in the message regardless of the medium in which it is to be transmitted' (op. cit.: 4).
4. The communicative pressure or stress (Candlin, 1987; Skehan, 1996). The language and information processing conditions under which pupils are expected to perform a learning task may influence the task outcome. These conditions include the amount of time available, speed of presentation or delivery, type of response, and in a group task, the number of participants and the types of social interactions. The assumption here is that, other things being equal, when a large amount of information has to be organised and presented quickly in a complex form with little opportunity to slow down interactions, it is difficult to attend to language forms. The need to communicate content meaning may take priority.

Suitability of tasks

Once the various demands of a task have been analysed, the evaluator will have to decide whether the task, as it is conceived within the curriculum, is suitable and appropriate for the second language pupils at any given time. The following questions may be useful in establishing the suitability of a task:

1. *Do the pupils have the necessary background content and language knowledge and skills to understand and engage with the task?*
2. *Are the learning activities involved familiar to the pupils? (Do they know what to do?)*
3. *Are the learning activities appropriately presented and organised to promote the desired understanding and sharing of thinking (in the case of a collaborative task)?*
4. *Does the language use required to perform the task contribute to the pupils' further language development?*

(It should be pointed out that while the above questions are analytically distinct, in real life they are likely to be interrelated and manifested at the same time.)

Evaluating the scaffolding of tasks

It is quite likely that the questions raised in the previous section will highlight the need for scaffolding and adjustment of the tasks. In the language socialisation perspective a novice learns by joining in and sharing an activity with others who are more knowledgeable or more expert.[8] Initially the expert would take full responsibility in the conduct of the activity; progressively, as the novice becomes more familiar with the proceedings, the expert hands over more and more of the responsibility. An example of this in primary socialisation would be when a mother accepts all her young child's one-word verbal efforts as meaningful utterances and expands them into meaningful and grammatically well-formed utterances. Such expansions in fact also serve as models for the child. In adult–child interaction, scaffolding may not be a conscious act. Gregory (1996: 21) offers a helpful example:

> *K (child): Mummy sock dirty.*
> *Mummy: Yes. They're all dirty.*
> *K: Mummy sock.*
> *Mummy: There.*
> *K: Mummy sock.*
> *Mummy: That's not mummy's sock. That's your sock. There.*
> *K: Kathryn sock.* (Italics in original.)

Perhaps at this point it would be useful to emphasise that socialisation does not mean *socialising the pupils into a fixed and immutable body of knowledge and skills.* Scaffolding, as part of the socialisation process, should not be seen as a fixed and mechanical process whereby joint activities involving the teacher and the pupil are transferred directly to the pupil's consciousness as a moment of learning. As Cazden (1988: 108) puts it: 'In teaching . . . we should not assume a one-to-one relationship between the components of mature performance and the ingredients of the most effective instruction . . . the models provided are samples to learn from, not examples to learn.' Furthermore, it would be important to bear in mind that all social activities are influenced by cultural norms concerning politeness and appropriate behaviour in respect of participants and context. Acts of scaffolding are subject to the same constraints. As Gregory (1996) shows, working with second language pupils may require the teacher to be conscious of the culture-boundedness of any scaffolding attempt; an attempt to provide opportunities for talk by asking general or display questions, for instance, may be baffling for those pupils who are not yet familiar with this kind of conversational strategy.

In the school situation the second language pupils are bound to encounter new or novel content and language. For such pupils it would be necessary to provide a certain amount of scaffolding of the learning activities. Effective scaffolding requires supportive teaching and school ethos. There are at least six key aspects of the teaching and learning situation to be considered: pupils' background knowledge and experience; transparency of learning task and learning activity; presentation of information and task; teacher–pupil and pupil–pupil language communication; task organisation; and school ethos. It would be true to say that while some of these considerations are equally applicable to all pupils, the needs of second language pupils require different understanding and specific interpretation.

(a) Evaluating background knowledge and experience

Second language pupils, like all other pupils, enter into the learning situation with certain background knowledge and experience. Their background knowledge, however, may or may not be relevant to the learning task at hand. It may also be partly or completely encoded in the first language. Insofar as this background knowledge is related or relevant to the learning task, it should be used for effective learning.

In a study of cognitive strategies used by second language pupils to engage learning tasks, O'Malley and Chamot (1990) found that many tried to relate new information to prior knowledge and to make meaningful personal associations to information presented. They formally refer to these cognitive strategies as *elaboration* and *transfer*. Elaboration is glossed as 'relating new information to prior knowledge, relating different parts of new information to each other, or making meaningful personal associations with the new information'. Transfer is glossed as 'using what is already known about language to assist comprehension or production' (op. cit.: 199).

This observation is consistent with the Vygotskyan view of the pupil as an active participant in the learning process. McDonell (1992: 57) argues that:

> (The pupils) . . . actively construct knowledge for themselves as they search for meaning. In order to construct this knowledge, pupils draw on what they already know. Learning does not occur in a vacuum. Drawing on prior knowledge, pupils generate hypotheses about the new, which they test out, alter, or refine on the basis of their experiences.

From the language processing point of view this general position is consistent with some aspects of schema theory. For instance, in respect of reading, Carrell and Eisterhold (1987) state that:

> ... a text only provides directions for listeners or readers as to how they should retrieve or construct meaning from their own, previously acquired knowledge, ... comprehending a text is an interactive process between the reader's background knowledge and the text. Efficient comprehension requires the ability to relate the textual material to one's own knowledge.

On this view, the more the pupil is able to activate the relevant background knowledge, the greater the comprehension of the task at hand. The use of a pupil's first language and the use of visual or graphic representation of content meaning can serve to activate the relevant background knowledge and to make learning more effective.[9]

(b) Evaluating transparency of learning task and activity

Related to the issues of background knowledge is the question of whether the learning tasks and activities are familiar to the pupils. Many learning tasks and activities seem to be 'obvious' and 'natural' to teachers and pupils with school routines. On the classroom level, reading a story with a teacher in a Key Stage 1 class (5–6-year-old children) often involves more than just reading in the sense of sounding the words; for instance, choosing a book, a discussion based on or derived from a book and repeating a model pronunciation offered by the teacher are often regarded as normal ingredients of a reading activity (Gregory, 1993, 1994). In this respect, a reading task, as seen from the point of view of the teacher, is in fact composed of a number of activities for the pupil. The conduct and sequence of these activities are culturally and socially constructed. Second language pupils without a shared experience with the teacher or the peers would not necessarily know what is involved initially.

On the level of organisation and management of performing a complex task, such as making a zigzag book, the relationship between the different activities may not be transparent. In this case, the making of a book would mean the following activities: reading a story together, re-telling the story by pupils in their own words, making a book out of sheets of thin card, illustrating the story in the form of drawings and pictures, writing the narrative, sequencing and matching the illustrations to the narrative, mounting the illustrations and the text and, finally, reading the book to the class. This task may take place over a period of three days (interspersed with other learning tasks and activities). A second language pupil without the necessary previous experience of doing this kind of extended task may find it difficult to link all the different activities together and to understand the purpose of the individual activities. Explicit modelling of each of the activities and their relationship with the final product would be helpful (Mohan and Marshall Smith, 1992).

(c) Evaluating context and cognitive demand

It is generally held that the language used in everyday interaction which has a high 'here-and-now' content is more easily understood (and learned) by second language pupils than the language used in formal communication, such as a lecture, which does not always relate to the 'here-and-now'. Thus the language used in ordering food in a canteen, where the food is visible and where the purpose is clear, is more easily understood and learned than the language used in a formal lecture on the nutritional values of different foods.

Cummins (1992) proposes a formal conceptual framework to distinguish these two types of language: basic interpersonal communication skills (BICS) and cognitive academic language proficiency (CALP). It is hypothesised that BICS typically occur in a context-rich environment where the communication involves relatively little cognitive demand, and CALP in a context-reduced environment where the communication involves a relatively high level of cognitive demand. These two dimensions are shown diagrammatically in Figure 11.1.

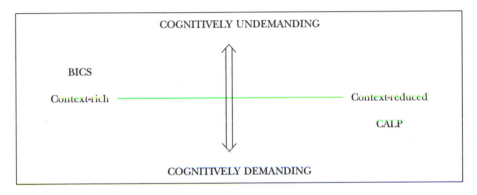

Figure 11.1   Distinguishing BICS and CALP

Cummins (1992: 21) argues that 'the more context-embedded the initial L2 input, the more comprehensible it is likely to be'. This argument is often interpreted to include all second language use, not just initial input. The earlier examples of ordering food in a canteen and listening to a lecture on nutritional values of different foods may be developed to demonstrate this point. In a canteen situation where the purpose of the interaction between the staff and the customer is mutually understood – and where the language communication is supported by real-life referents and paralinguistic clues, such as the food on display and gestures – it is relatively easy to make the intended meaning understandable, but the same transaction would be less context-embedded if all participants are required to communicate by means of written orders and there is no food on display. Likewise, a formal lecture on the nutritional values of foods may be made more or less context-embedded by the amount of visual illustrations, diagrams, pictures and realia used in the presentation. In both situations the relationship between the degree or extent of context-embeddedness and comprehension is not fixed; the pupils' comprehension depends on their current level of language knowledge and skills as well as their prior knowledge or experience in the relevant activities and subject matter. Pedagogically it is important to recognise that there is no mechanical way of calibrating context-embeddedness in terms of pupil comprehension. Teachers have to make case-by-case judgements. Context-embeddedness is therefore a relative concept: what is highly context-embedded for some pupils may be highly context-reduced for others, and vice versa. There is no universal defining criterion (Leung, 1996).

The key point here is that cognitive demand can be lowered by increasing contextual support. In a pedagogical sense, one may collapse Cummins' two-dimensional analytical framework into a one-dimensional pedagogical continuum: the degree or extent of context-embeddedness. On this view, one may argue that, in principle, the content of learning activities may be made more or less comprehensible to second language pupils; it is a matter of the degree or extent of contextualisation. Contextual support is therefore an important consideration in scaffolding tasks.

Furthermore, the notion of context is widely reified in second language studies and, more generally, as being simply a 'given'. For a discussion of this fallacy and a demonstration of how context is not 'given' but is 'interpreted' and even 'learned', see Mohan and Helmer (1988), which examines young second language learners' developing interpretations of gestures.

One way of providing contextual support in the learning activities is to make consistent and principled use of graphic representation of the key information in the learning task or materials. The discussion in Chapters 6 and 7, this volume, has shown that there are some common cross-curricular knowledge structures which occur in a great deal of the teaching/learning tasks and materials. These knowledge structures can be represented graphically to help pupils to grasp the important meanings involved and to produce work. Mohan (1986) uses the term 'key visuals' to refer to these graphic representations. Perhaps it is important to emphasise here that the key visuals, as conceived by Mohan and his colleagues, are different in nature, if not in appearance, from other kinds of visuals which one finds in textbooks and in classrooms generally. Key visuals are developed to represent both the shape or pattern of the structure of the text (spoken or written) and the content knowledge at the same time. Put differently, the key visuals show the meaning relationship as they are represented in the text. They are meant to lower the language barrier. Pupils are thus given a greater opportunity to access the content meaning. The key visuals themselves can be used as scaffolding devices for language learning activities (Early and Tang, 1991; also Chapter 7, this volume).

The types of scaffolding offered to pupils will depend on the pupils' needs. This has to be judged on a case-by-case basis. From the evaluation point of view, Table 11.1 indicates some of the areas of scaffolding where questions may be raised.

Table 11.1   Areas of scaffolding

Issue	Scaffolds
Background knowledge	• *Is there use of pupils' L1 to unlock relevant previous knowledge and to facilitate L1–L2 transfer?* • *Does the teacher use realia and other contextual clues to help make connections with previous learning and current knowledge?*
Familiarity with learning activities	• *Does the teacher show pupils the taken-for-granted ingredients of classroom activities? (For instance, reading may involve discussion.)* • *Does the teacher make explicit the components of a task? (Often a task is made up of a number of activities. It may be helpful to show, by example and by task organisation, how the various parts are related to form a whole.)*
Presentation and organisation of tasks	• *Does the teacher use graphics to show key knowledge structures and language embedded in the content material?* • *In a group task situation, does the teacher ensure that the second language pupils have an active role to play, e.g. as a holder of key information for task completion, and that only one joint task outcome is allowed in order to increase the probability of discussion and exchange of view?*
Further language development	• *Does the teacher provide adequate opportunities for pupils to attend to language forms involved in doing tasks?*[10] • *Does the teacher adjust the use of language when interacting with pupils to achieve greater comprehension of meaning and to provide language models?*

LANGUAGE SOCIALISATION[11]

Much of the discussion in this chapter has been articulated within a broad language socialisation perspective. The concern is to focus on the ididvidual learner without losing sight of the social nature of learning. The remarks in this section are intended to elaborate on some particular aspects of this position which are still subject to debate.

A great deal of the current professional discussion in ESL within the mainstream context tends to be grounded in the innatist view of language development. At the heart of the innatist view of language development is the central notion of the innate human capacity to learn language. For instance, Krashen's (1985) formulation of comprehensible input for a second language argues that all a language pupil needs is the right environment where the target language is made understandable. On this view pupils create their own language knowledge in the course of communicating with others. They draw on their innate language learning facilities and construct a grammar. Language, in this conception, is seen to be primarily made up of vocabulary and sentence level syntax. Successful language acquisition essentially means successful acquisition of grammatical principles and forms, albeit non-consciously. This fundamental assumption is often invisible in the professional literature. The discourse of mainstreaming has tended to obscure this underlying view of language which is undifferentiated for context and curriculum content.

The language socialisation perspective, while acknowledging the role played by internal language processing factors, builds on the basis of a common human learning and meaning-making capacity. Language acquisition is seen within a wider process of socialisation; it does not regard language acquisition as just a phenomenon of internal psychological and cognitive processes on the individual level. Following Vygotsky's view on human development (Vygotsky, 1962; Davidov, 1995), an individual acquires his or her consciousness through social interaction. 'Vygotsky saw the transformation of elementary processes into higher order ones as possible through the mediating function of culturally constructed artefacts including tools, symbols and more elaborate sign systems such as language' (Lantolf and Appel, 1994: 6). More specifically, individuals acquire meaning and knowledge, including language knowledge, through participation in social or collective activities with others. Ochs (1988: 15) argues that 'Novices are able to acquire cognitive skills through participation in joint activities (which require these skills) with more knowledgeable persons . . . Quite important here is the impact of socially and culturally organised language practices in activity settings.' In the school context this means that teachers, as the more 'knowledgeable' persons, clearly have a critical role to play and language is seen as a system of linguistic resources that people use to represent and create meaning (Halliday, 1973, 1985).

Perhaps it would be important to re-emphasise at this point that the socialisation perspective does not necessarily assume static achievement norms or uniform outcomes. The emphasis here is on the socially interactive nature of learning. Therefore we are not assuming, nor are we suggesting that it is desirable to have, a fixed and immutable body of knowledge and skills into which learners and novices are socialised. Teachers and pupils can jointly decide on new ways of working/learning and generate novel outcomes which transcend existing norms and expectations.

This view of learning locates language in a social context where meaning is generated and negotiated. In this sense, the conception of language acquisition is not restricted to learning vocabulary and sentence level syntax, either consciously or non-consciously; it is also concerned with discourse, i.e. how people make meaning using chunks of language in context. The issue of content meaning of the discourse is now an integral part of language learning. In the school situation this means that one will need to look at how language is used in different curriculum tasks and what second language pupils have to do to accomplish these tasks. Put differently, we are interested in the content and the activity involved in the tasks and how language is used in the doing of the tasks.

The language socialisation standpoint raises the question of the connections between discourse and its cultural context. This results in a very different view and analysis of task, and one that raises questions that extend far beyond a second language acquisition perspective. From an evaluative point of view, this means that one looks at a task not simply as an occasion where the grammar of the language is in play, but as the construction of meaning through discourse and communication within a cultural context, where culture includes the culture of the school. What values underpin classroom tasks and practices? How does the teacher interpret the task? Does the pupil interpret the task differently? How were tasks done in the pupils' previous schooling experience? How are they done in the current school culture? And how does the discourse of the task reflect these meanings?

The discussion in this chapter has focused on content-language integration issues within the classroom context from an evaluative standpoint. There are wider structural questions within the education system which we need to examine. We will turn to these wider questions in the next chapter.

NOTES

1. It is interesting to note that a moment's reflection will show that many of these apparently ordinary real-world tasks have their counterparts in the curriculum and in school activities generally (e.g. pupils acting as guides on parents evenings). Even the most unlikely tasks such as booking a hotel room may occur in role play and drama.
2. Following Kumaravadivelu's (1993) argument, a hierarchy is assumed here. A pedagogical task may include one or more than one activity; an activity may include one or more than one exercise.
3. There are cross-curricular thinking skills, e.g. describing or predicting, and text types, e.g. reports or letters. The point here is that these thinking skills and text types often take on a subject-specific character and appearance.
4. One of the definitions of register, offered by Richards et al. (1985: 242), is as follows: 'a speech variety used by a particular group of people, usually sharing the same occupation (e.g. doctors, lawyers) or the same interests (e.g. stamp collectors, baseball fans). A particular register often distinguishes itself from other registers by having a number of distinctive words, by using words or phrases in a particular way (e.g. in tennis: deuce, love, . . .), and sometimes by special grammar constructions (e.g. legal language).' It is, however, important to note that a register is not an immutable phenomenon; it can vary depending on the context and the participants involved in any communication situation and it changes over time.
5. 'A text type is a general category that refers to labels we apply to texts as products or things. Text types would therefore include particular products such as reports, expositions, stories, procedures, etc.' (Knapp and Watkins, 1994: 12).
6. It should be pointed out that the outcome of such assessment should be interpreted locally with reference to teacher input and classroom organisation. One has to be cautious in any attempt to generalise the outcome of such contextualised assessment. (For a discussion, see McNamara, 1996.)
7. For a discussion on the need to map long-term ESL development, see McKay (1992). See Gipps (1994) for a discussion on educational assessment.
8. It is not suggested here that all learning activities are collaborative or group-based in the real-time sense. Some activities, which are collaborative and interactive in

nature, may contain components which are carried out individually. A teacher working with an individual pupil can be seen in this socialisation perspective.

9. A pupil's ability to participate in the task will also be dependent on whether he or she has the requisite background knowledge to make sense of the information in the first place. For instance, a decision-making task involving the choice of the best value for a family holiday may be quite a difficult concept for those pupils who may have little experience of a 'holiday' as it is understood in, say, Britain. The lack of this kind of background knowledge often makes some tasks very difficult. Where this is the case it may be necessary to provide the background knowledge as part of the presentation of the task.

10. The idea is to exploit where possible the opportunities for accelerated acquisition of syntax and morphology. It is generally understood that there is a universal sequence of acquisition as far as *naturalistic use* is concerned. For instance, questions in the SVO? pattern (He is home?) tend to occur before the copula inversion (Is he home?). Teaching the copula inversion when the pupils are already producing the SVO? pattern may accelerate the acquisition process. But teaching the same pupils to insert an auxiliary verb in the second position (Where have you put it?) is likely to be counter-productive. This is because the Auxiliary 2nd pattern tends to emerge at a much later stage. (For a discussion, see Pienemann and MacKey, 1992).

11. This view is consistent with some aspects of a number of psycholinguistic principles: language learning is a developmental process; it is a process of negotiation; it is not linear; it is in part incidental and in part a subconscious activity. (For a review of literature, see Ellis, 1994.)

Chapter 12

Curriculum identity and professional development: system-wide questions

Constant Leung and Charlotte Franson

INTRODUCTION

In the previous chapter we discussed some of the key pedagogical issues at the classroom level. For ESL to achieve a proper curriculum and professional status it is, however, important to address some of the whole-system issues which are fundamental to any future development. In this final chapter on the English system we will briefly draw attention to six interconnected issues: conceptualisation of the learner; conceptualisation of ESL as a discipline; curriculum development; teacher education and professional development; assessment; and the nature of funding and provision. We argue that for ESL pedagogy to develop and respond to the whole range of changing pupil needs, the current thinking behind these six issues has to be examined and the related policy and practice re-articulated accordingly.

CONCEPTUALISATION OF THE LEARNER

We have already referred to the fact that discussion on ESL pedagogy in England has tended to be limited to issues of classroom organisation and participation in learning processes. One of the reasons which made this narrowness of focus possible is the implicit assumption that there is an ideal-type universal ESL learner, with the corollary that all learners go through similar learning processes and have similar learning needs. This conceptualisation of the putative learner is highly problematic. Classroom teaching experience and demographic changes in recent years have pointed to the need to move away from this kind of assumption. Since the 1950s the ESL learner has been perceived primarily as a linguistic and social outsider. This conceptualisation has been reflected in a number of official documents. In the Plowden Report (DES, 1967: 72), for instance, the immigrant (ESL) pupil was seen as in need of social familiarisation and lamented that '. . . there has been little opportunity for teachers to learn how to teach English to foreigners'. The more integrationist Swann Report (DES, 1985b: 8) promoted a pluralist view founded on firm assumptions of fixed ethnic boundaries: 'Whilst we are *not* looking for the assimilation of the minority communities with an unchanged dominant way of life, we are perhaps looking for the 'assimilation' of *all* groups within a redefined concept of what it means to live in British society today' (italics in original). It is perhaps understandable that, in the 1950s and 1960s when there was a relatively large-scale inward migration from the Common-wealth and Pakistan, the education system viewed the new pupils as outsiders, or indeed as foreigners, to an assumed homogeneous British culture and English language. (This point has been challenged; for a wider discussion see Harris, 1997 and Leung et al., 1997.) But such a time-bound and falsely sim-plified view of the learners cannot be sustained. Linguistic and ethnic diver-sity in many English schools, particularly in the urban areas, is considerably more complex. The bilingual pupil population is in fact made up of a number of different groups:

• pupils with an overseas background, including those coming from the European Union member states, who are new to English (all ages);
• pupils from ethnic/linguistic minority communities in England (or Britain generally) with a home experience in a language other than English who are learning to use English in school (particularly nursery/reception year children);
• pupils from ethnic/linguistic minority communities in England (or Britain generally) who are fluent in vernacular spoken English for everyday social purposes and familiar with the local culture (all ages), but they may not be conversant with academic uses of English;
• pupils from ethnic/linguistic minority communities in England (or Britain more generally) whose ability to use English for social and academic pur-poses is comparable to that of the monolingual English native speakers; these pupils are also familiar with the local culture.

It should be pointed out that all these pupils are generally assumed to be bilingual in a vague and general sense. The kinds and degrees of bilingual-ism among these pupils have in fact been never clearly identified and docu-mented in any systematic way. Recent classroom-based studies suggest that ethnic minority bilingual pupils' first language and literacy in their first or home languages vary enormously; some are fluent in both the spoken and written modes, others are only able to understand some routinised expressions in familiar contexts and yet others are straddled somewhere between these extremes (see Harris, 1997, for a more detailed discussion).

These different types of learner clearly have different language learning needs and they require different responses. They, in turn, require the teacher to differentiate appropriateness of different teaching strategies and focus on different aspects of second language development. For instance, teachers may choose to focus on the development of second language reading and writing for academic purposes for those pupils who are already familiar with the local spoken English and cultural practices; whereas for the beginners who are new to both English and local culture they may choose to put priority on the development of spoken language for both everyday social interaction and classroom learning purposes in the initial period. Another aspect of the heterogeneous nature of the pupil language profile, which has direct influence on the teaching strategies, is the extent to which a pupil is able to use his or her first language to learn English and curriculum content; the general assumption that all bilingual pupils will benefit from teaching support using their first language is not very helpful on the individual level. All available classroom and school level evidence point to an intergenerational language shift towards English (Harris, 1997; Mobbs, 1997). These and other similar observations clearly show the importance and the need to achieve a higher level of precision in our conceptualisation of the learner.

CONCEPTUALISATION OF ESL AS A DISCIPLINE

The discussion in Chapters 9 and 10 suggests that ESL is conceptualised as a diffused curriculum concern and not as a distinct discipline within the curriculum. Chapter 11 argues that some of the pedagogic principles that have grown out of this conceptualisation require critique and further development. Thus there is a good case for taking a fresh look at the conceptualisation itself. Bernstein's (1996) discussion on the linked concepts of competence and performance, as two pervasive cross-disciplinary ideas in Western European and North American contexts in the past 30 years or so, is useful heuristically in that it helps to illuminate the underlying character of the current conceptualisation of ESL. These concepts are not representations of actual policies or models of practice; they are abstracted values and beliefs on which actual policies and practices are based. Competence, as an abstract concept, is characterised as follows[1]:

- it is 'intrinsically creative and tacitly acquired' (op. cit.: 55)
- it is a 'practical accomplishment' (loc. cit.)
- it is socially constituted through negotiation, in the broadest sense of 'social order as practice, cognitive structuring, language acquisition' (loc. cit.) and such negotiations are not culture specific (or exclusive) in that all may participate
- its acquisition is not subject to the influence of the power differentials between participants.

Bernstein (1996) argues that a social logic inheres in this concept of competence. By social logic Bernstein is referring to a set of founding assumptions which shape and form the concept. In the case of ESL, Bernstein's postulations can be interpreted to include:

- All (ESL) students can achieve and acquire this universally accessible competence; there are no 'deficits' (op. cit.: 56) in the acquirers. Age and other individual personal characteristics are not regarded as salient; different first and second language developmental trajectories and pathways are not regarded as significant.

- The student is active in creating meaning and is creative in the use of current knowledge or resources, e.g. the use of a limited set of syntactical rules to create new meaning. There is some sort of invariant approach to acquisition.
- The acquisition is tacit and immanent. It is 'not advanced by formal instruction' nor is it subject to 'public regulation' (op. cit.: 56), e.g. a subject syllabus; only facilitation and context management are required.
- The acquisition does not require or involve hierarchical power relations among the parties concerned. Social class, ethnicity, gender, age as well as institutional positions are not regarded as salient.
- The present tense is the 'temporal perspective' (op. cit.: 56); the past and the future are revealed through the moment of realisation. Starting positions and learning outcomes do not bear on pedagogy or acquisition in any explicit way.

This conceptualisation of competence can be contrasted with that associated with what Bernstein (1996) refers to as performance. He glosses performance as a practice which '. . . places . . . emphasis upon a specific output of the acquirer, upon a particular text the acquirer is expected to construct, and upon the specialised skills necessary to the production of this specific output, text or product' (op. cit.: 57–8). Indeed, by construing the opposite of the above discussion on competence, one may extend this general characterisation to suggest a 'social logic' of performance for ESL in the following way:

- All may enter into the development process but the outcome depends on a large number of considerations including types and contexts of educational provision, age and context of learning, types/definitions of language attainment, background educational experience, individual differences in aptitude, cognitive style and motivation (August and Hakuta, 1997; Davies et al., 1997; Dörnyei, 1998; Ellis, 1994; Skehan, 1998; Spolsky, 1989; Thomas and Collier, 1997, among others). Learner differences are not ignored; there is no automatic universal outcome.
- There is variability in the use of language by learners. Such variability may be influenced by a large number of factors such as conditions of language use and types of task (Foster, 1998, among others) and form-function relations (see Ellis, 1994, ch. 4, for a general summary).
- Explicit teaching and conscious analysis have a role to play in second language development (Schmidt, 1990; Spolsky, 1989, among others). Language learning is not always tacit, there is a role for noticing and hypothesis-testing (Swain, 1995; cf. Truscott, 1998).
- The distinction between native speaker and second language learner suggests one dimension of power differential and, in the context of formal teaching and schooling, the teacher–learner distinction suggests another (Cummins, 1996). The unequal inter-ethnic and inter-communal relations between majority language and minority language communities within the

context of 'official' social integration may be yet another dimension of power differential (Bourdieu, 1991; Tosi, 1996).

- Second language development is seen as a process of progressive approximation towards the ideal, the benchmark or the norm; hence there are stages or a sequence of learning, and at any one point learners may show deficits (as measured against the expected achievement). All ESL scales (indeed any norm or criterion referenced scale for any subject) make this assumption.

For the purpose of this discussion, the main differences between competence and performance have been summarised in Table 12.1.

Table 12.1 Main differences between competence and performance

Aspect of social logic (assumptions)	Competence	Performance
1. Recognition of individual/group differences in acquisition pathways and outcomes	Not important	Important
2. Variations in styles/manners of acquisition and language use	Not important	Important
3. Explicit pedagogy and curriculum	Not important	Important
4. Hierarchical/unequal power relationships	Not important	Important
5. Development measured in stages/outcomes	Not important	Important

The current conceptualisation of ESL is clearly associated with the assumptions underpinning Bernstein's (1996) competence. Many of the issues raised earlier in Chapter 10 can now be seen in an interrelated way. It can be argued that these assumptions have coalesced to form networks of ideas which Kuhn (1962/70: 46) might refer to as community paradigms in which

> [members of the professional community] work from models acquired through education and ... exposure to the literature often without quite knowing or needing to know what characteristics have given these models the status of community paradigms. And because they do so they need no full set of rules.

To the extent that some key aspects of the current conceptualisation have been found to be problematic, there is a need for rethinking at this level. The corpus of theoretical and empirical work cited above in conjunction with the discussion on performance can serve as useful pointers in this critique of reasoning.

CURRICULUM DEVELOPMENT

Under the current statutory arrangements, schools in the state sector can only offer limited curriculum accommodation to ESL pupils. The officially stated view is that the National Curriculum as a whole is able to accommodate the learning needs of all pupils, including those of ESL pupils. Implicit in this view is the assumption, as suggested earlier, that there is a universal language learning model or process for all pupils irrespective of their language background. The English (subject) National Curriculum (DfEE, 1999a: 6) states that:

> The programme of study set out what pupils should be taught, and the attainment targets set out the expected standards of pupil's performance. It is for schools to choose how they organise their school curriculum to include the programmes of study for English.

The Science (subject) National Curriculum (1999c: 69) states that:

> Pupils should be taught in all subjects to express themselves correctly and appropriately and to read accurately with understanding . . .

There is no specific mention of the second language learning needs of individual ESL pupils in the curriculum description. We would argue that the use of English within the National Curriculum, in the absence of any evidence to the contrary, is predicated on a set of idealised native speaker competencies and norms. (For a wider discussion on the conceptualisation of English, see Bourne and Cameron, 1996.) Indeed, the official policy document on ESL (SCAA, 1996) recommends the use of the National Curriculum programmes of study as a basis for ESL work. Few would take issue with the ideal that all pupils should be expected to achieve at the highest level, the question here is whether a non-ESL-sensitive curriculum framework provides the necessary support for schools and teachers to work with pupils with ESL needs. Some of the recent attempts by ESL professionals in the USA and the Victorian state government in Australia to provide more rigorous and systematic support in this field are of interest for us here.

In the USA the TESOL Standards for ESL (TESOL, 1997) attempt to highlight the areas of language knowledge and skills, ESL pupils in primary and secondary schools need to become proficient in English; the document also asserts the need for pupils to have access to grade-appropriate instruction in the curriculum subjects. The standards have been developed to complement work in other curriculum content areas to meet the needs of ESL pupils and to provide a bridge to general educational standards. The document identifies three broad goals for ESL pupils: personal, social and academic uses of English. Each goal has content standards, descriptors and sample progress indicators of pupils' achievement. The sample progress indicators are grouped by grade levels. The standards are illustrated by classroom vignettes intended to help teachers to see how the descriptors could be realised in the teaching and learning process. There is, however, no detailed specification of language learning outcomes. The document sets out to offer guidelines on the development of an ESL curriculum by individual states and invites teachers to use the sample progress indicators to develop their own judgements of pupil performance. Thus the intention is to provide a framework which teachers can use to plan teaching and to chart ESL pupils' progress in the curriculum areas.

The Board of Studies in the state of Victoria, Victoria (Board of Studies, 2000; see also chapter 2), produced an ESL Companion to the mandated English Curriculum and Standards Framework. The purpose of this document is to set out, for both ESL and mainstream teachers, teaching and learning contexts conducive to second language development as well as learning outcomes in different phases of education. The ESL learning outcomes are explicitly related to the mainstream English curriculum. It is recognised that as ESL pupils progressively develop their English language knowledge and skills, the mainstream English curriculum goals and demands will become more relevant and appropriate.

The key distinguishing feature between the United States' TESOL, the Victoria state curriculum documents and the English National Curriculum is that both the USA and the state of Victoria in Australia try to acknowledge the presence of the second language learner while the content specifications of the National Curriculum in England does not. In this situation both the ESL specialist and the main stream teacher are left with the task of doing what they can to help the ESL pupils to 'get on' with the curriculum content and language learning, as we have shown in Chapter 10. There are examples of effective teaching (cf. OFSTED, 1994) but the education system clearly has a need, indeed a social responsibility, to recognise ESL as a distinct issue of learning and teaching and to set out some explicit requirements and guidance on curriculum provision.

TEACHER EDUCATION AND PROFESSIONAL DEVELOPMENT

At present ESL is not offered as a specialist subject in initial teacher education. Indeed, no professional credential is required for ESL teaching; all teachers with a statutory teaching qualification (in any subject area or phase of education) may undertake ESL teaching. In a recent survey, two-thirds of the student teachers in the sample indicated that they felt 'poorly prepared' for ESL work (Gardiner, 1996). This state of affairs cannot be sustained on a permanent basis. Current official figures suggest that half a million pupils do not speak English as a first language (DfEE, 1997b). In some inner city areas the percentage can exceed 50 per cent of the school population, e.g. the London borough of Brent. Some individual populations consist of 80 per cent or more linguistic minority pupils. The European Union projects that by the year 2025, 15–20 per cent of the school population in all member states will be from ethnic and linguistic minority backgrounds (Tosi, 1996). As the European Commission (1994: 1) states, 'cultural and linguistic diversity of the public schools is becoming the norm'. All teachers are likely to encounter ESL pupils in their classrooms. This means that ESL, both as a subject specialism and as a part of a wider agenda for teacher education (for all subject specialisms), has to be given urgent recognition.

It is, however, important to recognise the need to differentiate between what is needed by non-ESL teachers and ESL specialists. Our experience suggests that for non-specialists at the pre-service training stage the programme of study should include, as a minimum, some knowledge of the formal features and patterns of discourse of the English language in the curriculum or subject context (not just knowledge of English[2]) and knowledge of second language acquisition in school settings. Pre-service trainee teachers will also need to have some practical knowledge and understanding of classroom actions – which Hargreaves (1993) might refer to as recipe knowledge – that would begin to take account of the learning needs of ESL learners. Furthermore, they will need to develop a knowledge of the ways of collaborating with a specialist ESL teacher in the same classroom and curriculum space.

For experienced mainstream teachers of ESL pupils there is a need to provide long-term recursive in-service training. The training should aim at building on their professional experiences and enhancing their willingness to learn to apply new knowledge and strategies to their classrooms. Apart from introducing the new knowledge about the English language, the range of educational and cultural experiences of ESL pupils, second language acquisition and classroom practices, the in-service training may need to address the questions of changing a teacher's beliefs and conceptualisation of teaching. Pennington (1995) suggests that for teachers to change their beliefs and practice they will have to go through a cycle of four practical and intellectual stages which encompass three areas of change, procedural, interpersonal and conceptual. Teachers need to be willing to:

- accept a problem
- grapple with the use of new information or techniques or materials (procedural)
- try to understand their own and pupils' reactions to the new practice and how to ensure a positive outcome (interpersonal)
- explain how the teaching method and process influence the learning process (conceptual).

All this suggests that in-service training cannot be regarded as a quick-fix solution focused on behavioural changes only. It is a long-term developmental process. (For a discussion, see Leung and Teasdale, 1997.)

For ESL specialists, an in-depth knowledge about language learning and the English language is required. They will also need expert knowledge and skills to assess the ESL pupil's learning needs in terms of the English language and curriculum content, and how to promote learning in the mainstream classroom context. Effective teaching demands sensitively judged application of methods and techniques informed by relevant theory in diverse circumstances; this is true of all teaching but is particularly true of ESL teaching because of the mainstreamed nature of the practice (Eraut, 1994; Elliot, 1993). It would be unwise to set a fixed and universal teaching model or method (in the sense of, say, the direct method, in foreign language teaching) since there are no easily definable standard contexts for ESL work. All ESL teachers work in diverse teaching situations in respect of types of pupil, ages, curriculum areas, pupil groupings, teaching partnerships, staff room cultures and schools. As all lessons are dynamic and the patterns of activities and interactions are variable; so too are the ESL teaching and learning aspects of the lesson. Furthermore, ESL teaching in the mainstream classroom, unlike other subjects such as science, cannot be said to have an established procedure. The learning outcome is not as predictable as in other subjects because of the wide range of pupils' differences. In this professional context, much depends upon the teacher's previous knowledge and experience, and quick interpretation and responsiveness to each situation as it develops. The application of a formulaic teaching method will not suffice. What is needed is a thorough knowledge of a range of teaching approaches and strategies and the requisite skills to select and apply such knowledge in context. However, it is possible to state the type of knowledge and skills required to deliver the necessary teaching. Our experience and work developed by colleagues else where (e.g. Strong and Hogan, 1994; TESOL, 1997) suggest that the areas of knowledge and skills presented in Figure 12.1 (overleaf) may be regarded as key ingredients.

In the longer run, an explicit statement about the minimum requirements for an ESL specialist teaching training would provide the basis for a uniform recognition of ESL teachers' qualifications and raise the professional standing of those working in ESL. It would contribute towards improving the quality of provision for ESL pupils by extending the range of knowledge and classroom methodology in the field.

ASSESSMENT

At present there are two separate systems of language assessment: the National Curriculum assessment and the local education authority/school assessment. Under the current statutory arrangements all pupils, including ESL pupils, are assessed according to the level descriptors set out in the English (subject) National Curriculum (DfEE, 1999a). The statutory assessment is concerned with formative and summative purposes. In addition to the statutory assessment, local education authorities and/or schools carry out their own ESL assessment. The locally organised assessment serves a number of different purposes:

- to identify the pupils' language learning needs (diagnostic purpose)
- to determine whether a pupil requires ESL support and the level of support required (how much time) (staff allocation and teaching purposes)
- to report progress (formative purpose)
- to report achievement at end points of study periods, e.g. at the end of an academic year (summative purpose)
- to attract staff funding from the state (funding purpose).[3]

The current uncoordinated dual-system practice is problematic for a number of reasons:

1. The English (subject) National Curriculum assumes mother-tongue speaker developmental norms set out in a scale of eight levels. This automatically

Structural features of English	Language form/meaning/function relationship	Language and curriculum content relationship	Principles of second language acquisition in the mainstream classroom context	Principles of second language assessment	Interpersonal management skills
For example: Sentence-level syntax, intonation	*For example:* The pragmatics (formality and politeness) of English language use	*For example:* Use of English in subjects such as science and maths	*For example:* Interpretation and application of major second language acquisition theories and the role of L1	*For example:* Use of formative language assessment within the curriculum context to promote effective teaching	*For example:* Ways of building a working relationship with colleagues at classroom and school level

KNOWLEDGE AND SKILLS

Figure 12.1 Knowledge and skills of L2 teachers

raises the fundamental question whether such a scale is appropriate for ESL pupils. Furthermore, the level descriptors are meant to cover the age range of 5 to 14. While it is claimed that the levels (1 to 8) are not age-specific, in practice the assessment system does relate levels to age groups. For instance, the descriptors in levels 1 to 3 are used to assess pupils at the age of 7. The level 1 descriptors for speaking and listening (DfEE, 1999a: 55) state that:

> Pupils talk about matters of immediate interest. They listen to others and usually respond appropriately. They convey simple meanings to a range of listeners, speaking audibly, and begin to extend their ideas or accounts by providing some detail.

Quite clearly this description of listening and speaking befits young primary school pupils' language use. It would, however, be inappropriate to use such descriptors to assess an ESL beginner at the age of 13 who has been to school elsewhere.[4] It is commonly accepted that primary school teachers have to stretch the meaning of 'appropriately' and 'begin to extend their ideas' liberally in order to make these descriptors work for pupils from linguistic minority communities who are at the beginning stages of learning to use English in school. The need to interpret the descriptors indicates a critical issue of consistency and stability of interpretation and application. (Local education authority ESL assessments in this phase of education tend to use descriptors such as 'may echo words and phrases' and 'may label familiar object', which indicates a more second language-oriented conceptualisation of language development.) For formative reasons the lack of overall system-wide consistency, while undesirable, may not seem to be crucial since the main purpose of the assessment is to chart individual pupil progress within a specific local school context. But it raises issues of what constitutes valid evidence of attainment as construed by teachers (Leung and Teasdale, 1997). In any case, consistency of application across the whole system is vital for summative assessment since the purpose here is to establish accountability and reliability of results (Gipps, 1994).

2. ESL assessment, developed and organised by local education authorities and schools, embodies a wide range of conceptualisations and practices (Leung, 1996). There are two fundamental issues:

* purpose of assessment and
* selection of and consistency in the knowledge and skills being sampled.

Local authorities and schools assess pupils' ESL development in order to identify their language learning needs and to allocate teaching staff for support teaching purposes. They also use ESL assessment results to establish the overall level of need in their local area or school at specific times, normally tied to funding cycles. This information is then used as a basis of grant application to the central government for specialist ESL provision. The same descriptors are often used for all the different purposes. There are problems associated with this multiple use of the same descriptors; for instance, for funding application purposes one is concerned with a snapshot of the overall level of needs at a specific moment. The funding agencies are not interested in detailed accounts of individual pupil development; therefore, a relatively brief set of descriptors providing a summative picture would suffice. However, diagnostic assessment carried out to identify pupil needs and to aid the planning of teaching would need to be detailed and contextualised within a specific curriculum setting. These two purposes, therefore, cannot be served by a single set of universal descriptors.

The types of language knowledge and skills sampled by the different local education authorities tend to vary. In a recent national survey, Leung (1996) reports that the knowledge and skills sampled by the different local ESL assessment schemes include grammar, learning strategies, functional use, first language literacy and use, and language sensitivity. The local authority assessment schemes show a range of different foci. In the absence of any national initiative to discuss ESL assessment issues, it is inevitable that there is local diversity. One of the consequences of the current situation is that pupils are assessed by different criteria in different parts of the country. Given that the amount of ESL support offered to pupils is, at least partly, determined by local assessment, there is a serious question about equity of access to educational opportunity. Furthermore, there is evidence that the descriptors associated with particular areas of knowledge and skills do not appear consistently across the different stages. For instance, in a scheme with five stages a descriptor concerned with learning strategies may only appear once in stage 3 (listening and speaking) and none of the reading and writing descriptors cover this area of knowledge and skill. This lack of systematicity in the sampling raises a troubling question of how pupil progress is charted.

3. Most of the local authority ESL assessment schemes are not explicitly and formally linked to the mainstream curriculum. Since ESL pupils have to learn to use English for academic purposes in the mainstream curriculum, it would be important to assess pupils' second language development accordingly. A curriculum-sensitive ESL assessment scheme would provide both contextually valid information as to pupils' ability to deal with the language demands of the classroom at any one time and the different demands in different phases of schooling. For instance, the collaborative, hands-on and experiential nature of many of the classroom tasks for 5- or 6-year-old pupils is likely to generate different language demands from an examination-bound history class for 15-year-old pupils. In the former there is likely to be a need, among other things, to use spoken language to work with others to explore meaning; in the latter the language use is likely to be more decontextualised and formal, with emphasis on reading and writing. A curriculum-sensitive ESL assessment system would need to take such differences into account. (For a further discussion, see Cameron and Bygate, 1997.)

THE NATURE OF FUNDING AND PROVISION

The ESL provision in England is – unlike other areas of curriculum provision – mainly organised as time-limited projects. The local education authorities and/or schools have to apply for funding based on evidence of need.[5] While the central government appears to recognise the educational importance of ESL (Squires, 1996; DfEE, 1998b), it has treated the funding of this provision as 'discretionary' and not mandatory (Bangs, 1994). One of the reasons for this short-term thinking may be historical. When funding for ESL, and other educational provisions for ethnic minorities generally, was first introduced in 1964, it was conceived as part of a response to assimilate immigrants into the host community.

> . . . the origins of . . . [this funding] lie in the assimilationist phase of educational thinking in that the underlying aim appears to be to overcome the perceived 'differences' of the ethnic minority groups with a view to their eventual absorption into the majority community.   (DES, 1985b: 358)

There was an implicit assumption that once assimilation had successfully taken place, there would not be a need for such arrangements. Events in the subsequent 30 years have shown that while the composition of the bilingual pupil population may have changed, the need for ESL has not disappeared.

The unstable and short-term nature of the ESL provision has led to a number of professional difficulties concerning employment, training and career development. For many ESL teachers, especially those who work in several schools on a fractional basis, employment as an 'ESL support' teacher continues to carry a pervasive aura of impermanence and lower status. This background of financial uncertainty has, for many teachers, reduced their sense of professional confidence. In the report 'Recent Research on the Achievements of Ethnic Minority Pupils', Gillborn and Gipps (1996: 79), in making explicit the benefits of ESL teaching, state that '[s]uch work may be weakened by the insecurity of [short-term contract] posts and new budgetary arrangements that cannot ring-fence resources to ensure spending on bilingual support'. Professional experience indicates that ESL teachers are taking up mainstream classroom teaching positions in order to secure what is perceived as more permanent employment. This can only reduce the pool of ESL teaching expertise available and deter new entrants to the field.

Professional development for ESL teachers continues to be problematic. We have already pointed out that there is no pre-service ESL (as a subject discipline) teacher training. Many ESL teachers gain their expertise and knowledge through on-the-job experience and local in-service education programmes. At the national level, the Grants for Educational Support and Training (GEST) Scheme had periodically included an in-service programme for training mainstream class and subject teachers in recent years. However, this funding was not available for ESL specialists. This was and continues to be a paradoxical situation. ESL teachers are often called upon to provide in-service training and yet they themselves are not given any pre-service specialist training and there is little long-term, qualification-based in-service training. At the same time, the education system itself seems to take the availability of ESL expertise for granted. For example, the initial teacher training curriculum which sets out 'Standards for the Award of Qualified Teacher Status' requires qualified teachers to demonstrate that they can 'plan their teaching to achieve progression in pupils' learning through . . . identifying pupils who are . . . not fluent in English and knowing where to get help in order to give positive and targeted support' (DfEE, 1998c: 12).

One result of the lack of a systematic, nationally recognised approach to ESL professional development has been a lack of career development for ESL teachers. In many ways becoming an ESL teacher is seen as a negative career decision. The lack of a recognised school-based professional identity (and promotion opportunities) such as that achieved by Special Educational Needs coordinators and the diverse teaching backgrounds of those working as ESL teachers have also contributed to this view of ESL teaching. Given the structure of ESL provision, there are often only a very few positions for career advancement. This lack of a career structure cannot appear attractive to young teachers. Taken in conjunction with the continuing uncertainties regarding the nature of ESL provision and funding, it is difficult to envisage how sufficient numbers of ESL teachers will be retained or new teachers recruited to the discipline. Positive action with regard to training, recruitment and career development within mainstream education will be necessary to ensure continued commitment to the discipline and the profession.

FUTURE DEVELOPMENTS

Our discussion has shown that ESL in England has gone through some profound changes both in terms of conceptualisation and classroom practice. The advances made in opening up access to the school curriculum by mainstreaming ESL students are significant for the development of equal opportunities in education. However, the mainstream process has also been accompanied by a loss of curriculum status, pedagogic focus and professional identity.

The main question before us now is this: How can we develop ESL as a distinctive discipline within the mainstream context? The pedagogic and structural issues raised in the previous chapter and earlier in this chapter would suggest that:

- At the classroom level there is a need to identify and sharpen the second language teaching and learning agenda within subject domains; participation in the mainstream curriculum activities does not necessarily lead to efficient content and language learning.
- At the subject discipline level there is a need to identify what is to be taught and learned – a set of theoretically explicit and empirically validated ESL learning outcome statements would greatly assist this process; the acquisition of general communication skills is only a part of second language development.

- At the educational provision level there is a need to rethink the nature of second language development and the types of learner in an ethnically and culturally diverse society; conceptualisations based on a historical view of ESL learners serve to limit our response to changing circumstances and pupil populations.

In terms of immediate action, four initiatives are needed urgently and they may act as a trigger for further development:

- the introduction (or re-introduction) of pre-service specialist ESL teacher education and a mandatory professional credential for teachers
- the introduction of differentiated but systematic and accredited in-service professional development for all teachers who work with ESL pupils and ESL post-holders
- the development of a set of mainstream curriculum-related ESL learning outcomes statements and attainment scales
- the development of funding arrangements which are based on needs and entitlements integrated with the more general educational provision.

These four initiatives, once put in process, would draw attention to all the issues raised in this discussion. ESL in England has been at the forefront of the movement towards equal access to the mainstream educational provision. This ideological commitment to an increased degree of equal opportunity and multiculturalism should be supported by an equally strong effort to develop a theoretically well-informed and empirically validated pedagogy.

NOTES

1. Note that Bernstein is using the terms 'competence' and 'performance' in a very different sense than the one adopted in a great deal of the recent discussion in vocational education, which tends to regard competence as comprising a much more bounded and technically defined set of knowledge and skills or behaviours. For a discussion, see Bates (1995), Gonczi (1994), and Jones and Moore (1995) among others. It should also be noted that these terms have been used differently in applied linguistics. For an example, see McNamara (1996), ch. 2.
2. There is a mention of subject-specific terminology in relation to the teaching of vocabulary in the National Curriculum for initial teacher training for primary phase English (DfEE, 1997a).
3. There is speculation that a set of National Curriculum (subject English)-derived assessment criteria may be introduced for funding (teacher staffing) application purposes. No details are available at this time.
4. The central curriculum authorities have recently presented two 'step descriptors' (QCA, 1998b) which are meant to be used to assess the developing English of ESL beginners not covered by the main English scale. At present the relationship between these descriptors and the main English scale is not clear.
5. ESL provision is organised on the basis of match-funding partnership between local and central government. The central government funding cycle has ranged between three and five years. The process has been less than straightforward. The

experience of the recent rounds of application was instructive. The length of time to prepare and submit the initial local education authorities (LEA) bids for ESL funding in 1992 in itself generated anxiety among staff and not all projects received the funding they requested. Some projects had to re-bid for funding within three years. In the same time period, central government grants to LEAs were much more tightly controlled and, increasingly, LEAs had less money to provide the matched funding. For example, one London education authority was unable to take up the total of its grant allocation because it was unable to provide the requisite matched funding. There was anecdotal evidence to suggest that many projects had to restructure and reduce their service as a result of financial restrictions. Even though another source of funding for ESL provision had been made available to LEAs through the Department of the Environment, many of the new bids were not successful and the general perception of having to 'jump' insurmountable hurdles was reinforced. In 1999 a new set of funding arrangements was administered by the DfEE; under the new arrangements the schools are responsible for appointing ESL staff directly. Further changes are being introduced for the years 2000 and 2001. This is an example of the constant changes in this field of work.

Conclusion

The general features of the situation of ESL learners in schools in England, Vancouver and Victoria, like the USA, are:

- ESL students are served by educational systems which claim to be inclusive but are in fact indifferent and insensitive to the full range of their language and learning needs; government policy does not sufficiently acknowledge their significant presence, particularly in urban schools.
- Policies and practices for ESL learners are inadequately coordinated with other aspects of school and curriculum practices.
- Reform tends to be rhetorically driven with too little attention paid to pedagogic and resource issues; it lacks a comprehensive vision.

In effect ESL students have been marginalised, paradoxically often within a mainstreamed context.

It is, however, important to recognise that, as the three case studies here have shown, all linguistic, cultural and educational practices are shaped to a great extent by the sociocultural and political context. There are different histories and different perceptions of issues in each country because of different approaches to immigration, to settlement, to inter-ethnic affairs, to teacher preparation, to education and to public accountability. These differences are manifested by different policies and actions, and they, accordingly, call for different responses.

For instance, Canada has 'long been regarded as a model bilingual society' (Fieras and Elliot, 1992: 152) but it does not yet have a policy that adequately acknowledges the place of ESL learners in the multicultural and multilingual nature of education in major urban centres. While Canada has a national multiculturalism policy, being the first country to have a multiculturalism law, and a national bilingual policy, with internationally respected work in French immersion, and in programmes for adult ESL learners, there is no national responsibility for the education of ESL learners in schools. As our historical review shows, because K–12 education is a provincial responsibility, but immigration is a federal responsibility, there has always been opportunity to argue that the education of immigrant ESL school learners is someone else's responsibility. This reinforces tendencies to overlook ESL school learners in educational policy and planning. It is therefore hardly surprising that there has been an inadequate government response.

Along with tendencies to overlook ESL school learners in public policy there are negative public perceptions which are not supportive of ESL learners or mainstreaming initiatives. These negative perceptions view the needs of ESL learners as an unnecessary burden on school finances and as part of a zero-sum game which takes away from the needs of students who are native speakers of English. When these perceptions are given weight, mainstreaming initiatives (and, in fact, programmes for ESL learners in general) are very vulnerable to budget cuts and re-prioritisation of funds. Years of cumulative institutional and professional progress may also be lost in the process, as recent experience in Vancouver, England and Australia would testify.

At least one recent Canadian policy recommendation appears to reflect such negative perceptions. *Not Just Numbers* (Davis et al., 1997: 45), an important advisory review submitted to the Canadian Minister of Immigration, provides an instance in its Recommendation 35 that immigrants who are 6 years or older should be required to pay the cost of their language training. The recommendation was abandoned after stormy public debate, and we would argue that language training in English or French is a fundamental democratic right of all Canadians (including new Canadians), based on Section 23 of the Canadian Constitution Act. But given the considerable public support it attracted, we wish to draw attention to the way in which the financial assumptions behind this recommendation stress the short-term costs of immigrants, ignore any gains, and fail to take a comprehensive view of the full costs of education over a school career. Take the case of an immigrant ESL child entering school in Vancouver in the second grade. It is true that the cost of a typical three years of ESL support is not negligible, but that cost is considerably less than the saving of the cost of the first year of the child's education. For older immigrant children entering with more years of schooling, the saving is correspondingly more. (In 1997 the province of British Columbia funded Vancouver (an extra) $955 per ESL student per year for ESL support, in addition to the funding that every student gets. So the cost of three years of ESL support is $2,865. In Vancouver in 1997, the average per pupil cost of education was approximately $5,800 per year.) Recommendation 35 is symptomatic of a narrow view that affects a wide range of issues.

In the case of England, the strong policy commitment to mainstreaming of ESL students has led to a curious and unwarranted complacency which has rendered ESL 'invisible'. Perhaps one of the most obvious signs of ESL issues being at the periphery of policy concerns is the fact that almost invariably new educational policies tend to have little regard for the language learning needs of second language students or to treat ESL issues as an afterthought. For instance, the current policy drive to raise the standards of literacy in primary schools, under the aegis of the National Literacy Strategy, is a case in point. The official framework of teaching (DfEE, 1998a) provides a prescription of the teaching syllabus and methodology involved, which includes an emphasis on the rule or pattern-governed aspects of the written language system; it also assumes a native-speaker knowledge of spoken English and cultural meaning. There is very little doubt that this notion of literacy has been conceptualised with the native-speaking child in mind and this is directly acknowledged when a policy document addresses the position of ESL students:

> The issues covered in this report have implications for the teaching of bilingual pupils who are not . . . an homogeneous group . . . For bilingual learners, fluent literacy in English takes time to learn . . . Children who have arrived recently from abroad may need longer to reach the target . . .   (DfEE, 1997a: 34)

Even so, the report goes on to assert confidently that 'we believe that our overall proposals will facilitate their acquisition of literacy' (op. cit.: 34). The point here is not that ESL students will necessarily be excluded from the benefits of such an approach to literacy but that its appropriateness is simply asserted without any supporting evidence or additional ESL curriculum provision. This is quite clearly a case of a strongly constructed and privileged discipline claiming generalised curriculum relevance and, by implication, displacing a weakly constructed one.[1]

The fringe status of ESL has also led to some self-referencing circular reasoning which downplays the need for separate and additional curricular provision; for instance, an official report on the current practice in assessing the language development of linguistic minority students argues that:

> The advent of the National Curriculum introduced a common assessment programme for all pupils, including bilinguals, through which their language competence could be mapped using the NC English levels. This has called into question the need for the continued use of the pre-existing language [ESL] scales rather than relying upon the NC English levels.   (OFSTED, 1997: 2)

This is clearly a case of policy relevance by proclamation.

The experience in Australia suggests that although progressive pedagogies, such as curriculum negotiation, process writing, whole language, natural learning and cooperative learning, appear to be more inclusive, their 'invisibility' (Bernstein, 1990) and focus on student-centred individual learning and participation may have created more and different barriers for ESL learners than traditional transmissional teaching approaches. However, a visible pedagogy does not necessitate a return to parsing and traditional grammatical exercises.

Systemic educational reform is needed, and the mainstreaming of ESL learners should be part of a more comprehensive vision which, at the least, should address the issues of culture and language relations, language as a medium of learning, and the coordination of general reforms with ESL reforms.

A more comprehensive vision needs to take greater account of the relations between culture and language, and between multiculturalism and multilingualism. It has been widely recognised (e.g. August et al., 1994) that the pursuit of greater competence in foreign language at a national level begins with a recognition that ESL learners represent an unmatched resource. For instance, two-way bilingual programmes (Christian, 1996), where students learn each other's language, provide a clear example of the coordination of ESL programmes with modern language programmes with mutual benefits for students of each language. Correspondingly, it needs to be more widely recognised that ESL learners similarly represent an unmatched resource in any form of multicultural education that aims to improve intercultural sharing, understanding and communication.

A more comprehensive vision needs to take greater account of 'language as a medium of learning', broadly conceived. We noted in the introduction how general educational reforms, responding to the growth of a 'knowledge-based' economy and the need for 'symbol-analysis' skills, asked schools to prepare students to read and write at a sophisticated level, to think critically, to solve problems, and to work collaboratively. There is general recognition that this change requires the development of higher literacy, but there is not yet sufficient awareness of the connections between communication, reasoning, teamwork and language development, or between learning language and language as a medium of learning.

Earlier, educators were more prepared to accept a simplistic view that saw a deep division between ESL students who were acquiring a language and native-speaker students who were acquiring an education. It is also unfortunate that some discussions of language and content integration have taken a limited second language specialist perspective which sees content merely as a means of maintaining student interest, and has given little recognition of common elements that might be shared between language and particular disciplines, or across the curriculum as a whole. Now there is more recognition of areas of common ground: that, differences notwithstanding, both ESL learners and native speakers are learning language for academic purposes, and both groups are using language to learn.

One example of the coordination of ESL work with discourse development in the English programme for native speakers is provided by the Disadvantaged Schools Research Program (Veel, 1998) which was developed in a group of inner city schools in Sydney, Australia, with a mixed population of ESL learners and native speakers. Here the focus of the writing programme was on the genres that were required for literacy in school, and the language features that characterise them. This focus is of great value to both ESL learners and native speakers, but one that is, as the Sydney researchers point out, detrimentally underplayed in language development for native speakers of English in many school systems. Here is a case where the needs of ESL learners draw attention to a fundamental problem of the education system as a whole.

Other cross-curriculum movements relating learning and discourse have a similar potential for common cooperation: examples include Reading in the Content Areas, Cooperative Learning, visual representations for critical thinking (Hyerle, 1996), and the educational development of computers as information organisers and multimedia devices. The 'knowledge structure' approach described in the Vancouver chapters was developed in the belief that there were convergences between movements such as these and that these convergences could be mutually strengthened through their connections with discourse and language. The approach is, of course, to be taken not as a terminus but as a starting point, an attempt to point to some connections and convergences that could serve as a basis for future exploration. The chapters on Victoria and England have similarly indicated the need to find ways of integrating and coordinating mainstream curriculum and ESL pedagogy urgently, even though differences in the educational environment and curriculum developments in these places have led to a set of different arguments.

A more comprehensive vision also needs to coordinate general reforms and reforms for ESL learners. Reforms which overlook ESL learners are unacceptable. It is difficult to see how general reforms of education can succeed in urban school systems with large numbers of ESL learners if general reforms are not coordinated with changes to address the needs of ESL learners. Any general reform intended to raise educational achievement is likely to be significantly and negatively affected by educational underachievement on the part of ESL learners. Similarly, ESL reforms need to be coordinated with general reforms in order to be fully effective. Tikunoff et al. (1991) studied the significant features of exemplary programmes for ESL learners that used English as the primary medium of instruction. The study found that programmes were notable for the extent to which they were integrated with the whole-school programme. Berman et al. (1995) identified eight schools in the USA that have created exemplary learning environments for LEP students. A major feature of each exemplary school was significant whole-school restructuring that included innovative methods of organising teaching, governance, and usage of time. These schools also exhibited high-quality language, arts, mathematics, science, and English language acquisition programming for LEP students. Commenting on these studies, Anstrom and Kindler (1996) remind us that although it is important to identify what is and what is not effective programming for language minority students, it is also imperative to have an understanding of the effective implementation of such programming within the context of whole-school educational reform.

Our experience of working with teachers in Australia, England and Canada, both mainstream 'content' teachers and ESL specialists, suggests that effective ESL pedagogy built on a clear concern for content learning and communication skills is beneficial for ESL and native-speaking English students alike. Readers will recall that the large-scale Vancouver implementation initiative described in the Canadian section was not limited to ESL teachers, but had school teams that included mainstream teachers with expertise in social studies, science and computers as well as an administrator. Similarly, many of the classrooms which the initiative reached were not second language classrooms consisting solely of ESL students but were mainstream classrooms with a 'content' teacher and a mixture of ESL learners and English-speaking students. Teachers frequently remarked that the teaching strategies discussed in the initiative applied generally and were not only of value to ESL learners. Thus, while the initiative was not directed at whole-school educational reform, it was not restricted to ESL learners and ESL teachers, and indeed it is hard to see how any initiative directed at mainstream urban classrooms could be restricted in that way. In sum, it is desirable to coordinate and harmonise whole-school reforms and ESL reforms if both are to succeed, particularly in view of the mix of students in the mainstream urban classroom and the long-term commitment that these complex changes require.

NOTE

1. There is now some official supplementary in-service training material on ethnic monitoring and inclusive teaching strategies designed to enable teachers to work more effectively with ESL students within the National Literacy Strategy teaching programme (DfEE, 1999d). This attempt to assist teachers is to be welcomed but it does not address the issues raised here.

References

Adamson, H. (1993) *Academic competence.* New York: Longman.

Aird, E. and Lippmann, D. (eds) (1983) *English is their right: strategies for teachers in the multilingual classroom.* Melbourne: AE Press.

Allen, J. and Widdowson, H. (1974) *English in physical science.* London: Oxford University Press.

Allwright, D. and Bailey, K.M. (1991) *Focus on the language classroom.* Cambridge: Cambridge University Press.

Anastos, J. and Arcowitz, R. (1987) A teacher-directed peer coaching project. *Educational Leadership,* **45** (3).

Anstrom, K. and Kindler, A. (1996) *Federal policy, legislation, and education reform: the promise and the challenge for language minority students* (NCBE Resource Collection Series No. 5). Washington DC: National Clearinghouse for Bilingual Education. (website: www.ncbc.gwu.edu)

Arkoudis, S. (1995) *Clash of cultures: mainstream teachers' working knowledge and English as a second language (ESL) pedagogy.* Unpublished MEd Minor Thesis, University of Melbourne.

Ashworth, M. (1975) *Immigrant children and Canadian schools.* Toronto: McClelland & Stewart.

Ashworth, M. (1988) *Blessed with bilingual brains: education of immigrant children with English as a second language.* Vancouver: Pacific Press, University of British Columbia.

Ashworth, M. (1992) *The first step on the longer path: becoming an ESL teacher.* Markham, Ontario: Pippin Publishing.

Ashworth, M. (1993) *Children of the Canadian mosaic: a brief history to 1950.* Toronto: OISE Press.

Ashworth, M. (1997) *Report on the external evaluation of the Victoria School Board's ESL/ESD program.* Victoria: Victoria School Board.

Ashworth, M., Cummins, J. and Handscombe, J. (1989) *Report of the external review team on the Vancouver School Board's ESL programs.* Vancouver: Vancouver School Board.

Ashworth, M. and Wakefield, H.P. (1994) *Teaching the world's children: ESL for ages three to seven.* Markham, Ontario: Pippin Publishing.

August, D. and Hakuta, K. (eds) (1997) *Improving schooling for language-minority children: a research agenda.* Washington, DC: National Academy Press.

August, D., Hakuta, K. and Pompa, D. (1994) *For all students: Limited English proficient students and goals 2000* (NCBE FOCUS: Occasional Papers in Bilingual Education, No. 10). Washington, DC: National Clearinghouse for Bilingual Education. (website: www.ncbc.gwu.edu)

Australian Ethnic Affairs Council (AEAC) (1977) *Australia as a multicultural society* (Submission to the Australian Population and Immigration Council on the Green Paper: Immigration Policies and Australia's Population). Canberra: Australian Government Printing Service.

Australian Language and Literacy Council (1995) *Teacher education in English language and literacy*, Canberra: Australian Government Printing Service.

Bachman, L. (1990) *Fundamental considerations in language testing.* Oxford: Oxford University Press.

Bangs, J. (1994) Funding for race equality in education: looking for the future. *Multicultural Teaching*, **13** (1): 7–9, 13.

Barlow, A. (1985) A voice from the mainstream. In M. Poole, P. de Lacey & B. Randhawa (eds) *Australia in transition: culture and life possibilities.* Sydney: Harcourt Brace Jovanovich, pp. 184–5.

Barnes, D. (1976) *From language to communication.* Harmondsworth: Penguin.

Barrs, M., Ellis, S., Hestor, H. and Thomas, A. (1990) *Patterns of learning: the primary language record and the National Curriculum.* London: Centre for Language in Primary Education.

Bates, I. (1995) The competence movement: conceptualising recent research. *Studies in Science Education*, **25**: 39–68.

BC Ministry of Education (1981) *English as a second language/dialect resource book for K-12.* Victoria, BC: Ministry of Education.

BC Ministry of Education (1986) *ESL resource book, Volumes I and II.* Victoria, BC: Ministry of Education.

BC Ministry of Education (1993) *Implementation guide for heritage languages in British Columbia.* Victoria, BC: Heritage Language Consortium.

BC Provincial Ministry Responsible for Multiculturalism and Immigration (1991) *Settlement services for immigrant children: a needs assessment.* Victoria, BC: Provincial Ministry.

Beazley, K. (1992) *Teaching counts: a ministerial statement.* Canberra: Australian Government Printing Service.

Benesch, S. (1993) ESL, ideology and the politics of pragmatism. *TESOL Quarterly*, **27** (4): 705–16.

Berman, P. et al. (1995) *School reform and student diversity: case studies of exemplary practices for LEP students.* Santa Cruz, CA: National Center for Research on Cultural Diversity and Second Language Learning.

Bernstein, B. (1990) *The structuring of pedagogic discourse: class, codes and control* (Vol. 4). London: Routledge.

Bernstein, B. (1996) *Pedagogy, symbolic control and identity.* London: Taylor & Francis.

Black, N.F. (1913) Western Canada's greatest problem: the transformation of aliens into citizens. *The Western School Journal*, **9** (5): 3.

Blair, M. and Bourne, J. (1998) *Making a difference: teaching and learning strategies in successful multi-ethnic schools.* Norwich: Dept for Education and Employment.

Board of Studies (1995) *Issues and options for VCE English: report of the VCE English Review Panel to the Board of Studies.* Melbourne: Board of Studies.

Board of Studies (1996) *The ESL companion to the English Curriculum and standards framework.* Melbourne: Board of Studies.

Board of Studies (2000) *The ESL companion to the English Curriculum and standards framework.* Melbourne: Board of Studies Second edition.

Bourdieu, P. (1991) *Language and symbolic power.* London: Polity Press.

Bourne, J. (1989) *Moving into the mainstream.* LEA provision for bilingual pupils. Windsor, Berkshire: NFER-Nelson.

Bourne, J. (1997) The continuing revolution: teaching as learning in the mainstream multilingual classroom. In C. Leung and C. Cable (eds) *English as an additional language: changing perspectives.* Watford: NALDIC, pp. 77–88.

Bourne J. and Cameron, D. (1996) Disciplining English: the construction of a national subject. In P. Woods (ed.) *Contemporary issues in teaching and learning.* London: Routledge, pp. 10–19.

Bourne, J. and McPake, J. (1991) *Partnership teaching: co-operative teaching strategies for English language support in multilingual classrooms.* London: HMSO.

Branson, J. and Miller, D. (1993) Sign language, the deaf and the epistemic violence of mainstreaming. *Language and Education,* **7** (1): 21–42.

Breen, M., Barratt-Pugh, C., Derewianka, B., House, H., Hudson, C., Lumley, T. and Rohl, M. (eds) (1997) *Profiling ESL children: how teachers interpret and use National and State assessment frameworks.* Canberra: DEETYA.

Brinton, D., Snow, M. and Wesche, M. (1989) *Content-based language instruction.* Philadelphia: Newbury House.

Britton, J. (1970) *Language and learning.* Harmondsworth: Penguin.

Britton, J. (1975) *The development of writing abilities.* London: Macmillan.

Britton, J. (1979) *Language and learning.* Harmondsworth: Penguin.

Bruner, J. (1983) *Child's talk: learning to use language.* London: Oxford University Press.

Bullock, A. (1975) *A language for life.* London: HMSO.

Burns, A. (1992) Teacher beliefs and their influence on classroom practice. *Prospect,* **7** (3): 56–65.

Calderhead, J. (1991) *Reflective teaching and professional development* (Unpublished seminar paper). Schools Program Division, Ministry of Education and Training, Victoria.

Callaghan, M. and Knapp, P. (1989) *The discussion genre.* Sydney: Metropolitan East Disadvantaged Schools Program.

Callan, V. (1986) *Australian minority groups.* Sydney: Harcourt Brace Jovanovich.

Cambourne, B. (1986) Process writing and non-English speaking background children. *Australian Journal of Reading,* **9** (3): 126–38.

Cambourne, B. (1988) *The whole story.* Auckland: Ashton Scholastic.

Cameron, L. and Bygate, M. (1997) Key issues in assessing progression in English as an additional language. In C. Leung and C. Cable (eds) *English as an additional language: changing perspective.* Watford: NALDIC, pp. 40–52.

Campbell, W.J. and McMeniman, M. (1985) *Bridging the language gap: ideals and realities pertaining to learning English as a second language (ESL).* Canberra: Commonwealth Schools Commission.

Campbell, W., Barnett, J., Joy, B. and McMeniman, M. (1984) *A review of the Commonwealth's English-as-a-second-language (ESL) program.* Canberra: Commonwealth Schools Commission.

Canadian School Boards' Association (1989) *Scholastic adaptation and cost effectiveness of programs for immigrant/refugee children in Canadian schools.* Ottawa: Canadian School Boards' Association.

Canale, M. and Swain, M. (1980) Theoretical bases of communicative approaches to second language teaching and testing. *Applied Linguistics,* **1** (1): 1–47.

Candlin, C.N. (1987) Towards task-based language learning. In C.N. Candlin and

D.F. Murphy (eds) *Language learning tasks.* London: Prentice-Hall International, pp. 5–22.

Cantoni-Harvey, G. (1987) *Content area language instruction.* Reading, MA: Addison Wesley.

Carrasquillo, A.L. and Rodriguez, V. (1995) *Language minority students in the mainstream classroom.* Clevedon: Multilingual Matters.

Carrell, P.L. and Eisterhold, J.C. (1987) Schema theory and ESL reading pedagogy. In M.H. Long and J.C. Richards (eds) *Methodology in TESOL.* Boston, MA: Heinle & Heinle, pp. 218–32.

Carrell, P.L. (1988) SLA and classroom instruction: reading. *Annual Review of Applied Linguistics,* **9**: 223–42.

Carrell, P.L., Devine, J. and Eskey, D.E. (eds) (1988) *Interactive approaches to reading.* New York: Cambridge University Press.

Castles, S., Kalantzis, M. and Cope, B. (1986) The end of multiculturalism? *Australian Society,* October.

Cazden, C. (1988) *Classroom discourse.* Portsmouth: Heinemann.

Chamot, A. and O'Malley, M. (1992) The cognitive academic language learning approach: a bridge to the mainstream. In P. Richard-Amato and M.A. Snow (eds) *The multicultural classroom: readings for content area teachers.* New York: Longman, pp. 39–57.

Chamot, A. and O'Malley, M. (1994) *The CALLA handbook.* Reading, MA: Addison Wesley.

Chaudron, C. (1988) *Second language classrooms.* Cambridge: Cambridge University Press.

Christian, D. (1995) *Program in immigrant education* (booklet) Washington, DC: Center for Applied Linguistics.

Christian, D. (1996) Language development in two-way immersion: trends and prospects. In James E. Alatis (ed.) *Georgetown University round table 1996.* Washington, DC: Georgetown University Press.

Christie, F. (1987a) Genres as choice. In I. Reid (ed.) *The place of genres in learning: current debates.* Geelong: Centre for Studies in Literary Education, Deakin University, pp. 22–34.

Christie, F. (1987b) The morning news genre. *Language in Education,* **4** (3): 161–79.

Christie, F. (1987c) Young children's writing: from spoken to written genres. *Language and Education,* **1** (1): 3–13.

Christie, F., Freebody, P., Devlin, A., Luke, A., Martin, J., Threadgold, T. and Walton, C. (eds) (1991) *Teaching English literacy: a project of national significance on the preservice preparation of teachers for teaching English literacy* (Vol. 3). Darwin: Centre for Studies of Language in Education, Northern Territory University.

Christie F., Gray, P., Gray, B., Macken, M., Martin, J. and Rothery, J. (1990–1991) *Language as a resource for meaning: reports, procedures, and explanations.* Sydney: Harcourt Brace Jovanovich.

Christie, F., Gray, B., Gray, P., Macken, M., Martin, J. and Rothery, J. (1992) *Exploring explanations: teachers' book, Levels 1–4.* Sydney: Harcourt Brace Jovanovich.

Christie, F. and Rothery, J. (1989) Exploring the written mode and range of factual genres. In *Writing in schools: study guide.* Geelong, Victoria: Deakin University, pp. 49–90.

Cleland, B. and Evans, R. (1984) *ESL topic books: learning English through general science.* Melbourne: Longman.

Cleland, B. and Evans, R. (1985) *ESL topic books: learning English through topics about Australia.* Melbourne: Longman.

Cleland, B. and Evans, R. (1988) *ESL topic books: learning English through topics about Asia.* Melbourne: Longman.

Cline, T. and Frederickson, N. (eds) (1996) *Progress in curriculum related assessment with bilingual pupils.* Cleveland: Multilingual Matters.

Coelho, E. (1992) Co-operative learning: foundation for a communicative curriculum. In C. Kessler (ed.) *Cooperative language learning.* New Jersey: Prentice Hall, pp. 31–49.

Collier, V.P. (1995a) *Promoting academic success for ESL students.* New Jersey: New Jersey Teachers of English to Speakers of Other Languages – Bilingual Educators (NJ TESOL-BE).

Collier, V. (1995b) Acquiring a second language for school. *Directions in Language and Education. National Clearing House of Bilingual Education,* **1** (4): entire issue.

Collier, V. (1987) Age and rate of acquisition of second language for academic purposes. *TESOL Quarterly,* **21** (3): 617–41.

Collier, V. (1989) How long? A synthesis of research on academic achievement in a second language. *TESOL Quarterly,* **21** (4): 509–31.

Collier, V.P. (1987) Age and rate of acquisition of second language for academic purposes. *TESOL Quarterly,* **21**: 617–41.

Collins, C. (1991) Teacher development: achievements and challenges. In P. Hughes (ed.) *Teachers' professional development.* Melbourne: Australian Council of Educational Research, pp. 10–24.

Commonwealth Department of Education (1967) *Situational English.* Canberra: Australian Government Printing Service.

Commonwealth Schools Commission (CSC) (1975) *Report for the Triennium 1976–1978.* Canberra: Australian Government Printing Service.

Commonwealth Schools Commission (CSC) (1979) *Education for a Multicultural Society.* Report by the Committee on Multicultural Education, Canberra.

Commonwealth Schools Commission (CSC) (1981) *Report for the Triennium 1982–1985.* Canberra: Australian Government Printing Service.

Connors, R.D. (1987) *Teacher rating of professional development needs: Implications for decision-making at the individual and system level.* Paper presented at the First Joint AARE/NZARE Conference, Christchurch, New Zealand.

Connors, R.D. (1991) Teacher development and the teacher. In P. Hughes (ed.) *Teachers' professional development.* Melbourne: Australian Council of Educational Research, pp. 53–81.

Cope, W. and Kalantzis, M. (1993) *The powers of literacy: a genre approach to teaching writing.* London: Falmer Press.

Corbel, C. (1986) *Using the system.* Melbourne: AE Press.

Costello, R. (1991) Government policy for the future development of teachers. In P. Hughes (ed.) *Teachers' professional development.* Melbourne: Australian Council of Educational Research, pp. 129–46.

Cox, D. (1976) Pluralism in Australia. *The Australian and New Zealand Journal of Sociology,* **12** (2).

Crandall, J. (1987) *ESL through content-area instruction.* Englewood Cliffs, NJ: Prentice-Hall Regents.

Crandall, J. and Tucker, R. (1989) *Content-based language instruction in second and foreign languages.* Paper presented at the RELC Regional Seminar: Language Teaching Methodology for the Nineties, Singapore.

Crandall, J., Spanos, G., Christian, D., Simich-Dudgeon, C. and Willetts, K. (1987)

Integrating language and content instruction for language minority students. National Clearing House for Bilingual Education.

CRE (1986) *Teaching English as a second language* (The Calderdale Report). London: Commission for Racial Equality.

Crookes, G. (1986) *Task classification: A cross-disciplinary review.* Centre for Second Language Classroom Research, Social Science Research Institute, University of Hawaii; cited in B. Kumaravadivelu (1993).

Crookes, G. and Gass, S.M. (eds) (1993) *Tasks and language learning.* Clevedon: Multilingual Matters.

Crookes, G. and Gass, S.M. (eds) (1993) *Tasks in a pedagogical context.* Clevedon: Multilingual Matters.

Crowhurst, M. (1994) *Language and learning across the curriculum.* Scarborough, Ont.: Prentice-Hall, Canada.

Cuban, L. (1986) *Teachers and machines: the classroom use of technology since 1920.* New York: Teachers College Press.

Cumming, A. (1989) Student teachers' conceptions of curriculum: towards an understanding of language teacher development. *TESL Canada Journal,* **7** (1): 33–51.

Cumming, A. (1995) *A review of ESL services in the Vancouver School Board.* Vancouver: Vancouver School Board.

Cummins, J. (1980) The cross-lingual dimensions of language proficiency: implications for bilingual education and the optimal age issue. *TESOL Quarterly,* **14** (1): 175–87.

Cummins, J. (1984) *Bilingualism and special education: issues on assessment and pedagogy.* Clevedon: Multilingual Matters.

Cummins, J. (1988) From multiculturalism to anti-racist education: an analysis of programmes and policies in Ontario. In T. Skutnabb and J. Cummins (eds) *Minority education: from shame to struggle.* Clevedon, Philadelphia: Multilingual Matters.

Cummins, J. (1991) Conversational and academic language proficiency in bilingual contexts. In J. Hulstijn and J. Matter (eds) *Reading in two languages. AILA Review,* **8**: 75–89.

Cummins, J. (1992) Language proficiency, bilingualism and academic achievement. In P.A. Richard-Amato and M.A. Snow (eds) *The multicultural classroom.* New York: Longman, pp. 16–26.

Cummins, J. (1993) Bilingualism and second language learning. In W. Grabe (ed.) *Annual review of applied linguistics* (Vol. 13). Cambridge: Cambridge University Press, pp. 51–70.

Cummins, J. (1996) *Negotiating identities: education for empowerment in a diverse society.* Ontario, CA: California Association for Bilingual Education.

Cummins, J. and Swain, M. (1986) *Bilingualism in education.* New York: Longman.

Curriculum Corporation (1995) *ESL scales.* Melbourne: Curriculum Corporation.

Davidov, V.V. (1995) The Influence of L.S. Vygotsky on education theory, research and practice. *Educational Researcher,* **24** (3): 12–21.

Davies, A., Grove, E. and Wilkes, M. (1997) Review of literature on acquiring literacy in a second language. In P. McKay, A. Davies, B. Devlin, J. Clayton, R. Oliver and S. Zammit (principal researchers) *The bilingual interface project report.* Canberra, Australia: Department of Employment, Education, Training and Youth Affairs, pp. 17–74.

Davis, S., Kunin, R. and Trempe, R. (1997) *Not just numbers.* Ottawa: Minister of Public Works and Government Services Canada.

Davison, C. (1992) Look out! Eight fatal flaws in team and support teaching. *TESOL in Context*, **2** (1): 39–41.

Davison, C. (1993a) Integrating ESL into the mainstream: Australian perspectives. *Multicultural Teaching*, **12** (3): 35–40.

Davison, C. (1993b) *Language and content: Have you got the right balance?* Paper presented at the VATME Miniconference: TESOL, LOTE and Multicultural Education; Enduring and Improving, Footscray College of TAFE.

DEET (1988) *Teachers' learning: improving Australian schools through inservice teacher training and development. Report of Inservice Teacher Education Project.* Department of Employment, Education and Training, Canberra: Australian Government Publishing Service.

DEET (1991) *Australia's language: the Australian language and literacy policy.* Department of Employment Education and Training, Canberra: Australian Government Publishing Service.

Dempsey, J. (1994) *Collaborative planning to integrate language and content; a case study.* Unpublished masters thesis, University of British Columbia, Vancouver, BC.

Department of Education (1975) *Report of the inquiry into schools of high migrant density.* Canberra: Department of Education.

Department of Education (Victoria) (1997) *The ESL report 1996.* Melbourne: LOTE, ESL and Multicultural Education Branch, Department of Education.

Derewianka, B. (1991) *Exploring how texts work.* Sydney: Primary English Teaching Association.

Derewianka, B. and Hammond, J. (1991) The pre-service preparation of teachers of students of non-English speaking background. In F. Christie, P. Freebody, A. Devlin, A. Luke, J. Martin, T. Threadgold and C. Walton (eds) *Teaching English literacy: a project of national significance on the preservice preparation of teachers for teaching English literacy* (Vol. 3). Darwin: Centre for Studies of Language in Education, Northern Territory University, pp. 28–68.

Derrick, J. (1977) *Language needs of minority group children.* Slough: NFER.

Derry, S. (1989) Putting learning strategies to work. *Educational Leadership,* January: 4–10.

DES (1965) *The education of immigrants* (Circular 7/65). Department of Education and Science, London: HMSO.

DES (1967) *Children and their primary schools: a report of the Central Advisory Council for Education* (Plowden Report). Department of Education and Science, London: HMSO.

DES (1971) *The education of immigrants. Education Survey 13.* Department of Education and Science, London: HMSO.

DES (1972) *The continuing needs of immigrants. Education Survey 14.* Department of Education and Science, London: HMSO.

DES (1975) *A language for life* (Bullock Report). Department of Education and Science, London: HMSO.

DES (1985a) *Better schools.* London: HMSO.

DES (1985b) *Education for all: the report of the committee of inquiry into the education of children from ethnic minority groups* (Swann Report). Department of Education and Science, London: HMSO.

DES (1988) *A survey of the teaching of English as a second language in six LEAs.* Department of Education and Science, London: HMSO.

DES (1989) *English for ages 5 to 16* (Cox Report). Department of Education and Science, London: HMSO.

Destino, T. (1996) *Juxtaposing 'language and content teaching' and 'second language science'.* TESOL conference presentation, Chicago.

DFE (1995a) *English in the National Curriculum.* Department for Education, London: HMSO.

DFE (1995b) *Geography in the National Curriculum.* Department for Education, London: HMSO.

DfEE (1997a) *The implementation of the National Literacy Strategy.* London: Department for Education and Employment.

DfEE (1997b) *Excellence in schools.* Department for Education and Employment, London: The Stationery Office Ltd.

DfEE (1997c) *Initial teacher training National Curriculum* (Circular 10/97). London: Department for Education and Employment.

DfEE (1998a) *The National Literacy Strategy: framework for teaching.* London: Department for Education and Employment.

DfEE (1998b) *Supplement to circular 13/98 the Standards Fund 1999–2000.* London: Department for Education and Employment.

DfEE (1998c) Teaching: high status, high standards (Circular 4/98). London: Department for Education and Employment.

DfEE (1999a) English: the National Curriculum for England. London: Department for Education and Employment.

DfEE (1999b) The Standards Fund 2000–2001 (Circular 16/99). London: Department for Education and Employment.

DfEE (1999c) Science: the National Curriculum for England. London: Department for Education and Employment.

DfEE (1999d) *The National Literacy Strategy: supporting pupils learning English as an additional language.* London: Department for Education and Employment.

Donato, R. (1994) Collective scaffolding in second language learning. In J.P. Lantolf and G. Appel (eds) *Vygotskian approaches to second language research.* New Jersey: Ablex Publishing Corporation, pp. 33–56.

Dörnyei, Z. (1998) Motivation in second and foreign language learning. *Language Teaching* **31**: 117–35. Doyle, M. and Reinhardt, J. (1992) The mainstreaming of ESL at Burwood Girls' High School. *TESOL in Context,* **2** (1): 35–9.

Doughty, C. (1991) Instruction does make a difference: the effects of instruction on the acquisition of relativisation in English as a second language. *Studies in Second Language Acquisition,* **13** (4): 431–69.

Doyle, W. (1983) Academic work. *Review of Educational Research,* **53** (2): 159–199.

Doyle, W. and Carter, K. (1984) Academic tasks in classroom. *Curriculum Enquiry,* **14** (2): 129–49.

Doyle, M. and Reinhardt, J. (1992) The mainstreaming of ESL at Burwood Girls' High School. *TESOL in Context,* **2** (1): 35–9.

Dulay, H., Burt, M. and Krashen, S. (1982) *Language two.* London: Oxford University Press.

Dunn, E. (1992) *Evaluation of the English as a second language pilot project.* Research Report 92–01, Student Assessment and Research, Vancouver School Board.

Early, M. (1989) Using key visuals to aid ESL students' comprehension. *Reading-Canada-Lecture,* **7** (4): 202–12.

Early, M. (1990) Enabling first and second language learners in the classroom. *Language Arts,* **67**: 567–75.

Early, M. (1991) Language and content learning, K-12: the Vancouver School Board Project. *Cross Currents,* **18**: 179–82.

Early, M. (1992) Aspects of becoming an academically successful ESL student. In

B. Burnaby and A. Cummings (eds) *Sociopolitical aspects of ESL in Canada*. Toronto: OISE Press, pp. 266–75.

Early, M. and Hooper, H. (in press) *ESL students in content classrooms: a task-based resource book*. Victoria, BC: Ministry of Education.

Early, M., Mohan, B.A. and Hooper, H.R. (1989) The Vancouver School Board language and content project. In J.H. Esling (ed.) *Multicultural education and policy: ESL in the 1990s*. Ontario: The Ontario Institute for Studies in Education, pp. 107–22.

Early, M. and Tang, G. (1991) Helping ESL students cope with content-based texts. *TESL Canada Journal*, **8** (2): 34–43.

Early, M., Thew, C. and Wakefield, P. (1986) *English as a second language. K-12: Resource book, Vol. 1*. Victoria, BC: Ministry of Education, British Columbia.

Education Department of South Australia (1991) *ESL in the mainstream, Workshops 1–5*. Adelaide, SA: Government Printer.

Edwards, V. and Redfern, A. (1992) *The world in a classroom: language in education in Britain and Canada*. Clevedon: Multilingual Matters.

Eisner, E. (1988) The ecology of school improvement. *Educational Leadership*, **45** (5): 24–9.

Elliot, J. (1993) Professional education and the idea of a practical educational science. In J. Elliot (ed.) *Reconstructing teacher education*. London: Falmer Press, pp. 65–85.

Ellis, R. (1994) *The study in second language acquisition*. London: Oxford University Press.

Enright, S. and McCloskey, M. (1988) *Integrating English: developing English language and literacy in the multilingual classroom*. Reading, MA: Addison-Wesley.

Eraut, M. (1986) Inservice teacher education. In M.J. Dunkin (ed.) *The international encyclopaedia of teaching and teacher education*. Oxford: Pergamon Press, pp. 730–43.

Eraut, M. (1994) *Developing professional knowledge and competence*. London: Falmer Press.

Erickson, F. (1987) Transformation and school success: the politics and culture of educational achievement. *Anthropology and Education Quarterly*, **18**: 335–56.

Eurocities (1994) *DIECEC Project: cooperation between cities in the field of intercultural education: final evaluation report*. Brussels: Eurocities.

European Commission (1994) *Report on the education of migrants' children in the European Union*. Luxembourg: Office for Official Publications of the European Communities.

Evans, M.A., Watson, C. and Willows, D.M. (1987) A naturalistic inquiry into illustration in instructional textbooks. In D.M. Willows and H.A. Houghton (eds) *The psychology of illustrations* (Vol. II). New York: Springer-Verlag.

Fenstermacher, G. and Berliner, D. (1985) Determining the value of staff development. *The Elementary School Journal*, **85** (3): 281–314.

Ferguson, T. (1991) What's so special about TESOL anyway? *TESOL in Context*, **1** (1): 5–7.

Fielding, N. (1983) Models of teacher development. *The Australian Journal of Teacher Education*, **8** (2): 10–21.

Fieras, A. and Elliot, J. (1992) *Multiculturalism in Canada*. Scarborough, Ontario: Nelson Canada.

Flaherty, L. and Woods, D. (1992) Immigrant refugee children in Canadian schools: educational issues, political dilemmas. In B. Burnaby and A. Cumming (eds) *Socio-political aspects of ESL*. Toronto: OISE Press, pp. 182–92.

Flanders, N.A. (1970) *Analyzing teaching behaviour*. Reading, MA: Addison-Wesley.

Foster, P. (1998) A classroom perspective on the negotiation of meaning. *Applied Linguistics*, **19** (1): 1–23.

Freedman, A. and Medway, P. (eds) (1994) *Genre and the new rhetoric*. London: Taylor & Francis.

Fullan, M. (1982) *The meaning of educational change*. Ontario Institute for Studies in Education. Toronto, Ontario: OISE Press.

Fullan, M. (1991) *The new meaning of educational change* (2nd edn). London: Cassell.

Fullan, M. (1993) *Changing forces: probing the depth of educational reform*. New York: Falmer Press.

Fullan, M. and Hargreaves, A. (1992) Teacher development and educational change. In M. Fullan and A. Hargreaves (eds) *Teacher development and educational change*. London: Falmer Press.

Galbally, F.C. (1978) *Report of the review of post arrival programs and services for migrants*. Canberra: Australian Government Printing Service.

Galton, M. et al. (1980) *Inside the primary classroom*. London: Routledge.

Gardiner, J. (1996) Recruits braced for the basics. *Times Educational Supplement*, 27 October.

Gaskell, P.J., Fleming, R., Fountain, R. and Ojelel, A. (1993) *British Columbia assessment of science 1991: technical report III: socioscientific component*. Victoria, BC: Queen's Printer for British Columbia.

Gattegno, C. (1972) *The common sense of teaching foreign languages*. New York: Educational Solutions.

Gattegno, C. (1976) *Teaching foreign languages in schools the Silent Way*. New York: Educational Solutions.

Gee, J. (1992) Socio-cultural approaches to literacy (Literacies). *Annual Review of Applied Linguistics*, **12**: 31–48.

Gibbons, P. (1998) Classroom talk and the learning of new registers in a second language. *Language and Education*, **12** (2): 99–118.

Gillborn, D. and Gipps, C. (1996) *Recent research on the achievement of ethnic minority pupils*. London: HMSO.

Gipps, C.V. (1994) *Beyond testing*. London: Falmer Press.

Golding, F. (1987) *Mainstreaming: a fourth phase*. Melbourne: Multicultural Education Services.

Gonczi, A. (1994) Competency based assessment in the professions in Australia. *Assessment in Education*, **1** (1): 27–44.

Goodlad, J. (1983) The school as workplace. In G. Giffin (ed.) *Staff development*. Chicago: University of Chicago Press.

Goodlad, J. (1984) *A place called school*. New York: McGraw-Hill.

Gregory, E. (1993) Sweet and sour: learning to read in a British and Chinese school. *English in Education*, **27** (3): 53–9.

Gregory, E. (1994) Cultural assumptions and early years' pedagogy: the effect of the home culture on minority children's interpretation of reading in school. *Language, Culture and Curriculum*, **7** (2): 111–23.

Gregory, E. (1996) *Making sense of a new world: learning to read in a second language*. London: Paul Chapman.

Halliday, M.A.K. (1973) *Exploration in the functions of language*. London: Edward Arnold.

Halliday, M.A.K. (1978) *Language as social semiotic: the social interpretation of meaning*. London: Edward Arnold.

Halliday, M.A.K. (1985) *An introduction to functional grammar*. London: Edward Arnold.

Halliday, M.A.K. (1986) Language and socialisation: home and school. In L. Gerot,

J. Oldenburg and T. Van Leeuwen (eds) *Proceedings from the Working Conference on Language in Education.* Macquarie University.

Halliday, M.A.K. (1994) *An introduction to functional grammar* (2nd edn). London: Edward Arnold.

Halliday, M.A.K. and Hasan, R. (1985) *Language context and text: aspects of language in a social-semiotic perspective.* Geelong: Deakin University Press.

Halliday, M.A.K. and Martin, J.R. (1993) *Writing science.* London: Falmer Press.

Hammond, J. (1987) An overview of the genre-based approach to the teaching of writing in Australia. *Australian Review of Applied Linguistics,* **10** (2): 163–81.

Hammond, J., Wickert, R., Burns, A., Joyce, H. and Miller, A. (1992) *The pedagogical relations between adult ESL and adult literacy.* Sydney: University of Technology.

Hampshire County Council (1996) *Bilingual learners' support service – service guidelines.* Hampshire County Council.

Hargreaves, A. (1992) Cultures of teaching: a focus for change. In A. Hargreaves and M.G. Fullan (eds) *Understanding teacher development.* Teacher College Press, pp. 219–42.

Hargreaves, D.H. (1993) A common sense model of the professional development of teachers. In J. Elliot (ed.) *Reconstructing teacher education.* London: Falmer Press, pp. 86–92.

Harklau, L. (1994) ESL versus mainstream classes: contrasting L2 learning environments. *TESOL Quarterly,* **28** (2): 241–72.

Harley, B., Allen, P., Cummins, J. and Swain, M. (eds) (1987) *The development of bilingual proficiency: social context and age* (Vol. 3). Toronto: Modern Languages Center, OISE.

Harris, R. (1979) Anglo-conformism, interactionism and cultural pluralism: a study of Australian attitudes to migrants. In P. de Lacey and M. Poole (eds) *Mosaic or melting pot?* Sydney: Harcourt Brace Jovanovich.

Harris, R. (1997) Romantic bilingualism? Time for a change? In C. Leung and C. Cable (eds) *English as an additional language: changing perspectives.* Watford: NALDIC, pp. 14–27.

Hawkes, N. (1966) *Immigrant children in British schools.* London: Pall Mall Press.

Hawkins, M. and Irujo, S. (1993) Paradoxes and perspectives. *TESOL Matters,* April–May: 13.

Helmer, S. (1995) *Joint work between ESL and subject area teachers: a case study at the secondary level.* Unpublished doctoral dissertation, University of British Columbia, Vancouver, BC.

Herber, H.L. (1970) *Teaching reading in content areas.* Englewood Cliffs, NJ: Prentice Hall.

Herriman, M. (1991) *An evaluative study of the Commonwealth ESL program.* Unpublished report for Department for Education and Training.

Ho, L. (1993) Language and content in context: towards a social ecology of language in immigrant education. *TESL Canada Review,* **10** (2): 31–54.

Hodge, R. and Kress, G. (1988) *Social semiotics.* Oxford: Polity Press/Basil Blackwell.

Hogan, S. (1994) *TESOL teacher competencies document.* Sydney: Association of TESOL NSW.

Holliday, W.G. (1975) What's in a picture? *The Science Teacher,* **42**: 21–2.

Hooper, H.R. (1988) *Computers and content-based language learning.* Unpublished masters thesis, University of British Columbia, Vancouver, BC.

Hooper, H.R. (1990) *A four year plan for Vancouver school board's ESL programs.* Implementation plan and presentation to Vancouver School Board Trustees, Vancouver, BC.

232   *References*

Hooper, H.R. (1996) Mainstream science with a majority of ESL learners: integrating language and content. In J. Clegg (ed.) *Mainstreaming ESL: case studies in integrating ESL students into the mainstream curriculum.* Clevedon: Multilingual Matters, pp. 217–36.

Hooper, H.R. and Hurren, P. (1992) *The Vancouver school board ESL pilot project.* Symposium presented at the 1992 TESOL Conference, Vancouver, BC.

Howatt, A. (1984) *A history of English language teaching.* Oxford: Oxford University Press.

Huang, J. (1991) *A knowledge framework approach to beginning Mandarin for elementary students.* University of British Columbia, Master's thesis.

Hunt, H., Miller, C. and Shaw, W. (1991) *Key visual dictionary.* Vancouver School Board, Lord Selkirk Elementary School.

Hunter, B., Crismore, A. and Pearson, P.D. (1987) Visual displays in basal readers and social studies textbooks. In D.M. Willows and H.A. Houghton (eds) *The psychology of illustration* (Vol. II). New York: Springer-Verlag, pp. 116–35.

Hurren, P. (1993) Exploring the collaborative planning model. *Emergency Librarian,* **20** (5; May/June): 8–12.

Hurren, P. (1994) How an ESL specialist and a classroom teacher collaboratively plan instruction which integrates language and content demands of tasks. MA thesis, University of British Columbia, Vancouver, Canada.

Hutchinson, T. and Waters, A. (1987) *English for specific purposes: a learning-centred approach.* Cambridge: Cambridge University Press.

Hyerle, D. (1996) *Visual tools for constructing knowledge.* Alexandria, Virginia: Association for Supervision and Curriculum Development.

Hymes, D. (1972) On communicative competence. In J.B. Pride and J. Holmes (eds) *Sociolinguistics.* London: Penguin.

Hymes, D. (1974) *Foundations in sociolinguistics.* Philadelphia: University of Philadelphia Press.

Ingvarson, L. and MacKenzie, D. (1988) Factors affecting the impact of inservice courses for teachers: implications for policy. *Teaching and Teacher Education,* **4** (2): 139–55.

Jakubowicz, A. (1984) *Education and ethnic minorities: issues of participation and equity. Discussion Paper No. 1.* Canberra: NACCME.

Jakubowicz, A. (1985) Ethnic affairs policy in Australia: the failure of multiculturalism. In M. Poole, P. de Lacey & B. Randhawa (eds) *Australia in transition: culture and life possibilities.* Sydney: Harcourt Brace Jovanovich, pp. 271–8.

Janks, H. and Paton, J. (1990) English and the teaching of literature in South Africa. In B.J. Janks and H. Janks (eds) *Teaching and learning English worldwide.* Clevedon: Multilingual Matters.

Jayasurija, L. (1984) Ethnicity and equality. *Education News,* **18** (11): 42–3.

Johnston, J. & Johnston, M. (1990a) *Content points A: science, mathematics and social studies activities.* Reading, MA: Addison-Wesley.

Johnston, J. & Johnston, M. (1990b) *Content points B: science, mathematics and social studies activities.* Reading, MA: Addison-Wesley.

Johnston, J. & Johnston, M. (1990c) *Content points C: science, mathematics and social studies activities.* Reading, MA: Addison-Wesley.

Johnston, J. & Johnston, M. (1990d) *Content points D: science, mathematics and social studies activities.* Reading, MA: Addison-Wesley.

Joint Review of Teacher Education (1986) *Improving Teacher Education.* Canberra: Commonwealth Tertiary Education Commission and Commonwealth Schools Commission.

Jones, L. and Moore, R. (1993) Education, competence and the control of expertise. *British Journal of the Sociology of Education*, **14** (4): 385–97.

Jones, L. and Moore, R. (1995) Appropriating competence: the competency movement, the New Right and the 'culture change' project. *British Journal of Education and Work*, **8** (2): 78–92.

Joyce, B. (1986) *Improving America's schools*. New York: Longman.

Kagan, S. (1990) *Cooperative learning: Resources for teachers*. University of California, Riverside.

Karmel, P. (1985) *Quality of Education in Australia: Report of the Review Committee*. Canberra: Australia Government Printing Office.

Kay, A. (1991) The ESL in the mainstream. *TESOL in Context*, **1** (1): 7–10.

Kennedy, P. (1993) *Preparing for the twenty-first century*. New York: HarperCollins.

Knapp, P. and Watkins, M. (1994) *Context, text, grammar. Teaching the genre and grammar*. Broadway, NSW: Text Productions.

Knight, T. (1977) The migrant and the remedial child: are they necessarily one and the same? *Polycom*, **15**: 18–28.

Krahnke, K. (1987) *Approaches to syllabus design for foreign language teaching*. Washington, DC: Center for Applied Linguistics.

Kramsch, C. (1993) *Context and culture in language teaching*. Oxford: Oxford University Press.

Krashen, S. (1985) *The input hypothesis*. New York: Longman.

Krashen, S. (1993) The effect of formal grammar teaching: still peripheral. *TESOL Quarterly*, **27** (4): 722–5.

Krashen, S. and Terrel, T. (1983) *The natural approach*. Oxford: Pergamon Press.

Kress, G. and van Leeuwen, T. (1996) *Reading images: the grammar of visual design*. London: Routledge.

Kuhn, T.S. (1962/70) *The structure of scientific revolutions*. Chicago: University of Chicago Press.

Kumaravadivelu, B. (1993) The name of the task and the task of naming: methodological aspects of task-based pedagogy. In G. Crookes and S.H. Gass (eds) *Tasks in a pedagogical context*. Clevedon: Multilingual Matters, pp. 69–96.

Langer, J. and Applebee, A. (1987) *How writing shapes thinking*. Urbana, IL: National Council of Teachers of English.

Lantolf, J.P. and Appel, G. (1994) Theoretical framework: an introduction to Vygotskian perspective on second language research. In J.P. Lantolf and G. Appel (eds) *Vygotskian approaches to second language research*. New Jersey: Ablex Publishing Corporation, pp. 1–32.

Lapkin, S. (ed.) (1998) French: second language education in Canada. Toronto: University of Toronto Press.

Lemke, J. (1995) *Textual politics: discourse and social dynamics*. London: Taylor & Francis.

Leung, C. (1993) National Curriculum: ESL in primary education in England. *Language and Education*, **7** (3): 163–80.

Leung, C. (1995) English as an additional language in schools: the role of higher education accrediting bodies in professional development. In P. Skehan (ed.) *Thames Valley University Working Papers in English Language Teaching* (Vol. 3, pp. 48–66).

Leung, C. (1996) English as an additional language within the national curriculum: a study of assessment practices. *Prospect*, **11** (2): 58–68.

Leung, C., Harris, R. and Rampton, B. (1997) The idealised native speaker, reified ethnicities and classroom realities. *TESOL Quarterly*, **31** (3): 543–60.

Leung, C. and Teasdale, A. (1997) What do teachers mean by speaking and listening?

A contextualised study of assessment in multilingual classrooms in the English National Curriculum. In A. Huhta, V. Kohonen, L. Kurki-Suonio and S. Luoma (eds) *Current developments and alternatives in language assessment.* Finland: University of Jyväskylä, pp. 291–324.

Leung, C. and Teasdale, A. (1998) ESL teacher competence: professionalism in a social market. *Prospect,* **13** (1): 4–23.

Levin, J.R., Anglin, G.J. and Carney, R.N. (1987) On empirically validating functions of pictures in prose. In D.M. Willows and H.A. Houghton (eds) *The psychology of illustration* (Vol. I). New York: Springer-Verlag, pp. 51–85.

Liang, X. (1999) Dilemmas of cooperative learning: Chinese students' experiences. Unpublished doctoral dissertation. University of British Columbia, Vancouver, BC.

Lightbown, P. and Spada, N. (1990) Focus-on-form and corrective feedback in communicative language teaching: effects on second language learning. *Studies in Second Language Acquisition,* **12** (4): 429–48.

Lingard, B., Knight, J. and Porter, P. (eds) (1993) *Schooling reform in hard times.* London: Falmer Press.

Linguistic Minorities Project (1985) *The other languages of England.* London: Routledge & Kegan Paul.

Little, J. (1984) Seductive images and organisational realities in professional development. *Teachers College Record,* **86** (1): 84–102.

Lo Bianco, J. (1987) *The national policy on languages.* Canberra: Australian Government Printing Service.

Lo Bianco, J. (1998) ESL: Is it migrant literacy? Is it history? *Australian Language Matters,* **6** (2): 1, 6–7.

Logan, L. and Sachs, J. (1988) Inservice education in Queensland: some lessons. *The South Pacific Journal of Teacher Education,* **16** (1): 63–9.

Long, M.H. (1983) Native speaker/non-native speaker conversation in the second language classroom. In M.A. Clark and J. Handscombe (eds) *On TESOL 82 Pacific perspectives on language learning and teaching.* Washington, DC: TESOL.

Long, M. (1985) Input and second language acquisition. In S. Gass and C. Madden (eds) *Input in second language acquisition.* Rowley, MA: Newbury House, pp. 377–93.

Long, M.H. (1989) Task, group, and task-group interactions. *University of Hawaii Working Papers in ESL,* **8** (2): 1–26.

Long, M. and Crookes, G. (1992) Three approaches to task-based syllabus design. *TESOL Quarterly,* **26** (1): 27–56.

Long, M.H. and Porter, P.A. (1985) Group work, interlanguage talk and second language acquisition. *TESOL Quarterly,* **19** (2): 207–27.

Love, K. (1996) Unpacking arguments: the need for a metalanguage. *Idiom,* **1**: 60–75.

Macías, R.F. et al. (1998) *Summary report of the survey of the states' Limited English Proficient students and available education programs and services, 1996–97.* Washington, DC: National Clearinghouse for Bilingual Education. (website: www.ncbc.gwu.edu)

Marland, M. (1977) *Language across the curriculum.* London: Heinemann.

Martin, J.R. (1978) *The migrant presence.* Sydney: George Allen & Unwin.

Martin, J.R. (1984) Types of writing in infants and primary school. In L. Unsworth (ed.) *Reading, writing, spelling. Proceedings of the Fifth Macarthur Reading/Language Symposium.* Sydney: Macarthur Institute of Higher Education, pp. 34–55.

Martin, J.R. (1985) *Factual writing: exploring and challenging social reality.* Victoria: Deakin University.

Martin, J.R. (1986) Intervening in the process of writing development. In C. Painter and J.R. Martin (eds) *Writing to mean: teaching genres across the curriculum*

(Occasional Papers No. 9). Sydney: Applied Linguistics Association of Australia, pp. 11–43.

Martin, J.R. (1992) *English text.* Amsterdam: John Benjamins.

Martin, J.R., Christie, F. & Rothery, J. (1987) Social processes in education. In I. Reid (ed.) *The place of genre in learning: current debates.* Geelong: Deakin University Press.

Martin, J., Matthiessen, C. and Painter, C. (1997) *Working with functional grammar.* London: Edward Arnold.

Maude, B. and Bourne, J. (1988) *Making a difference: teaching and learning strategies in successful multi-ethnic schools.* Suffolk: Department for Education and Employment.

McCarthy, M. and Carter, R. (1994) *Language as discourse: perspective for language teaching.* London: Longman.

McDonell, W. (1992) Language and cognitive development through cooperative group work. In C. Kessler (ed.) *Cooperative language learning.* New Jersey: Prentice Hall Regents, pp. 51–64.

McGroarty, M. (1989) The benefits of cooperative learning arrangements in second language instruction. *NABE Journal,* **13**: 127–43.

McKay, P. (1992) *ESL development: language and literacy in schools* (Vols 1 and 2). Melbourne: National Languages and Literacy Institute of Australia.

McKay, P. (1994) Two ESL scales at the national level? What has happened and why? *Australian Language Matters,* **2** (2): 1, 18.

McKay, P. and Scarino, A. (1991) *The ESL framework of stages.* Melbourne: Curriculum Corporation.

McLaughlin, B. (1992) *Myths and misconceptions about second language learning: what every teacher needs to unlearn.* National Centre for Research on Cultural Diversity and Second Language Learning, University of California, Santa Cruz, CA.

McLeod, B. (1996) *School reform and student diversity: exemplary schooling for language minority students* (NCBE Resource Collection Series, No. 4). Washington DC: National Clearinghouse for Bilingual Education. (website: www.ncbc.gwu.edu)

McNamara, T.F. (1995) Modelling performance: opening Pandora's Box. *Applied Linguistics,* **16** (2): 159–79.

McNamara, T.F. (1996) *Measuring second language performance.* London: Longman.

Meiers, M. (1994) Exploring the English statement and profile – a project of the Australian Literacy Federation: Some TESOL connections. *TESOL in Context,* **4** (1): 16–19.

Meyer, B.J.F. (1985) Prose analysis: purposes, procedures, and problems. In B.K. Britton and J.B. Black (eds) *Understanding expository text.* Hillsdale, NJ: Erlbaum, pp. 269–304.

Ministry of Education (1963) *English for immigrants.* London: HMSO.

Ministry of Education (1981) *Language/dialect resource book for K-12.* Victoria, BC: Ministry of Education.

Ministry of Education (1987) *The teaching of English as a second language (ESL): guidelines for primary and post-primary schools.* Melbourne, Victoria: Ministry of Education.

Ministry of Education (1988) *Teaching English as a second language: a support document for the English language framework.* Melbourne, Victoria: Ministry of Education.

Mobbs, M. (1997) *Children's other languages: expertise, affiliation and language use amongst second-generation British South Asian pupils.* National Association for Language Development in the Curriculum. Occasional Paper No. 9. Watford: NALDIC.

Mohan, B. (1986) *Language and content.* Reading, MA: Addison-Wesley.

Mohan, B. (1989a) Knowledge structures and academic discourse. *Word,* **40** (1–2): 99–105.

Mohan, B.A. (1989b) Language socialization. *Word,* **4** (1–2): 100–14.

Mohan, B. (1991) LEP students and the integration of language and content: knowledge structures and tasks. In C. Simich-Dudgeon (ed.) *Proceedings of the First Research Symposium on Limited English Proficient Students' Issues.* Washington, DC: Office of Bilingual Education and Minority Languages Affairs.

Mohan, B. and Early, M. (1996) *Conversation about change; interviews with teachers.* Unpublished paper, University of British Columbia, Vancouver, BC.

Mohan, B. and Helmer, S. (1988) Context and second language development: preschoolers' comprehension of gestures. *Applied Linguistics,* **9** (3): 275–92.

Mohan, B. and Low, M. (1985) Academic writing and Chinese students. *TESOL Quarterly,* **19** (3): 515–34.

Mohan, B. and Low, M. (1995) Collaborative teacher assessment of ESL writers: conceptual and practical issues. *TESOL Journal,* **5** (1): 28–31.

Mohan, B. and Marshall Smith, S. (1992) Context and cooperation in academic tasks. In D. Nunan (ed.) *Collaborative language learning and teaching.* Cambridge: Cambridge University Press.

Mohan, B., Early, M. and Tang, G. (unpublished) *Integration and 'Thinking Skills': a review of British Columbia Curricular Frameworks K-12.* Report to the Ministry of Education, British Columbia.

Mohan, B. and Wong, A. (1992) *Language socialisation in theory and practice: a business case.* Paper presented at the 1992 International Systemic Functional Congress, Sydney, Australia.

Moore, H. (1992) *Rethinking the role of eclecticism in teacher development.* Paper presented at the ACTA-VATME National Conference, University of Melbourne.

Moore, H. (1995) Telling the history of the 1991 Australian Language and Literacy Policy. *TESOL in Context,* **5** (1): 6–20.

Moore, H. (1996) Telling what is real: competing views in assessing English as a second language development. *Linguistics and Education,* **8** (2): 189–228.

Morris, A. and Stewart-Dore, N. (1984) *Learning to learn from text.* Ryde, NSW: Addison Wesley.

Nance, D. and Fawns, R. (1993) Teachers' working knowledge and training: the Australian agenda for reform of teacher education. *Journal of Education for Teaching,* **19** (2): 159–73.

Nation, P. (1991) *Teaching and learning vocabulary.* New York: Newbury House.

Naylor, C. (1994) Research and Technology, BC Teachers' Federation. Research Reports on ESL. *Classroom Teachers' Focus Group responses: What is adequate ESL/ ESD support? The Views of ESL teachers.* Vancouver, BC: Teachers' Federation.

Neering, R. and Grant, P. (1986) *Other places, other times.* Toronto: Gage Educational.

Nieto, S. (1996) *Affirming diversity: the sociopolitical context of multicultural education* (2nd edn). New York: Longman.

NLLIA (1994) *ESL development: language and literacy in schools* (Vol. 1). National Languages and Literacy Institute of Australia. Canberra: Department of Employment, Education and Training.

Novak, J.D. and Gowin, D. (1984) *Learning how to learn.* Cambridge: Cambridge University Press.

NSW Department of School Education (1992) *Language & Social Power.* Erskineville, NSW: Metropolitan East Disadvantaged Schools Program.

Nunan, D. (1989) *Designing tasks for the communicative classroom.* Cambridge: Cambridge University Press.

Nunan, D. (1991) Communicative tasks and the language curriculum. *TESOL Quarterly,* **25** (2): 279–95.

O'Malley, J.M. and Chamot, A.U. (1990) *Learning strategies in second language acquisition.* Cambridge: Cambridge University Press.

Ochs, E. (1988) *Culture and language development: language acquisition and language socialisation.* Cambridge: Cambridge University Press.

OFSTED (1994) *Educational support for minority ethnic communities: a survey of educational provision funded under Section 11 of the 1966 Local Government Act.* London: Office for Standards in Education.

OFSTED (1997) *The assessment of the language development of bilingual pupils.* London: Office for Standards in Education.

Ogbu, J.U. (1987) Variability in minority school performance: a problem in search of an explanation. *Anthropology and Education Quarterly,* **18** (4): 312–34.

O'Malley, J. (1988) The Cognitive Academic Language Learning Approach (CALLA). *Journal of Multilingual and Multicultural Development,* **9** (1 and 2): 43–60.

O'Malley, J. and Chamot, A. (1989) *Learning strategies in second language acquisition.* Cambridge: Cambridge University Press.

O'Toole, M. (1989) *Science Exercises,* Sydney: Nelson Press.

Oxford, R. (1990) *Language learning strategies.* New York: Newbury House.

Oxford, R. (1996) *Language learning strategies around the world: cross-cultural perspectives.* Honolulu: University of Hawaii Press.

Paikeday, T. (1985) *The native speaker is dead!* Toronto: Paikeday Publishing Inc.

Peeck, J. (1987) The role of illustrations in processing and remembering illustrated text. In D.M. Willows and H.A. Houghton (eds) *The psychology of illustration* (Vol. I). New York: Springer-Verlag, pp. 115–51.

Peirce, B.N. (1995) Social identity, investment and language learning. *TESOL Quarterly,* **29** (1): 9–32.

Pennington, M. (1989) Faculty development for language programs. In R. Johnson (ed.) *The second language curriculum.* Cambridge: Cambridge University Press.

Pennington, M. (1995) The teacher change cycle. *TESOL Quarterly,* **29** (4): 705–30.

Pennycook, A. (1990) Critical pedagogy and second language education. *System,* **18** (3): 303–14.

Peters, R.S. (1966) *Ethics and education.* London: Allen & Unwin.

Pica, T. (1994) Research on negotiation: what does it reveal about second-language learning conditions, processes and outcomes? *Language Learning,* **44** (3): 493–527.

Pica, T., Kanagy, R. and Falodun, J. (1993) Choosing and using communication tasks for second language instruction. In G. Crookes and S.H. Gass (eds) *Tasks and language learning.* Clevedon: Multilingual Matters, pp. 9–34.

Pichards, J.D. (1992) Executive summary of the final report: longitudinal study of structured English immersion strategy, early exit and late exit transitional bilingual programs for language minority children. *Bilingual Research Journal,* **16**: 1–61.

Pienemann, M. (1989) Is language teachable? Psycholinguistic experiments and hypotheses. *Applied Linguistics,* **10** (1): 52–79.

Pienemann, M. and Johnston, M. (1987) Factors affecting the development of language proficiency. In D. Nunan (ed.) *Applying second language acquisition research.* Adelaide: National Curriculum Resource Centre.

Pienemann, M. and Lightbown, P. (1993) Comments on Stephen D. Krashen's 'Teaching issues: formal grammar instruction'. Two readers react. *TESOL Quarterly,* **27** (4): 717–21.

Pienemann, M. and Mackey, A. (1992) An empirical study of children's ESL development and rapid profile. In P. McKay (ed.) *ESL development: language and literacy in schools* (Vol. 2). Melbourne: National Languages and Literacy Institute of Australia, pp. 115–259.

Prabhu, N.S. (1987) *Second language pedagogy*. Oxford: Oxford University Press.

QCA (1998a) *Describing progression in learning English*. London: Qualifications and Curriculum Authority.

QCA (1998b) *Step descriptors*. London: Qualifications and Curriculum Authority.

Ramirez, J.D. (1992) Executive summary of the final report: Longitudinal study of structured English immersion strategy, early exit and late exit transitional bilingual programmes for language minority children. *Bilingual Research Journal*, **16**: 1–61.

RCBB (1969) *Book IV – The cultural contribution of the other ethnic groups*. Royal Commission on Bilingualism and Biculturalism, Ottawa: Queen's Printer.

Reeder, K., Hasebe-Ludt, E. and Thomas, L. (1995) *Taking the next steps toward a coherent language education policy for British Columbia*. Paper. Vancouver: Language Education Department, University of BC.

Reich, R. (1992) *The work of nations*. New York: Vintage Books.

Reid, L. (1987) *The place of genre in learning: current debates*. Geelong: Centre for Studies in Literary Education, Deakin University.

Reinking, R. (1986) Integrating graphic aids into content area instruction: the graphic information lesson. *Journal of Reading*, **30** (2): 146–51.

Richards, J. and Hurley, R. (1990) Language and content: approaches to curriculum alignment. In J. Richards (ed.) *The language teaching matrix*. Cambridge: Cambridge University Press, pp. 144–59.

Richmond, BC School District (1995) *Report of the review of English as a Second Language program*. Richmond, BC: School District.

Rosen, C. & Rosen, H. (1973) *The language of primary school children*. London: Penguin Education.

Rothery, J. (1984) The development of genres – primary to junior secondary school. *Children writing: Study Guide (ECT 418 Language Studies)*. Deakin University, Geelong, Victoria, pp. 67–114.

Rothery, J. and Stenglin, M. (1994) *Writing a book review: a unit of work for junior secondary English (write it right resources for literacy and learning)*. Sydney: Metropolitan East Disadvantaged Schools Program.

Rueda, R., Goldenberg, C. and Gallimore, R. (1992) *Rating instructional conversations: a guide*. National Center for Research on Cultural Diversity and Second Language Learning. http://www.ncbe.gwu.edu/miscpubs/ncrcdsll/epr4.html

Ryan, S.T.H.S. (1986) *Guidelines to Commonwealth Schools Commission for 1987*. Statement by the Commonwealth Minister for Education.

Savignon, S. (1991) Communicative language teaching: the state of the art. *TESOL Quarterly*, **25** (2): 261–77.

Saville-Troike, M. (1984) What really matters in second language learning for academic achievement? *TESOL Quarterly*, **18** (2): 199–219.

SCAA (1996) *Teaching English as an additional language: a framework for policy*. London: School Curriculum and Assessment Authority.

Scarino, A., McKay, P. and Vale, D. (1988) *The Australian language levels, Books 1–4*. Curriculum Corporation; Canberra.

Schmidt, R.W. (1990) The role of consciousness in second language learning. *Applied Linguistics*, **11** (2): 129–58.

Schön, D. (1971) *Beyond the stable state*. New York: Norton.

Schön, D.A. (1987) *Educating the reflective practitioner*. London: Jossey-Bass.

Schools Council Project in English for Immigrant Children (1969) *Scope, stage 1: An introductory English course for immigrant children*. London: Schools Council.

Schwartz, R.J. and Parks, S. (1994) *Infusing the teaching of critical and creative thinking into content instruction*. Pacific Grove, CA: Critical Thinking Press.

Seesahai, M., Sander, A., Yonemoto, Y. and Fong, G. (1993) *The views of parents of ESL students concerning the B.C. education system.* A BCTF Focus Group. Vancouver: British Columbia Teachers' Federation.

Senge, P. (1990) *The fifth discipline: the art and practice of the learning organization.* New York: Doubleday.

Short, D., Crandall, J. and Christian, D. (1989) *How to integrate language and content instruction: a training manual.* Center for Language Education and Research, University of California; Los Angeles.

Skehan, P. (1996) A framework for the implementation of task-based instruction. *Applied Linguistics,* **17** (1): 38–62.

Skehan, P. (1998) *A cognitive approach to language learning.* Oxford: Oxford University Press.

Skutnabb-Kangas, T. (1988) Multilingualism and the education of minority children. In T. Skutnabb-Kangas and J. Cummins (eds) *Minority education: from shame to struggle.* Clevedon, Philadelphia: Multilingual Matters.

Smolicz, J. (1985) Multiculturalism and an overarching framework of values. In M. Poole, P. de Lacey and B. Randhawa (eds) *Australia in transition: culture and life possibilities.* Sydney: Harcourt Brace Jovanovich, pp. 76–87.

Snow, C.M., Met, M. and Genesee, F. (1989) A conceptual framework for the integration of language and content in second/foreign language instruction. *TESOL Quarterly,* **23** (2): 201–19.

Snow, M.A., Met, M. and Genesee, F. (1992) A conceptual framework for the integration of language and content instruction. In P.A. Richard-Amato and M.A. Snow (eds) *The Multicultural Classroom.* New York: Longman, pp. 27–38.

South Australian Teaching and Curriculum Centre (1995) *An evaluation of the ESL in the mainstream professional development course.* Adelaide: National Languages and Literacy Institute of Australia.

Spolsky, B. (1989) *Conditions for second language learning.* Oxford: Oxford University Press.

Squires, R. (1996) Equal opportunities in education. In C. Leung and P. Barnett (eds) *Managing equality of opportunity in education into the 21st century.* London: Commission for Racial Equality and Thames Valley University, pp. 1–7.

Stern, H. (1992) *Issues and options in language teaching.* Oxford: Oxford University Press.

Strevens, P. (1977) *New Orientations in the teaching of English.* Oxford: Oxford University Press.

Strong, R. and Hogan, S. (1994) *TESOL teacher competencies document.* Paper presented at the 28th Annual TESOL Convention, Baltimore.

Sullivan, B.M. (1988) Q.C. Commissioner. *A legacy for learners. The report of the Royal Commission on Education.* Victoria, BC: Ministry of Education.

Swain, M. (1985) Communicative competence: some roles of comprehensible input and comprehensible output in its development. In S. Gass and C. Madden (eds) *Input in second language acquisition.* Rowley, MA: Newbury House, pp. 235–56.

Swain, M. (1991) The immersion experience in Canada: is it relevant to Hong Kong? In V. Bickley (ed.) *Where from here? Issues relating to the planning, managing and implementation of language teaching and training programmes in the 90s.* Hong Kong Government Education Department.

Swain, M. (1995) Three functions of output in second language learning. In G. Cook and B. Seidlhofer (eds) *Principle and practice in applied linguistics* Oxford: Oxford University Press, pp. 125–44.

Swales, J. (1990) *Genre analysis.* Cambridge: Cambridge University Press.

Swann, M. (1985) *Education for all: a brief guide to the main issues of the report.* London: HMSO.

Tang, G. (1989) *Graphic representations of knowledge structures in ESL student learning.* Unpublished doctoral dissertation, University of British Columbia, Vancouver, BC.

Tang, G.M. (1991a) The role and value of graphic representation of knowledge structures in ESL student learning: an ethnographic study. *TESL Canada Journal,* **9** (1): 29–41.

Tang, G.M. (1991b) ESL student perception of student-generated graphics as a reading strategy. *Reflections on Canadian Literacy,* **9** (1): 2–9.

Tang, G.M. (1992) The effect of graphic representation of knowledge structures on ESL reading comprehension. *Studies in Second Language Acquisition,* **14**: 177–95.

Tang, G.M. (MS) Graphic representation of knowledge structures across languages and cultures: an ethnographic study of secondary students.

TESOL (1997) *ESL standards for pre-K-12 students.* Alexandria, VA: Teachers of English to Speakers of Other Languages.

Teunissen, F. (1992) Equality of educational opportunity for children from ethnic minority communities. In E. Reid and H. Reich (eds) *Breaking the boundaries – migrant workers' children in the EC.* Clevedon: Multilingual Matters, pp. 88–111.

Thomas, W.P. and Collier, V. (1997) *School effectiveness for language minority students.* Washington, DC: National Clearinghouse for Bilingual Education.

Threadgold, T. (1988) Stories of race and gender: an unbounded discourse. In D. Birch and M. O'Toole (eds) *Functions of style.* London: Frances Pinter.

Tikunoff, W.J. (1985) *Developing strident functional proficiency: a teachers' casebook, Part I: Teacher Training Monograph 2.* Gainesville, Florida: Bilingual/ESOL Teacher Training Project.

Tikunoff, W.J. et al. (1991) *Final report: a descriptive study of significant features of exemplary special alternative instructional programs.* Prepared under contract for the US Department of Education by the Southwest Regional Educational Laboratory, Los Alamitos, CA.

Tizard, B., Blatchford, P., Burke, J., Farquhar, C. and Plewis, I. (1988) *Young children at school in the inner city.* Hove and London: Lawrence Erlbaum.

Tomlinson, S. and Tomes, H. (1983) *Ethnic minorities in British schools. A review of the literature 1960–82.* London: Heinemann.

Toohey, K. (1992) We teach English as a second language to bilingual students. In B. Burnaby and A. Cumming (eds) *Socio-political aspects of ESL.* Toronto: OISE Press, pp. 87–96.

Toronto School Board (1992) The growth of tolerance in Canada and Toronto. *Research Review* #21. Toronto: Toronto School Board, pp. 1–11.

Tosi, A. (1996) *Learning from diversity: language education and intercultural relations in the inner city.* Brussels: European Commission and Eurocities.

Townsend, H.E.R. (1971) *Immigrant pupils in England. The LEA response.* Slough: NFER.

Truscott, J. (1998) Noticing in second language acquisition: a critical review. *Second Language Research,* **14** (2): 103–35.

Tsolidis, G. (1985) Towards a definition of a second-phase learner. *Polycom,* **39** (April): 16–22.

Vacca, R.T. (1981) *Content area reading.* Boston: Little Brown & Company.

Vacca, R.T. and Vacca, J.L. (1993) *Content area reading.* New York: HarperCollins

Valdés, G. (1997) Dual-language immersion programs: a cautionary note concerning the education of language-minority students. *Harvard Educational Review,* **67** (3): 391–429.

Veel, R. (1998) *Exploring literacy in school science.* London: Rutherford.

Vygotsky, L.S. (1962) *Thought and language.* Cambridge, MA: MIT Press.

Wajnryb, R. (1992) Learning to help: An exploration into supervisory behaviour. *Prospect,* **7** (3): 32–41.

Walker, J. and Evers, C. (1984) Conflicts in consciousness: imperatives can lead to knots in thinking. In R. Halkes and J. Olsen (eds) *Teacher thinking: a new perspective on persistent problems in education.* Lisse: Swets & Zeitlangef.

Wallace, C. (1987) Issues in teaching English as a second language. In S. Abudarham (ed.) *Bilingualism and the bilingual.* Windsor: Berkshire NFER-Nelson.

Weinstein, C. and Meyer, R. (1985) The teaching of learning strategies. In M. Wittrock (ed.) *Handbook of research on teaching* (3rd edn). New York: Macmillan.

Werner, O. and Schoepfler, G. (1987) *Systematic fieldwork,* 2 Vols. Newbury Park, CA: Sage.

Wesche, M. (1993) Discipline-based approaches to language study. In M. Krueger and F. Ryan (eds) *Language and content: discipline- and content-based approaches to language study.* Lexington, MA: Heath, pp. 57–82.

White, D. and Hannan, B. (1986) *Some ideas about equality in education* (Unpublished paper): ACT Schools Authority.

Widdowson, H. (1978) *Learning language as communication.* Oxford: Oxford University Press.

Widdowson, H.G. (1983) *Learning purpose and language use.* Oxford: Oxford University Press.

Wilkins, D. (1976) *Notional syllabuses.* Oxford: Oxford University Press.

Williams, A. (1995) *Content-based language teaching: problems and promise.* Unpublished MEd Thesis, La Trobe University.

Williamson, J. and Woodall, C. (1996) A vision for English: re-thinking the revised National Curriculum in the light of contemporary critical theory. *English in Education,* **30** (3): 4–13.

Willis, D. (1991) *The lexical syllabus.* London: Collins.

Wilton, J. and Bosworth, R. (1984) *Old worlds and new Australia: the post-war migrant experience.* Ringwood, Victoria: Penguin.

Winn, W.D. (1987) Charts, graphs and diagrams in educational materials. In D.M. Willows and H.A. Houghton (eds) The psychology of illustration (Vol. I). New York: Springer-Verlag, pp. 152–98.

Winne, P.H. and Marx, R.W. (1989) A cognitive-processing analysis of motivation within classroom tasks. In C. Ames and P. Ames (eds) *Research on motivation in education* (Vol. 3). New York: Academic Press, pp. 223–57.

Write it Right (1995) *Exploring literacy in school English.* (Resources for Literacy series.) Disadvantaged Schools Program, Metropolitan East, NSW Department of School Education, Sydney.

Write it Right (forthcoming) *Exploring literacy in school science.* (Resources for Literacy series.) Disadvantaged Schools Program, Metropolitan East, NSW Department of School Education, Sydney.

Yaxley, B. (1991) Teaching, teacher thinking and teacher development. In P. Hughes (ed.) *Teachers' professional development.* Melbourne: Australian Council of Educational Research, pp. 82–94.

Zeichner, K. (1983) Alternative paradigms of teacher education. *Journal of Teacher Education,* **34** (3): 3–9.

Zimpher, N. (1988) A design for the professional development of teacher leaders. *Journal of Teacher Education,* **39** (1): 53–60.

Name Index

General Index